Quantum Computing with Silq Programming

Get up and running with quantum computing with the simplicity of this new high-level programming language

Srinjoy Ganguly

Thomas Cambier

BIRMINGHAM—MUMBAI

Quantum Computing with Silq Programming

Group Product Manager: Aaron Lazar

Publishing Product Manager: Shweta Bairoliya

Senior Editor: Storm Mann

Content Development Editor: Nithya Sadanandan

Technical Editor: Gaurav Gala

Copy Editor: Safis Editing

Project Coordinator: Deeksha Thakkar

Proofreader: Safis Editing

Indexer: Rekha Nair

Production Designer: Vijay Kamble

First published: April 2021

Production reference: 3090921

Published by Packt Publishing Ltd.
Livery Place
35 Livery Street
Birmingham
B3 2PB, UK.

978-1-80056-966-9

www.packt.com

I dedicate this book to God, my Guru, to my family, my teachers and tutors, and to my amazing friends for their consistent support and encouragement throughout the writing process.

– Srinjoy Ganguly

I would like to thank Prof. Dr. Martin Vechev for giving me the opportunity to write my Master's thesis at the SRI lab at ETH Zurich, and Benjamin Bichsel for his help on implementing quantum algorithms with Silq.

– Thomas Cambier

Contributors

About the authors

Srinjoy Ganguly is the founder and CEO of AdroitERA, an EdTech firm, and possesses a Master's in quantum computing technology from the Technical University of Madrid, and a Master's in artificial intelligence from the University of Southampton. He has over 4 years' experience in quantum computing and 5 years' experience in machine learning and deep learning. He currently leads the **Quantum Machine Learning (QML)** study space at QWorld. He has given an expert talk on QML at IEEE SPS. His research interests include QML, Quantum Image Processing, **Quantum Natural Language Processing (QNLP)**, machine learning, and deep learning.

Thomas Cambier is a French programmer and software developer. After studying top-level mathematics, physics, and computer science at Ecole Polytechnique, France's leading engineering school, he obtained a Master's degree in computer science at ETH Zürich on a broad range of subjects going from algorithmics and cryptography to object-oriented programming. Deeply interested in the promising possibilities resulting from quantum computing, he wrote his Master's thesis on the design of quantum algorithms with Silq, a brand-new high-level quantum language created by a research group at ETH Zürich.

About the reviewer

Alberto Maldonado is doing his Ph.D. on QML in computer science at the Center for Computing Research, IPN, Mexico. At his institute, he has collaborated with the Fermilab and CERN research centers for the GeantV project. Alberto has participated in different events, such as Xanadu's Qhack, and was a mentee of QOSF's mentor program. He is passionate about using new technologies and paradigms, such as quantum computing, and is self-taught and diligent.

Table of Contents

4
Physical Realization of a Quantum Computer

Section 2:
Challenges in Quantum Programming and Silq Programming

5
Challenges in Quantum Computer Programming

6

Silq Programming Basics and Features

7

Programming Multiple-Qubit Quantum Circuits with Silq

Section 3: Quantum Algorithms Using Silq Programming

8
Quantum Algorithms I – Deutsch-Jozsa and Bernstein-Vazirani

9
Quantum Algorithms II – Grover's Search Algorithm and Simon's Algorithm

13
Quantum Machine Learning

Other Books You May Enjoy

Index

Preface

Quantum computing is an emerging cutting-edge technology that has already started having an impact on various industries, along with academia. Quantum computers have proved that significant speed-ups are possible in different kinds of algorithms over the present classical algorithms. As Moore's law comes to an end, the importance of quantum computers is increasing for various applications, including finance, chemistry, optimization, and many more. One of the major challenges that people in the quantum computing space face is related to low-level circuit programming, which restricts industry and academia from developing quantum applications for deployment.

This book will introduce you to a high-level quantum programming language – Silq. We will utilize Silq to construct quantum circuits on our own, understand and develop important quantum algorithms, and learn about some significant applications of quantum computing, such as quantum error correction, quantum cryptography, and quantum machine learning. You will be learning hands-on Silq programming to understand its unique features, such as more intuitive syntax and automatic uncomputation compared to other quantum programming languages, such as Microsoft Q#.

Who this book is for

This Silq quantum computing book is for students, researchers, and scientists looking to learn quantum computing techniques and high-level quantum programming development. Quantum computing enthusiasts who want to explore this futuristic technology will also find this book useful. Beginner-level knowledge of any programming language, as well as mathematical topics such as linear algebra, probability, complex numbers, and statistics, is required.

What this book covers

Chapter 1, *Essential Mathematics and Algorithmic Thinking*, provides you with a basic foundational knowledge of mathematics and algorithms.

Chapter 2, *Quantum Bits, Quantum Measurements, and Quantum Logic Gates*, introduces the basics of quantum bits, measurements, and single-qubit quantum logic gates.

In *Chapter 3, Multiple Quantum Bits, Entanglement, and Quantum Circuits*, you will explore multiple qubits and their various quantum circuits using single- and multi-qubit quantum gates.

Chapter 4, Physical Realization of a Quantum Computer, takes you through various technologies that will enable you to build a real physical quantum computer.

Chapter 5, Challenges in Quantum Computer Programming, will introduce you to the various challenges faced in quantum programming.

In *Chapter 6, Silq Programming Basics and Features*, we will introduce Silq and help you to start programming with this high-level quantum programming language.

In *Chapter 7, Programming Multiple Qubit Quantum Circuits with Silq*, you will learn to tackle multiple qubits in Silq and construct various interesting quantum circuits using Silq.

In *Chapter 8, Quantum Algorithms I – Deutsch-Jozsa and Bernstein-Vazirani*, you will start coding your very first quantum algorithms using Silq – Deutsch-Jozsa, which identifies whether a function is constant or balanced, and Bernstein-Vazirani, which finds a secret string encoded in a function.

In *Chapter 9, Quantum Algorithms II – Grover's Search Algorithm and Simon's Algorithm*, you will see how to use Grover's search algorithm for unstructured database search, and Simon's algorithm for finding a hidden string.

In *Chapter 10, Quantum Algorithms III – Quantum Fourier Transform and Phase Estimation*, you will learn two of the most important algorithms – first, the **Quantum Fourier Transform** (**QFT**), which is a technique for linear transformations on qubits. Then you will use the QFT to learn about the quantum phase estimation algorithm.

Chapter 11, Quantum Error Correction, offers an introduction to classical error-correction techniques, and you will learn to implement different quantum error-correcting codes to prevent a potential bit-flip or phase-flip from occurring on a qubit.

In *Chapter 12, Quantum Cryptography – Quantum Key Distribution*, you will see an overview of classical cryptographical methods and learn to implement in Silq a quantum protocol useful to safely exchange keys: quantum key distribution.

In *Chapter 13, Quantum Machine Learning*, you will explore some important concepts regarding quantum machine learning and recent developments happening in the field of quantum computing.

To get the most out of this book

You will need the latest version of Microsoft Visual Studio Code installed on your Windows computer.

Software/hardware covered in the book
Visual Studio Code with the Silq plugin

If you are using the digital version of this book, we advise you to type the code yourself or access the code via the GitHub repository (link available in the next section). Doing so will help you avoid any potential errors related to the copying and pasting of code.

After you finish with the book, we recommend you try to solve the challenges hosted by Microsoft Q# using Silq language for more programming practice!

You can find those challenges in the following links:

- Microsoft coding contest 2018: `https://codeforces.com/contest/1002/`

- Microsoft coding contest 2019: `https://codeforces.com/contest/1116/`

- Some of the challenges, solved using Silq, have been given in the Silq documentation: `https://silq.ethz.ch/examples`

Download the example code files

You can download the example code files for this book from GitHub at `https://github.com/PacktPublishing/Quantum-Computing-with-Silq-Programming`. In case there's an update to the code, it will be updated on the existing GitHub repository.

We also have other code bundles from our rich catalog of books and videos available at `https://github.com/PacktPublishing/`. Check them out!

Download the color images

We also provide a PDF file that has color images of the screenshots/diagrams used in this book. You can download it here: `https://static.packt-cdn.com/downloads/9781800569669_ColorImages.pdf`.

Conventions used

There are a number of text conventions used throughout this book.

`Code in text`: Indicates code words in text, database table names, folder names, filenames, file extensions, pathnames, dummy URLs, user input, and Twitter handles. Here is an example: "In the second line, the `coerce` keyword forces the secret string to be a classical unsigned integer on four qubits."

A block of code is set as follows:

```
def scal[n:!N](const x:uint[n], const y:uint[n])qfree:uint[n] {
    count := 0:uint[n];
    for k in [0..n) {
        count += x[k] && y[k];
    }
    return count;
}
```

When we wish to draw your attention to a particular part of a code block, the relevant lines or items are set in bold:

```
def scal[n:!N](const x:uint[n], const y:uint[n])qfree:uint[n] {
    count := 0:uint[n];
    for k in [0..n) {
        count += x[k] && y[k];
    }
    return count;
}
```

Bold: Indicates a new term, an important word, or words that you see onscreen. For example, words in menus or dialog boxes appear in the text like this. Here is an example: "In the world of quantum computing we use the term **qubit** or **quantum bit** to represent the bits."

> **Tips or important notes**
> Appear like this.

Get in touch

Feedback from our readers is always welcome.

General feedback: If you have questions about any aspect of this book, mention the book title in the subject of your message and email us at customercare@packtpub.com.

Errata: Although we have taken every care to ensure the accuracy of our content, mistakes do happen. If you have found a mistake in this book, we would be grateful if you would report this to us. Please visit www.packtpub.com/support/errata, selecting your book, clicking on the Errata Submission Form link, and entering the details.

Piracy: If you come across any illegal copies of our works in any form on the Internet, we would be grateful if you would provide us with the location address or website name. Please contact us at copyright@packt.com with a link to the material.

If you are interested in becoming an author: If there is a topic that you have expertise in and you are interested in either writing or contributing to a book, please visit authors.packtpub.com.

Reviews

Please leave a review. Once you have read and used this book, why not leave a review on the site that you purchased it from? Potential readers can then see and use your unbiased opinion to make purchase decisions, we at Packt can understand what you think about our products, and our authors can see your feedback on their book. Thank you!

For more information about Packt, please visit packt.com.

Section 1:
Essential Background and Introduction to Quantum Computing

This part deals with the mathematical prerequisites that are essential for understanding quantum computing and the challenges faced by users who perform quantum programming in their daily lives. The construction of a real quantum computer will also be touched upon briefly. After completing this part, you will feel confident in your mathematical abilities and understand the challenges faced by the quantum computing community.

This section comprises the following chapters:

- *Chapter 1, Essential Mathematics and Algorithmic Thinking*
- *Chapter 2, Quantum Bits, Quantum Measurements, and Quantum Logic Gates*
- *Chapter 3, Multiple Quantum Bits, Entanglement, and Quantum Circuits*
- *Chapter 4, Physical Realization of a Quantum Computer*

1
Essential Mathematics and Algorithmic Thinking

Quantum computing utilizes the phenomena and properties of quantum mechanics to perform computational tasks. This is done using a quantum computer, which is made using the principles of quantum physics. Today, quantum computers are still in their early stages, but the field is rapidly evolving as more and more communities from different backgrounds get involved in the field. Quantum computers will soon be able to solve challenges that are too complex for classical computers.

This chapter is intended to develop your understanding of the mathematical concepts that are required for quantum computing. This will help you to understand the ideas behind the applications of mathematical concepts to quantum computation. We will cover the following topics:

- Linear algebra
- Coordinate systems, probability, and complex numbers
- Computational thinking and computer algorithms
- The time and space complexity of algorithms

Introducing linear algebra for quantum computing

The concepts and techniques of linear algebra are so important and central to the field of quantum computing because almost all of the operations that take place in quantum computing use the language of linear algebra to describe the details and processes that happen within a quantum computer.

Linear algebra deals with the study of vector spaces and matrices. It primarily covers linear mapping and transformations of vectors and matrices. The geometric representation of linear algebra, such as in 2D Cartesian systems, makes it a lot easier to visualize operations happening on vectors and matrices.

In this section, we will cover the essential topics of linear algebra that are relevant to the world of quantum computing. The mathematical terms will be related to their equivalent quantum computing terms so that you can get a full understanding of the technical terms in quantum language. Let's start with the basic building blocks of linear algebra – vectors and vector spaces.

Vectors and vector spaces

In this section, you will develop a fundamental understanding of vectors and vector spaces. You will also learn about the relationship between vectors and the quantum computing world and will come to appreciate the practical nature of the mathematics involved. In quantum computing and quantum mechanics, vector spaces constitute all the possible quantum states, and they obey the rules of addition and multiplication. Vectors and vector spaces also play an important role in fluid mechanics, wave propagation, and oscillators.

Vectors

In the world of classical computation, we represent classical bits as **0**, which represents the voltage level being *off*, and **1**, which represents it being *on*. However, in the world of quantum computing, we use the term **qubit**, or **quantum bit**, to represent bits. Quantum bits comprise a two-level quantum system that forms the basic units of information in quantum computation, and they derive their properties from quantum mechanics. You may wonder why I am discussing **qubits** in the vectors section; this is because qubits can be represented as vectors!

Vectors are just collections or lists of numbers, and in a more geometric sense, they represent direction along with magnitude. Mathematicians refer to these as *vectors*, whereas quantum physicists and computer scientists call them *qubits*. I will use the term qubits instead of vectors. The notation to represent qubits is known as the **bra-ket** notation or **Dirac notation** and uses angle brackets, <>, and vertical bars, |, to represent the qubits. The paper by Dirac titled *A new notation for quantum mechanics* explains the bra-ket notation in more detail and can be found in the *Further reading* section. The basic qubits used most frequently in quantum computing are column vectors (2D).

The 0 qubit can be written as $|0>$ and 1 can be written as $|1>$; these are called ket 0 and ket 1, respectively. Qubits are quantum states, and a general quantum state can be denoted by $|\psi>$.

We can see a ket representation of qubits as follows:

$$|0> = \begin{bmatrix} 1 \\ 0 \end{bmatrix} \text{ and } |1> = \begin{bmatrix} 0 \\ 1 \end{bmatrix}$$

The bra notation, which is the transpose of ket, is given as follows:

$$<0| = \begin{bmatrix} 1 & 0 \end{bmatrix} \text{ and } <1| = \begin{bmatrix} 0 & 1 \end{bmatrix}$$

The important properties of the bra-ket notation is as follows:

- Every ket qubit will have a bra qubit.
- Constant multiple property – for a constant multiple c, $|c\psi> = c|\psi>$, and $<c\psi| = c^* <\psi|$.

Vector spaces

A **vector space** is a collection of vectors where two essential operations can take place, namely, vector addition and scalar multiplication. In quantum computing, you deal with complex vector spaces, $\mathbb{C}$, called **Hilbert spaces**, which means that vectors can consist of complex numbers, and all the rules of complex numbers can be applied in the calculations whenever we are carrying out operations and calculations with vectors and matrices. Hilbert spaces are usually denoted by the letter H. We will see this more in the next section.

Vector addition can be performed in the following way:

$$|\psi> = |0> + |1> = \begin{pmatrix} 1 \\ 0 \end{pmatrix} + \begin{pmatrix} 0 \\ 1 \end{pmatrix} = \begin{pmatrix} 1 \\ 1 \end{pmatrix}$$

Here, the corresponding elements of the vectors are added together. This can be easily extended to n dimensions as well, where n corresponding elements are added. The quantum state $|\psi>$ formed previously is also known as a **superposition** of quantum states, which means that not only can quantum states be present at $|0>$ or $|1>$, but they can also be present in the superposition of $|0>$ and $|1>$. This is a very important property in quantum computation. Superposition states are linear combinations of other quantum states.

According to quantum mechanics, quantum states always need to be normalized because the probabilistic description of wave functions in quantum mechanics means that all the probabilities add to 1, so normalizing the state $|\psi>$ will give us $\frac{1}{\sqrt{2}}(|0> +|1>)$, which is the proper definition of the state $|\psi>$. The modulus squared of the coefficients of the quantum states gives us the probability of finding that particular state. As an example, $(\frac{1}{\sqrt{2}})^2$ is the respective probabilities of finding $|0>$ and $|1>$ in the preceding case.

Scalar multiplication in vector spaces happens as follows:

$$2 \, |0> = 2 \begin{pmatrix} 1 \\ 0 \end{pmatrix} = \begin{pmatrix} 2 \\ 0 \end{pmatrix}$$

Here the scalar, which can be a real or complex number, is being multiplied by each of the elements present in the vector.

Whenever a vector can be written as a linear combination of other vectors, those vectors are known as linearly dependent vectors. Therefore, the **linear independence** of vectors implies that vectors cannot be written as a combination of other vectors. For example, the vectors $|0>$ and $|1>$ are *linearly independent*, but $\begin{pmatrix} 2 \\ 0 \end{pmatrix}$ is *linearly dependent* because $\begin{pmatrix} 2 \\ 0 \end{pmatrix}$ can be written as $|0> + |0>$. The vectors $|0>$ and $|1>$ form the basis vectors and are the most common computational basis used in quantum computation. Similarly, in terms of Cartesian coordinates, the vectors $(1, 0)$ and $(0, 1)$ form the basis vectors for the Cartesian plane.

Vectors and vector spaces are very important concepts and will be used frequently throughout the book. We will now describe some operations that are important for vectors.

Inner products and norms

Inner products is a useful concept for the comparison of closeness between two vectors or quantum states, which is frequently carried out in quantum computing. In this section, you will become familiar with the calculation of inner products and the norms of quantum states. Inner products are useful for identifying the distinguishability of two different quantum states, and this property can be used for clustering. Norms are useful for describing the stretch or range of a particular quantum state in the vector space.

Inner products

The most important difference between an inner product and a **dot product** is the space and the mapping process. For the dot product, you will be familiar with the fact that the process takes two vectors from the Euclidean space and operates on them to provide us with a real number. In the case of **inner products**, the two vectors are taken from the $\mathbb{C}^n$ space and the operations map it to a complex number. Inner products measure the closeness between two vectors. The notation <a|b> defines an inner product between two quantum states or two vectors.

For calculating, we have $< a|b > = a^T b$, where a^T is the transpose of vector a. If $< a|b > = 0$, then the vectors are known as orthogonal vectors. Since the output of the inner product is complex, $< a|b >^* = < b|a >$ holds true.

Let's solve an example to see the calculation of inner products:

$$< 0|0 > = (1\ 0)\begin{pmatrix}1\\0\end{pmatrix} = 1*1 + 0*0 = 1$$

$$< 0|1 > = (1\ 0)\begin{pmatrix}0\\1\end{pmatrix} = 1*0 + 0*1 = 0$$

Similarly, you can verify that $< 1|0 > = 0$ and $< 1|1 > = 1$. Since $< 1|0 > = < 0|1 > = 0$, it shows that $|0 >$ and $|1 >$ are **orthogonal**, but $< 0|0 > = < 1|1 > = 1$, which shows that they are normalized. This means that $|0 >$ and $|1 >$ are **orthonormal**!

For the calculation of the inner product whenever the elements are complex, the Hermitian conjugate of the vector is necessary to compute. To calculate the Hermitian conjugate, we take the complex conjugate of the elements of the vector and write it in a row vector form. For the computation of inner products, we then multiply the Hermitian conjugate by the column vector. The Hermitian conjugate is denoted by $(|a >)^\dagger = < a|$.

Norms

The **norm** of a vector gives us the length of that vector. This is a real number and is denoted as follows:

$$\|a\| = \sqrt{<a|a>}$$

The notion of the length of a vector is also known as the magnitude of the vector, which was mentioned at the beginning of the section on vectors. These operations are important for understanding various quantum algorithms in later chapters.

With inner products, norms, and vector spaces defined, let's now look at a few properties of Hilbert spaces, which are where all quantum computations happen.

Properties of Hilbert spaces

Let's look at some important properties of Hilbert spaces very briefly. You can try solving the proofs of these properties for yourself as a nice exercise:

- A Hilbert space is a linear vector space satisfying the inner product condition – $<\psi_1, \psi_2> \in \mathbb{C}$

- Hilbert spaces satisfy conjugate symmetry: $<\psi_1, \psi_2> = <\psi_2, \psi_1>^*$

- Hilbert spaces satisfy positive definiteness: $<\psi, \psi> = |\psi|^2 \geq 0$

- Hilbert spaces are separable, so they contain a countable dense subset.

- Hilbert spaces satisfy that they are linear with respect to the first vector:
  $<\psi_1, a\psi_2 + b\psi_3> = a <\psi_1, \psi_2> + b <\psi_1, \psi_3>$ where a and b are scalars.

- Hilbert spaces satisfy that they are anti-linear with respect to the second vector:
  $<a\psi_1 + b\psi_2, \psi_3> = a^* <\psi_1, \psi_3> + b^* <\psi_2, \psi_3>$

We have discussed the various characteristics of and operations for vectors. Now we will dive into matrices and their operations while describing their relevance to quantum computing.

Matrices and their operations

Matrices are a significant part of quantum computing and their importance can't be emphasized enough. The fundamental concept behind matrices is that they connect theoretical quantum computing with practical quantum computing because they are easily implemented on computers for calculations. In this section, you will learn about matrices and their operations.

A **matrix** is an array of numbers that are arranged in a tabular format, that is, in the form of rows and columns. Primarily, matrices represent linear transformations in a vector space, making them essentially a process of linear mappings between vector spaces. For example, a rotation matrix is a rectangular array of elements arranged in order to rotate a vector in a 2D or 3D space. From this, you should begin to grasp the idea that whenever a matrix acts on an object, it will create some effect, and the effect is usually in the form of the transformation of functions or spaces. So, matrices can be called **operators** in the language of quantum computation, or in other words, **operators** can be represented using matrices.

The general form of a matrix is as follows:

$$\begin{bmatrix} a_{1,1} & a_{1,2} & \cdots & a_{1,n} \\ a_{2,1} & a_{2,2} & \cdots & a_{2,n} \\ \vdots & \vdots & \ddots & \vdots \\ a_{m,1} & a_{m,2} & \cdots & a_{m,n} \end{bmatrix}$$

Here $a_{m,n}$ represents the element at the mth row and the nth column. When $m = n$, if the rows and the columns equal each other, then that matrix is known as a square matrix.

Since we are now familiar with the matrix notation, let's dive into some basic operations that are performed on matrices for simple calculations. Along the way, we will keep on seeing other forms of matrices that are important to the field of quantum computing.

Transpose of a matrix

We get the **transpose** of a matrix when we interchange the rows with the columns or the columns with the rows. For example, we can define a matrix A and calculate its transpose as follows:

$A = \begin{bmatrix} a & b & c \\ d & e & f \\ g & h & i \end{bmatrix}$. The transpose of A is given as $A^T = \begin{bmatrix} a & d & g \\ b & e & h \\ c & f & i \end{bmatrix}$, where T is the transpose.

It can be observed that by taking the transpose of matrix A, the diagonal entries – $a, e,$ and i – remain unchanged for A^T. If $= A^T$, then the matrix is a symmetric matrix. Now you can observe that symmetric matrices or operators are useful because they are able to represent the scaling of different axes, which can be the computational basis for our quantum computation. It is worth observing that $(A^T)^T = A$, which you can verify for yourself. For these reasons, the transpose of a matrix is an important concept to study in quantum computing.

Another important property to note here is that symmetric matrices represent the scaling of the computational basis, and asymmetric matrices represent the level of rotation of the computational basis. The rotation and scaling are the fundamental transformations that a matrix can represent.

If a matrix has complex entries such as $C = \begin{bmatrix} 1 & 2+i \\ 3-i & -i \end{bmatrix}$, then we always do

a **conjugate transpose or adjoint** of such matrices, which is denoted by $C^\dagger = \bar{C}^T$. We can perform the transpose of C first and then do the conjugation, or vice versa:

$$C^\dagger = \begin{bmatrix} 1 & 3+i \\ 2-i & i \end{bmatrix}$$

Just as we saw with the definition of a symmetric matrix, if $C = C^\dagger$, that is, the matrix is equal to its adjoint, then it is known as a Hermitian matrix.

Let's see how we can perform basic arithmetic operations on matrices such as addition and multiplication. Let's start with addition.

Matrix addition

Now, let's see how we can add two matrices. Let's define matrices A and B. Matrix addition is defined only for square matrices. We will look at a general case and then see an example:

$$A + B = \begin{bmatrix} a & b \\ c & d \end{bmatrix} + \begin{bmatrix} e & f \\ g & h \end{bmatrix} = \begin{bmatrix} a+e & b+f \\ c+g & d+h \end{bmatrix} = C$$

Our example for illustrating the addition of matrices is as follows:

$$A = \begin{bmatrix} 1 & 2 \\ 3 & 4 \end{bmatrix} \text{ and } B = \begin{bmatrix} 5 & 6 \\ 7 & 8 \end{bmatrix}, \text{ then } A + B = \begin{bmatrix} 1+5 & 2+6 \\ 3+7 & 4+8 \end{bmatrix} = \begin{bmatrix} 6 & 8 \\ 10 & 12 \end{bmatrix}$$

It can be observed that the corresponding elements are added together in matrix addition. The same method can be followed for matrix subtraction as well.

Let's see the properties of matrix addition. For A, B, and C matrices with size m x n, we have the following:

- Commutative: $A + B = B + A$

- Associative: $A + (B + C) = (A + B) + C$

- Additive identity: $A + O = A$, where O is a unique m x n matrix that, when added to A, gives back A

- Additive inverse: $A + B = O$, where $B = -A$

- Transpose property: $(A + B)^T = A^T + B^T$

Next, we will look at matrix multiplication.

Matrix multiplication

Let's look at the matrix multiplication process, which will later help us to understand multiple quantum gates applied to qubits in *Chapter 2*, *Quantum Bits, Quantum Measurements, and Quantum Logic Gates*. This is defined when the number of columns of the first matrix is equal to the number of rows of the second matrix. Let's take an example of a general case for matrix multiplication:

$$A * B = \begin{bmatrix} a & b \\ c & d \end{bmatrix} \begin{bmatrix} e & f \\ g & h \end{bmatrix} = \begin{bmatrix} a*e+b*g & a*f+b*h \\ c*e+d*g & c*f+d*h \end{bmatrix} = C$$

We take this example and multiply A and B together as shown here:

$$A * B = \begin{bmatrix} 1 & 2 \\ 3 & 4 \end{bmatrix} \begin{bmatrix} 5 & 6 \\ 7 & 8 \end{bmatrix} = \begin{bmatrix} 1*5+2*7 & 1*6+2*8 \\ 3*5+4*7 & 3*6+4*8 \end{bmatrix} = \begin{bmatrix} 5+14 & 6+16 \\ 15+28 & 18+32 \end{bmatrix}$$
$$= \begin{bmatrix} 19 & 22 \\ 43 & 50 \end{bmatrix}$$

Now, if we define an operator $K = \begin{bmatrix} 1 & 0 \\ 0 & -1 \end{bmatrix}$ and make it operate on the qubit $|0>$, which

is like $K|0>$, we can get $\begin{bmatrix} 1 & 0 \\ 0 & -1 \end{bmatrix}\begin{bmatrix} 1 \\ 0 \end{bmatrix} = \begin{bmatrix} 1*1+0*0 \\ 0*1+(-1*0) \end{bmatrix} = \begin{bmatrix} 1 \\ 0 \end{bmatrix}$. We see that $|0>$

remains unchanged by the operation of K. But if you apply $K|1>$, then you will get $-|1>$ and you can verify it yourself! This means that the operator K changes the sign of the qubit only when it is in the $|1>$ state.

It is useful to remember that $(AB)^T = B^T A^T$, and similarly, for complex matrices, $(AB)^\dagger = B^\dagger A^\dagger$. It will be a good exercise for you to prove that matrix multiplication is not commutative, which means that for any two matrices A and B, $A * B \neq B * A$.

Let's see the properties of matrix multiplication. For A, B, and C matrices with size $m \times n$, we have the following:

- Associative: $A(BC) = (AB)C$

- Distributive: $A(B + C) = AB + AC$ and $(A + B)C = AC + BC$

- Multiplicative identity: $I_m A = A I_n = A$

For two scalars c and d, a few properties on scalar multiplication are provided as follows:

1. $A(cB) = c(AB) = (cA)B$

2. $(c + d)A = cA + dA$

3. $c(A + B) = cA + cB$

4. $(cd)A = c(dA)$

5. $(cA)^T = cA^T$

We have now discussed some basic arithmetic operations on matrices. Now let's see how we can calculate the inverse of a matrix.

Inverse of a matrix

The **inverse** of a matrix represents the undoing of a transformation that has been done by a matrix. So, if the operator K transforms the vector space into some other space, then the inverse of K, denoted as K^{-1}, can be used to bring back the original vector space.

Let's see the calculation of an inverse of a 2x2 matrix. For a 2x2 matrix, the inverse is defined as follows: $A = \begin{bmatrix} a & b \\ c & d \end{bmatrix}$ then $A^{-1} = \frac{1}{ad - bc} \begin{bmatrix} d & -b \\ -c & a \end{bmatrix}$.

If we take $A = \begin{bmatrix} 1 & 2 \\ 3 & 4 \end{bmatrix}$, then its inverse can be calculated as shown:

$$A^{-1} = \frac{1}{1*4 - 2*3} \begin{bmatrix} 4 & -2 \\ -3 & 1 \end{bmatrix} = \frac{1}{-2} \begin{bmatrix} 4 & -2 \\ -3 & 1 \end{bmatrix}.$$

For an operator K, if $KK^{\dagger} = K^{\dagger}K = I$, which means $K^{-1} = K^{\dagger}$, then the operator is known as a **unitary** operator. I is the identity matrix whose diagonal entries are 1 and the rest are 0. The concept of a unitary operator and transformation are important because according to the postulate of quantum mechanics, time evolution in a quantum system is unitary. This means that these operators preserve the probabilities, and in a more mathematical sense, they preserve the length and angles of the vectors (quantum states). It is worth to note that eigenvalues of a unitary matrix is of a unit modulus.

Most of the time, a unitary matrix is denoted by U.

Some interesting properties of unitary matrices are as follows:

- For any two complex vectors a and b, the unitary preserves their inner product, so $< Ua, Ub > = < a, b >$.

- Since U commutes with its conjugate transpose ($U^*U = UU^*$), it is called a normal matrix.

- The columns of U form an orthonormal basis of $\mathbb{C}^n$.

- The rows of U form an orthonormal basis of $\mathbb{C}^n$.

- U is an invertible matrix with the property $U^{-1} = U^*$.

- The eigenvectors of a unitary matrix are orthogonal.

Next, we will discuss the determinant and trace of a matrix and show how they can be calculated.

The determinant and trace of a matrix

The **determinant** represents the volume of an n-dimensional parallelepiped formed by the columns of any matrix or an operator. The determinant is a function that takes a square matrix as an input gives a single number as an output. It tells us the linear transformation change for area or volume. For a 2x2 matrix, the determinant is calculated as follows:

$$A = \begin{bmatrix} a & b \\ c & d \end{bmatrix} \text{ then } \det(A) = \begin{vmatrix} a & b \\ c & d \end{vmatrix} = ad - bc.$$

For a 3x3 matrix, the determinant is calculated like this:

$$B = \begin{bmatrix} a & b & c \\ d & e & f \\ g & h & i \end{bmatrix} \text{ then }$$

$$\det(B) = a \begin{vmatrix} e & f \\ h & i \end{vmatrix} - b \begin{vmatrix} d & f \\ g & i \end{vmatrix} + c \begin{vmatrix} d & e \\ g & h \end{vmatrix} = a(ei - fh) - b(di - fg) + c(dh - eg)$$

It is worth pointing out that the determinant of a unitary matrix is 1, meaning

$|\det(U)| = 1$. As an exercise, prove that the matrix $U = \begin{bmatrix} \dfrac{1}{\sqrt{2}} & \dfrac{1}{\sqrt{2}} \\ \dfrac{1}{\sqrt{2}} & -\dfrac{1}{\sqrt{2}} \end{bmatrix}$ is a unitary matrix with a determinant of 1.

The **trace** of a matrix or operator is defined as the sum of all the diagonal elements. This is given as follows:

$$\text{If } A = \begin{bmatrix} a & b & c \\ d & e & f \\ g & h & i \end{bmatrix}, \text{then } Tr(A) = a + e + i$$

An interesting property to note is that the trace of a matrix also represents the sum of the eigenvalues of the matrix and is a linear operation.

Let's now dive into the expectation value of an operator and its usefulness.

The expectation value (mean value) of an operator

Suppose we prepare a quantum state $|\psi>$ many times and we also measure an operator K each time when we prepare that state. This means we now have a lot of measurements with us, so it is natural for us to determine the cumulative effect of the measurement results. This can be done by taking the **expected value** of the operator K. This is given as follows:

$$< K > = < \psi|K|\psi >$$

So, the expected value is the average of all the measurement results, which are weighted by the likelihood values of the measurement occurring.

Now that we've learned about the various operations that can be performed on operators, let's learn about some important calculations that are performed on operators: eigenvalues and eigenvectors.

The eigenvalues and eigenvectors of an operator

Eigenvalues and **eigenvectors** are among the most important topics covered in linear algebra literature as they have a lot of significant applications in various fields. Apart from quantum computing, eigenvalues and eigenvectors find applications in machine learning (for instance, in dimensionality reduction, image compression, and signal processing), communication systems design, designing bridges in civil engineering, Google's Page Rank algorithm, and more.

Conceptually, we search for those vectors that do not change directions under a linear transformation but whose magnitude can change. This is essentially the concept of eigenvectors and eigenvalues. Just as we try to find roots of a polynomial, which are those values of a polynomial that restrict the shape of the polynomial, eigenvectors are those vectors that try to prevent a linear transformation from happening in the vector space, and eigenvalues represent the magnitude of those eigenvectors. Now, since we have an intuitive understanding of the concept, we can look at the more mathematical elements and the calculation.

A vector is called an eigenvector of an operator K if the following relation is satisfied:

$$K|\psi> = \lambda|\psi>$$

Here, $|\psi>$ is the eigenvector and λ is the associated eigenvalue, which is also a complex number. If the eigenvectors of an operator represent the computational basis, then any state $|\psi>$ can be written as the linear combination of the eigenvectors associated with the operator K. This is true for diagonal matrices, where there are only diagonal entries and the rest of the elements are zero. The inverse of a diagonal matrix is as simple as just taking a reciprocal value of the diagonal elements. This makes a lot of practical applications simpler.

Now we will show the calculation process for eigenvalues and eigenvectors. Let's consider a 2x2 matrix; let's define a matrix A:

$$A = \begin{bmatrix} 5 & -3 \\ -6 & 2 \end{bmatrix}$$

The characteristic equation for A that is used to calculate eigenvalues is given by the following:

$$|A - \lambda I| = 0$$

We apply the values of A and the identity matrix:

$$\left| \begin{bmatrix} 5 & -3 \\ -6 & 2 \end{bmatrix} - \lambda \begin{bmatrix} 1 & 0 \\ 0 & 1 \end{bmatrix} \right| = 0$$

Simplifying further, we will get the following:

$$\left| \begin{bmatrix} 5 & -3 \\ -6 & 2 \end{bmatrix} - \begin{bmatrix} \lambda & 0 \\ 0 & \lambda \end{bmatrix} \right| = 0$$

Now, subtracting λ from A, we have the following:

$$\left| \begin{bmatrix} 5 - \lambda & -3 \\ -6 & 2 - \lambda \end{bmatrix} \right| = 0$$

Now we will use the following relation to gain the characteristic equation of this matrix by calculating the determinant:

$$\lambda^2 - Tr(A)\lambda + |A| = 0$$

Here $Tr(A) = 7$ and $|A| = -8$, so we get the equation as follows:

$$\lambda^2 - 7\lambda - 8 = 0$$

If we factorize the preceding characteristic equation, then we will get this:

$$\lambda_1 = -1, \lambda_2 = 8$$

These are the eigenvalues of the operator A.

Now we will move on to calculating the eigenvectors. Let $\lambda_1 = -1$, and let's put this value into the following equation:

$$(A - \lambda I)X1 = 0$$

$$\begin{bmatrix} 6 & -3 \\ -6 & 3 \end{bmatrix} \begin{bmatrix} x1 \\ x2 \end{bmatrix} = \begin{bmatrix} 0 \\ 0 \end{bmatrix}$$

The equations can be formed as follows:

$$6x1 - 3x2 = 0$$

$$-6x1 + 3x2 = 0$$

Since both the equations are the same, by simplifying and solving further, we will get the following:

$$2x1 - x2 = 0$$
$$x2 = 2x1$$

Now we can choose a value for $x1$ to have the eigenvectors. The simplest value is 1. Then, we will have the eigenvector $X1 = \begin{bmatrix} 1 \\ 2 \end{bmatrix}$. In a very similar process, $X2 = \begin{bmatrix} 1 \\ -1 \end{bmatrix}$; you can verify it yourself.

Let's now consider solving an example for a 3x3 matrix also. We will define a matrix called A:

$$A = \begin{bmatrix} 8 & -8 & -2 \\ 4 & -3 & -2 \\ 3 & -4 & 1 \end{bmatrix}$$

The characteristic equation for A that is used for calculating eigenvalues is as follows:

$$|A - \lambda I| = 0$$

We then apply the values of A and the identity matrix:

$$\left| \begin{bmatrix} 8 & -8 & -2 \\ 4 & -3 & -2 \\ 3 & -4 & 1 \end{bmatrix} - \lambda \begin{bmatrix} 1 & 0 & 0 \\ 0 & 1 & 0 \\ 0 & 0 & 1 \end{bmatrix} \right| = 0$$

Simplifying a bit gives us the following:

$$\left| \begin{bmatrix} 8 & -8 & -2 \\ 4 & -3 & -2 \\ 3 & -4 & 1 \end{bmatrix} - \begin{bmatrix} \lambda & 0 & 0 \\ 0 & \lambda & 0 \\ 0 & 0 & \lambda \end{bmatrix} \right| = 0$$

Subtracting λ from A, we have this:

$$\left| \begin{bmatrix} 8 - \lambda & -8 & -2 \\ 4 & -3 - \lambda & -2 \\ 3 & -4 & 1 - \lambda \end{bmatrix} \right| = 0$$

We will use a technique to simplify the calculations to calculate the determinant of this large matrix, which is as follows:

$$\lambda^3 - Tr(A)\lambda^2 + (Sum\ of\ Diagonal\ Minors)\ \lambda - |A| = 0$$

For calculating the minors, we just hide the rows and columns for the element for which we want to calculate the minor and then take the determinant of the remaining values.

Considering $a_{1,1} = 8$, we hide the first row and the first column, and the remaining elements become the following:

$$\begin{vmatrix} -3 & -2 \\ -4 & 1 \end{vmatrix} = -11$$

For $a_{2,2} = -3$, we hide the second row and the second column, and the remaining elements become this:

$$\begin{vmatrix} 8 & -2 \\ 3 & 1 \end{vmatrix} = 14$$

For $a_{3,3} = 1$, we get the following:

$$\begin{vmatrix} 8 & -8 \\ 4 & -3 \end{vmatrix} = 8$$

Therefore, the sum of the diagonal becomes $-11 + 14 + 8 = 11$. The trace of A is -6 and $|A|$ is 6.

The final relation is this:

$$\lambda^3 - 6\lambda^2 + 11\lambda - 6 = 0$$

A calculator can be utilized to calculate the roots of this polynomial, and by doing so, you will get the roots of this cubic polynomial as follows:

$$\lambda_1 = 1, \lambda_2 = 2 \ and \ \lambda_3 = 3$$

These are the eigenvalues of the operator A.

We will start by calculating the eigenvectors for A. We will start with $\lambda_1 = 1$ and put this value in the following equation:

$$(A - \lambda I)X1 = 0$$

$$\begin{bmatrix} 7 & -8 & -2 \\ 4 & -4 & -2 \\ 3 & -4 & 0 \end{bmatrix} \begin{bmatrix} x1 \\ x2 \\ x3 \end{bmatrix} = \begin{bmatrix} 0 \\ 0 \\ 0 \end{bmatrix}$$

We will now utilize Cramer's rule to solve the preceding system of linear equations.

Consider any two rows or columns in the preceding matrix where adding or subtracting the values does not give 0 as an answer:

$$7x1 - 8x2 - 2x3 = 0$$

$$4x1 - 4x2 - 2x3 = 0$$

We can write $x1, x2,$ and $x3$ as the numerators and then write the determinants as the respective denominators, where the entries are coefficients from the other variables. This can be done as follows:

$$\frac{x1}{\begin{vmatrix} -8 & -2 \\ -4 & -2 \end{vmatrix}} = \frac{-x2}{\begin{vmatrix} 7 & -2 \\ 4 & -2 \end{vmatrix}} = \frac{x3}{\begin{vmatrix} 7 & -8 \\ 4 & -4 \end{vmatrix}}$$

We observe that for $x1$, we take the coefficients of $x2$ and $x3$ as the determinant entries by hiding the $x1$ terms. A similar process is done for others as well.

Solving the equation further, we will get the following result:

$$\frac{x1}{16 - 8} = \frac{-x2}{-6} = \frac{x3}{-28 + 32}$$

After solving a bit more, we have the following equation:

$$\frac{x1}{8} = \frac{x2}{6} = \frac{x3}{4}$$

Therefore, the eigenvector $X1 = \begin{bmatrix} 8 \\ 6 \\ 4 \end{bmatrix}$, which can be simplified further to be

$$X1 = \begin{bmatrix} 4 \\ 3 \\ 2 \end{bmatrix} \text{ for } \lambda_1 = 1 \quad .$$

Similarly, for $\lambda_2 = 2, X2 = \begin{bmatrix} 3 \\ 2 \\ 1 \end{bmatrix}$ and $\lambda_3 = 3, X3 = \begin{bmatrix} 2 \\ 1 \\ 1 \end{bmatrix}$.

We saw how to calculate the eigenvalues and eigenvectors of matrices/operators. Next, we are going to discuss an important concept known as tensor products.

Tensor products

In quantum computing, we often have to deal with two, three, or multi-qubit systems instead of only one qubit. A two-qubit system would be $|00>$, for example. Similarly, a three-qubit system would be $|000>$. To deal with such composite systems, we use **tensor products**, which help us in performing various mathematical calculations on composite systems. The formal definition of a tensor product, as provided by *An Introduction to Quantum Computing*, is as follows:

> *The tensor product is a way of combining spaces, vectors or operators. An example is the union of two spaces H1 and H2 where each belongs to H, whose dimensions are n and m respectively. The tensor product of H1⊗ H2 generates a new spacetime H of dimension nxm.*

You can find the referenced text in the *Further reading* section.

Let's now look at the calculation of tensor products for column vectors, which is the most common way of denoting a quantum state. Let's define two quantum states:

$$|\psi> = \begin{bmatrix} a \\ b \end{bmatrix} \text{ and } |\alpha> = \begin{bmatrix} c \\ d \end{bmatrix}$$

The tensor product of the two states is as follows:

$$|\psi> \otimes |\alpha> = \begin{bmatrix} a \\ b \end{bmatrix} \otimes \begin{bmatrix} c \\ d \end{bmatrix} = \begin{bmatrix} ac \\ ad \\ bc \\ bd \end{bmatrix}$$

Using this, we can now describe the column vector representation of a two-qubit system. Suppose we consider $|00>$. This can be written like this:

$$|0> \otimes |0> = \begin{bmatrix} 1 \\ 0 \end{bmatrix} \otimes \begin{bmatrix} 1 \\ 0 \end{bmatrix} = \begin{bmatrix} 1 \\ 0 \\ 0 \\ 0 \end{bmatrix}$$

The tensor product has a distributive property, which is shown as follows:

$$|\psi> \otimes(|\alpha> + |\beta>) = |\psi> \otimes |\alpha> + |\psi> \otimes |\beta>.$$

For example, $\begin{bmatrix} 1 \\ 0 \end{bmatrix} \otimes \left(\begin{bmatrix} 0 \\ 1 \end{bmatrix} + \begin{bmatrix} 1 \\ 1 \end{bmatrix} \right) = \begin{bmatrix} 1 \\ 0 \end{bmatrix} \otimes \begin{bmatrix} 0 \\ 1 \end{bmatrix} + \begin{bmatrix} 1 \\ 0 \end{bmatrix} \otimes \begin{bmatrix} 1 \\ 1 \end{bmatrix}.$

Proving all the properties of tensor products requires knowledge of abstract algebra and is out of the scope of this book. I highly recommend that you check out the books *Finite-Dimensional Vector Space* and *Algebra* by S. Lang (see the *Further reading* section) to gain a better understanding of the properties of tensor products.

The calculation of tensor products for two operators is given here. Let's define two 2x2 operators:

$$A = \begin{bmatrix} a & b \\ c & d \end{bmatrix} \text{ and } B = \begin{bmatrix} e & f \\ g & h \end{bmatrix}$$

The tensor product of operators A and B is shown here:

$$A \otimes B = \begin{bmatrix} aB & bB \\ cB & dB \end{bmatrix} = \begin{bmatrix} ae & af & be & bf \\ ag & ah & bg & bh \\ ce & cf & de & df \\ cg & ch & dg & dh \end{bmatrix}$$

Tensor products are very useful to verify the **entanglement** of quantum states. Entanglement is a useful property in quantum mechanics where two or more quantum systems can have some properties correlated with each other. As a consequence, knowing the properties of the first system can help to decipher the properties of the second system instantly.

With the conclusion of our discussion of tensor products, we also conclude our discussion of linear algebra. From the next section onward, we will discuss the visualization aspects of quantum computing, such as coordinate systems and complex numbers. We will also discuss probability theory in relation to quantum computing.

Coordinate systems, complex numbers, and probability

In this section, we will dive into three crucial topics of mathematics that are used heavily in quantum computation – **coordinate systems**, **complex numbers**, and **probability**. Coordinate systems are useful for the graphical representation of quantum states and to describe mathematical calculations in a visual format. After a fundamental understanding of coordinate systems, we will move on to complex numbers and look at their relationship with coordinate systems. You will see the simplicity of calculations carried out using the complex plane. Finally, we will learn about some fundamental probability theory concepts that are useful to quantum computing. Let's start with coordinate systems.

Introducing coordinate systems

In this section, you will learn about visualizing **quantum states**, which are just vectors in a mathematical sense. This will be useful for visualizing the geometry of quantum states and the various operations that you have already learned about in the previous sections. We will start with **2D coordinate systems** and then move on to **3D coordinates** before learning about the **polar coordinate system**.

2D Cartesian coordinate systems

Cartesian coordinates are one of the most useful graphical ways of visualizing 2D and 3D planes. *Figure 1.1* shows the 2D coordinate system and displays the coordinates and vectors present in the space:

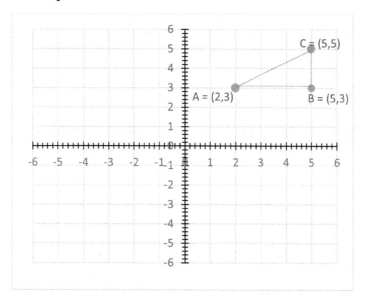

Figure 1.1 – A 2D Cartesian coordinate system

The coordinates in the Cartesian plane (Euclidean space) are denoted as (x,y), where the horizontal line is the x-axis and the vertical line is the y-axis; for example, in the preceding figure, three coordinates are represented as **A = (2,3)**, **B = (5,3)**, and **C = (5,5)**. The point **O = (0,0)** is the origin. Using these coordinate values and the Pythagoras theorem for right triangles, the length AC can be calculated as $AC^2 = AB^2 + BC^2$. The distances in the Cartesian plane are called the Euclidean distance. This can be used to plot various kinds of functions, such as polynomial curves, circles, hyperbola, and exponentials. Cartesian coordinates can also be written in column vector form as $\binom{2}{3}$.

We will now move on to 3D coordinate systems and understanding their usefulness.

3D Cartesian coordinate systems

In a 3D Cartesian system, we have 3 axes – the x-axis, the y-axis, and the z-axis. Often, we have to use 3D representations of vectors to understand the higher-dimensional aspect of quantum computing. *Figure 1.2* shows the 3D coordinate system, and this coordinate system turns out to be very useful for understanding and visualizing higher-dimensional computations:

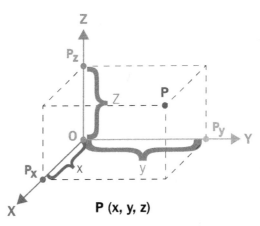

Figure 1.2 – A 3D Cartesian coordinates system

The coordinates can be denoted as (x,y,z). In this case, the x-axis is the tilted axis, the y-axis is the horizontal axis, and the z-axis represents the height or vertical axis. The mathematical calculations used for 2D systems can also be utilized for 3D systems. This 3D coordinate system will be very useful when we discuss **Bloch sphere** representations of qubits in *Chapter 2, Quantum Bits, Quantum Measurements, and Quantum Logic Gates*.

Next, we will introduce the polar coordinates system and discuss the conversion of coordinates between Cartesian and polar coordinate systems.

Converting Cartesian systems to polar coordinate systems

For simple calculations and complex numbers (covered in the next section), it is useful to convert Cartesian coordinates to polar coordinates, which involves using trigonometric functions. Polar coordinates are easily represented using a unit circle given in a 2D Cartesian plane. *Figure 1.3* shows the polar coordinate system:

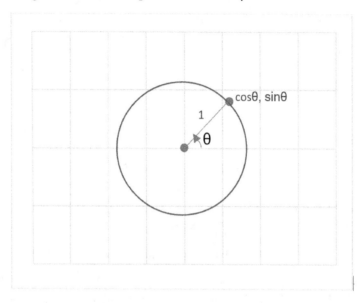

Figure 1.3 – Polar coordinate system

In a polar coordinate system, the (x,y) coordinates are represented as $(r\ cos\theta, r\ sin\theta)$, where r is the radius and is given as $r = \sqrt{x^2 + y^2}$ and $\theta = tan^{-1}\frac{y}{x}$ in degrees. To convert degrees into radians, multiply the degree value by $\frac{\pi}{180}$. To convert radians back into degrees, multiply by $\frac{180}{\pi}$. If you want to convert from polar to Cartesian, then you can use $x = r\ cos\theta$ and $y = r\ sin\theta$. The polar representation that we learned about will be very useful for the calculations related to complex numbers.

Complex numbers and the complex plane

Jerome Cardan introduced the concept of **complex numbers** when it was found that while solving the roots of a quadratic polynomial, the square roots of negative numbers were encountered, which were not covered by real numbers. Due to this, the imaginary unit $i = \sqrt{-1}$ was introduced. This helped to write numbers such as $\sqrt{-a} = \sqrt{a}i$

A complex number consists of real and imaginary parts. It is defined as follows:

$$z = a + ib$$

Here, a and b are real numbers. In this, a is the real component and $i\,b$ is the imaginary component, where b is the imaginary coefficient. Again, a complex number can be represented as a vector. In vector form, it $z = \begin{pmatrix} a \\ b \end{pmatrix}$. In *Figure 1.4*, the complex number $2 + 3i$ is shown:

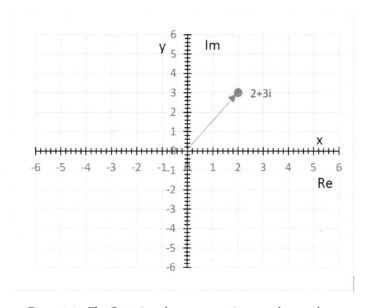

Figure 1.4 – The Cartesian plane representing complex numbers

In the preceding figure, you can see that the complex number $2 + 3i$ has been represented in a Cartesian plane, where the x-axis denotes the real component and the y-axis denotes the imaginary component, more specifically, the imaginary coefficient, which is a real number.

Performing arithmetic operations on complex numbers is fairly intuitive and usually follows the normal algebraic rules.

For example, let's see the addition of two complex numbers:

$$(-1 + 2i) + (3 + 4i) = (3 - 1) + (2 + 4)i = 2 + 6i = \binom{2}{6}$$

The addition of complex numbers is commutative and associative, as follows:

- Commutative: $z_1 + z_2 = z_2 + z_1$, for example,
  $(2 + i) + (1 - i) = (1 - i) + (2 + i)$

- Associative: $z_1 + (z_2 + z_3) = (z_1 + z_2) + z_3$, for example,
  $(2 + i) + [(1 - i) + (1 + i)] = [(2 + i) + (1 - i)] + (1 + i)$

Subtraction is similar to addition. Let's see the multiplication of two complex numbers:

$$(a + ib) * (c + id) = (ac - bd) + i(ad + bc)$$

Similar to addition, multiplication has commutative and associative properties, along with another property called the distributive property. This is shown as follows:

- Commutative: $z_1 * z_2 = z_2 * z_1$, for example,
  $(2 + i) * (1 - i) = (1 - i) * (2 + i)$

- Associative: $z_1 * (z_2 * z_3) = (z_1 * z_2) * z_3$, for example,
  $(2 + i) * [(1 - i) * (1 + i)] = [(2 + i) * (1 - i)] * (1 + i)$

- Distributive: $z_1 * (z_2 * z_3) = z_1 * z_2 + z_1 * z_3$, for example,
  $(2 + i) * [(1 - i) * (1 + i)] = (2 + i) * (1 - i) + (2 + i) * (1 + i)$

The complex conjugate of a complex number is given as follows:

$$\overline{(a + ib)} = a - ib$$

The complex conjugate shows us the reflection of the complex number in another part of the axis provided in the complex plane.

The modulus of a complex number is very similar to calculating the magnitude of a vector and is given as follows:

$$|(a + ib)| = \sqrt{a^2 + b^2}$$

We saw the polar coordinate system in the previous section and discussed how it is useful in the case of complex number representation. We will now look at using the polar coordinate system for complex number representation, which is a very important method to consider.

The main formula that connects polar coordinates with the **complex plane** is known as Euler's formula. The complex plane can be defined as a geometric visualization of the complex numbers in a 2D coordinate system, where the x-axis becomes the *real* part and the y-axis becomes the *imaginary* part. This is also known as the z-plane. *Figure 1.5* shows the complex plane along with the Euler's relation, where φ (phi) is the angle:

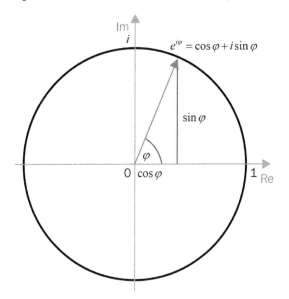

Figure 1.5 – Euler's formula representation using a unit circle

Euler's formula is given as follows:

$$e^{i\varphi} = \cos\varphi + i\sin\varphi$$

This formula helps connect the trigonometric relations with the complex exponentials. This helps us to represent a complex number in a polar representation. Let's define the complex number as follows:

$$z = x + iy$$

Here, putting $x = r\cos\varphi$ and $y = r\sin\varphi$ will give z as follows:

$$z = r\cos\varphi + ir\sin\varphi = r(\cos\varphi + i\sin\varphi) = re^{i\varphi} \text{ given as } \sqrt{x^2 + y^2} = |z| \text{ and}$$

$\varphi = \tan^{-1}\dfrac{y}{x}$ in degrees.

If you calculate $|e^{i\varphi}|$, you will see that it is always 1, and you can verify it yourself. It will require the usage of one of the most common trigonometric identities. Euler's identity is given as $e^{i\pi} + 1 = 0$ and is usually a good thing to know!

It is important to be familiar with some identities that make our mathematical calculations easier for the case of complex numbers. Two identities that are useful are these:

$$Cos\ \varphi = \frac{e^{i\varphi} + e^{-i\varphi}}{2} \text{ and } Sin\ \varphi = \frac{e^{i\varphi} - e^{-i\varphi}}{2}$$

These identities are essentially representations of common trigonometric functions in terms of their complex exponentials.

The complex conjugate of $e^{i\varphi}$ is $e^{-i\varphi}$. The complex exponential form makes the calculations a lot easier.

Let's now dive into the topic of probability and learn about its significance in the field of quantum computing.

Probability

The concept of **probability theory** has always found significance in almost every area of science and technology, and quantum computing is no exception. Probability is a useful tool for dealing with the inherent randomness of real-life situations. In this section, we will dive into the basics of probability, random variables, and the usefulness of probability in quantum computing. Let's start with the definition of probability and its basic axioms.

Probability basics and axioms

Probability, as you might have guessed, is a branch of mathematics that deals with the likelihood or chance of events occurring. It is helpful in representing the likelihood of events happening in a system in terms of mathematical language. Girolamo Cardan wrote a book called *Book on Games of Chance* that introduced the first systematic treatment of the theory of probability.

Today, the applications of probability are huge in number because probabilistic techniques are used to predict the outcomes of various situations. It is used in games, weather forecasting, sports predictions, machine learning methods, reinforcement learning in artificial intelligence, deep learning, and quantum mechanics and physics for quantum measurement theory.

In quantum measurement theory, we check and calculate the probabilities of a quantum state being collapsed to a certain state. This is where the tools of probability theory are very useful. To make a probabilistic model of an unknown situation, two important things need to be considered: **sample space** and the **law of probability**.

Let's understand sample space first. A sample space is a set or collection of all the possible outcomes of a particular event. It is usually denoted by Ω (pronounced as *omega*). For example, for an experiment of flipping a coin, we have a total of two possible outcomes, which are heads (H) and tails (T). So, the sample $space\ \Omega\ =\ \{H, T\}$.

The law of probability assigns a numerical value (non-negative) to a particular event that represents the likelihood of that event occurring out of all the possible events. This is usually given as follows:

$$Probability\ of\ event\ happening\ =\ \frac{Number\ of\ ways\ the\ event\ can\ happen}{Total\ number\ of\ outcomes}$$

For example, the probability that tails can occur when we flip a coin is as follows:

$$P(T) = \frac{1}{2}$$

Now we will look at some fundamental axioms of probability that are necessary for understanding the law of probability:

- **Probability can't be negative**: This means that the probability of events from the sample space must be greater than or equal to zero. $P(A) \geq 0$ for every A.

- **Probability addition**: For two disjointed events A and B, their probability of union is given by the sum of their individual probabilities. $P(A \cup B) = P(A) + P(B)$ when $P(A)$ and $P(B)$ are independent events. If events are not independent, then $P(A \cup B) = P(A) + P(B) - P(A$ disjoint $B)$.

- **The sum of all probabilities must be 1**: The probability of the entire sample space must be equal to 1. $P(\Omega) = 1$.

It is important to mention that $P(H) = 1 - \frac{1}{2} = \frac{1}{2}$, which is a complementary probability, and $P(H) + P(T) = 1$. Also, the probability values of a certain event

A from the sample space must be $0 \leq P(A) \leq 1$ so that the sum of all the probabilities of events present in the sample space adds up to 1. We observed that probabilities often have a numerical value, but many variables in the real world do not possess numerical values, so now we will discuss this issue in the next section by introducing random variables.

Discrete random variables and probability mass functions

Many times in the real world, the outcome of the events that we measure may not be numerical in nature. In those cases, **random variables** come to our rescue.

Random variables entail a mapping process that assigns a numerical value to the outcome of the events happening in a sample space. So, the random variable works as a function by taking outcomes from the sample space and giving them a numerical value taken in a real number line. In our case, we will be discussing **discrete random variables**.

Discrete random variables can be associated with a probability distribution, which is known as the **Probability Mass Function** (**PMF**). The PMF provides the probability of each of the numerical values that a discrete random variable can take. The sum of elements of the PMF always adds up to 1.

Let's consider a situation where a coin is flipped and every time heads comes up, you win $10, and every time tails comes up, you lose $10.

In random variable notation, this can be described as follows:

$$x = X(w) = \begin{cases} +10, & if\ w = H \\ -10, & if\ w = T \end{cases}$$

To describe the PMF for this coin flipping experiment, we have this:

$$f_X(x) = \begin{cases} \frac{1}{2}, if\ x = +10 \\ \frac{1}{2}, if\ x = -10 \end{cases}$$

Randomness, as we have seen, is a very useful phenomenon and has a wide variety of applications. In practical coding implementation, we have pseudo-random number generators that generate numbers between 0 and 1, but the process of generation is not truly random. This process is called sampling. One of the most useful benefits of a quantum computer would be to generate truly random numbers.

We will now focus our attention on calculating the mean and variance when data is provided to us.

Expectation (mean value) and variance calculation

The expectation is simply the mean of a random variable. It is the weighted mean of all the possible values of a random variable. The weights used for the purpose of expectation calculation are in proportion to the probabilities of the outcome of events. From the perspective of the PMF, the expected value of the PMF denotes the center of gravity of that PMF distribution. This is like calculating a linear combination of outcomes where the weights are the probabilities. Mean is also known as the first moment in statistics.

The formula that is used to calculate the expectation is as follows:

$$< X > = \mathbb{E}[X] = \sum_{x} x \, P(X = x)$$

As an example, for a 6-sided die toss, we have the probability of each side as $\frac{1}{6}$. Now, to calculate the expectation of this event, we need to multiply the probability by each of the numbered sides (the values of the outcomes), as shown here:

$$< X > = \frac{1}{6}(1) + \frac{1}{6}(2) + \frac{1}{6}(3) + \frac{1}{6}(4) + \frac{1}{6}(5) + \frac{1}{6}(6) = \frac{21}{6} = 3.5$$

Variance is the measure of dispersion around the mean value. Intuitively, variance is about measuring the expected value of dispersion or the spread of the random variables from their mean value. Variance is also known as the second moment in statistics.

Therefore, the formula for variance becomes as follows:

$$Var(X) = \mathbb{E}[(X - \mathbb{E}[X])^2] = \mathbb{E}[X^2] - \mathbb{E}[X]^2 = \sum_{x}(x - \mathbb{E}[X])^2 \mathbb{P}(X = x)$$

Again, by considering the same 6-sided die example, we can calculate its variance as follows:

$$Var(X) = \mathbb{E}[X^2] - \mathbb{E}[X]^2 = \frac{1}{6}(1^2 + 2^2 + 3^2 + 4^2 + 5^2 + 6^2) - 3.5^2 = \frac{91}{6} - 12.25$$
$$= 2.92$$

Essentially, variance defines the spread from the mean value, and in our case, the value is 2.92. In the next section, we will learn about the significance of the law of large numbers.

The law of large numbers

The law of large numbers states that the average or mean value of a large number of trials will be closer to the expected value and will tend to be closer and closer as the number of trials increases significantly.

In quantum computing, we perform measurements of probabilities of quantum states occurring after the quantum states are passed through a quantum circuit. This is done a number of times because the quantum computers that we have today are noisy and the quantum states that are prepared in the computer carry a lot of noise. So, to get accurate probability measurements, we run the measurements multiple times, and this is where the law of large numbers comes in. After a certain number of iterations of measurements, we start getting closer to the expected value, which is the ideal value.

With the conclusion of our discussion of probability, we also conclude our discussion of the essential mathematical concepts that are required for quantum computing. Let's now dive into the basics of algorithmic thinking and computer science that are essential for understanding quantum computing.

Defining computational thinking

The title of this book is *Quantum Computing with Silq Programming*, which means that quantum programming is at the heart of this book, and programming is a discipline that comes from computer science. Quantum computing is essentially a blend of many disciplines, including mathematics, quantum physics, quantum mechanics, and computer science. The concepts of quantum mechanics and physics will be introduced throughout the book as and when required. We have already covered the basic mathematics required for quantum computing, and now we are going to focus on another crucial aspect – computer science.

Computational thinking involves approaches to or methods of problem solving where we utilize ideas from computer science and express the problems and their solutions in such a way that the computer can execute them. This process involves breaking a large problem into smaller parts and then recognizing the pattern present in those small problems, finally developing a step-by-step solution to that problem. This is an efficient process to problem solving where once we convert a real-world complex problem so that a computer can understand it, a computer can then be used to solve the problem. This kind of thinking process is not only important to solve problems in science but is equally beneficial in other fields as well, such as social science, medical science, education, and business.

Computational thinking has four very important characteristics or skills associated with it:

- Decomposition
- Pattern recognition
- Data representation and abstraction
- Algorithmic design

In this section, we are going to discuss the first three skills, and then in the next section, we will discuss algorithms. Algorithms deserve a separate special section because they are a very significant aspect on their own, and covering them will later help us to understand various quantum algorithms. The algorithms covered here will be basic; discussing anything more advanced is beyond the scope of the book. In the next section, we will start our discussion of decomposition.

Decomposition

Decomposition is the first pillar of the computational thinking process. In the real world, problems are very complex to solve and require a lot of effort to reach a particular solution; therefore, it is much easier to divide a problem into smaller sub-problems and then work on them individually, because smaller ones are usually easier to solve. It may be that the smaller sub-problems are complex in themselves, and in that case, they can be divided into further smaller sub-problems. This process is also known as decomposition.

For example, suppose that you want to develop a mobile banking application so that offline transactions can be shifted completely to online. For this kind of problem, you can start by considering for which platform you would like to make your application, such as Android or iOS. Suppose you chose Android: you would then need to know some programming basics for Android as well. You will also be required to use Android tools to make the app. After all this, you might go about designing the app and its various functionalities step by step to complete the mobile banking application. That would all be a process of decomposition.

Now let's move on to pattern recognition and learn about its usefulness with regard to the computational thinking process.

Pattern recognition

Now we move on to another important pillar of the computational thinking process, **pattern recognition**. In the previous section, we discussed decomposition, where we divide a big problem into smaller sub-problems and then work on them. Often, we find some kind of pattern in the sub-problems that occurs frequently for most sub-problems. It's helpful to find this pattern to solve the sub-problems. Once we solve it once in one sub-problem, the rest becomes easy, because the same pattern is followed by other sub-problems as well. This then entails a repetitive process that can be followed until the problem is solved.

For example, consider the banking application we mentioned previously. Here, we want to include a feature where people can upload their photo and their proof of identity, and then the application will match the photo provided by the customer and the proof of identity to issue a bank passbook. This is where pattern recognition comes into the picture. The photo-matching technique consists of comparing the various pixels of the customer image with their proof of identity, and this process is repeated until a match of a person is accurately found. This is applied to a large number of customers in the bank who register for their banking application.

We have now looked at the first two pillars of computational thinking. Let's now move on to data representation and abstraction.

Data representation and abstraction

Now we will discuss the third component of the computational thinking process, that is, **data representation and abstraction**. When we are solving sub-problems, we will often find that some of the details are relevant to solving the problems and others are not. So, the process of data representation and abstraction involves the identification of those characteristics that are relevant to solving the problem and removing those characteristics that are not relevant. This process is also known as abstraction and is one of the most crucial elements in computer science and programming.

Considering the same bank application example, we can apply data representation and abstraction to the problem as explained. Every bank customer who registers for the banking application needs to provide some important details, such as their name, address, phone number, date of birth, income tax details, and email address. Now, in all of this data, there is a possibility that the name, date of birth, or address might be the same for two different customers. To differentiate customers, banks provide a unique account number to each of their customers to represent the data more efficiently so that registration can be performed easily. Also, data such as hobbies and food preferences does not hold any importance and can be filtered out.

There is another aspect of the computational thinking process that includes three characteristics – **abstraction**, **automation**, and **analysis**. These are very similar to the characteristics that we saw in the previous sections. *Abstraction* involves formulating the problem itself, such as constructing a banking application. Then, we move to *automation*, where the solution is expressed, such as coding various elements of the bank processes in the application using Android; and finally, we reach *analysis*, where the solution developed is executed on a computer and then evaluated for performance improvements.

The final pillar of computational thinking, algorithms, is discussed in the next section, as it is a significant part of computational thinking and programming.

Introducing computer algorithms

In the previous section, we discussed computational thinking and three of its primary pillars. The fourth and final pillar of computational thinking is **algorithms**. In this section, we will start with the definition of the linear search algorithm and see how it works. Then, we will discuss briefly the divide-and-conquer algorithms for searching. First, let's define what an algorithm is.

Defining an algorithm

An algorithm is a proper sequence of steps or rules that can be implemented in a computer to solve problems or perform calculations. It is like a recipe used to solve problems using computational thinking and is one of the most important parts of the computational process because this is where things start to get implemented in the real world. The algorithm is the very first step to writing a computer program!

Consider the example of making tea, which involves a sequence of steps that we need to follow in a certain order to make it successful. First of all, you will require the ingredients and resources, such as water, an electric kettle, a teabag, and a cup. Now we fill the kettle with water, switch it on, and let it boil. As soon as the kettle's boiled, we pour the water into the cup and then put the teabag into the cup. We let the teabag brew there for a few minutes and then we remove it. That's it – our tea is ready!

Now consider the steps for adding two numbers as performed by a computer. We know that for this, we would require the two numbers, and we will get an answer to our problem by the addition of the two numbers.

An algorithm for this would involve defining three variables that can store those two numbers and the answer. We would perform the addition and store the answer in the third variable. Finally, we could print the value of the third variable, which has the answer. You might wonder, *can the tea-making job be done by a computer?* And the answer is yes, it can! But the process is way more complex: for that, you have to teach a robot how to make tea! For a computer algorithm, we simply use the sequence of steps as instructions that are given to the computer to solve a particular problem.

Let's now learn about the way in which a **linear search algorithm** works. This is the most basic and simple of all the searching algorithms.

The linear search algorithm

Let's consider a searching problem where we have to search for a specific element in an array and return the index of the element when it is found. Some sample Python 3 code to do the searching is given as follows:

```python
a = ['t','u','t','o','r','i','a','l']
x = 'o'
def linearsearch(a, x):
    for i in range(len(a)):
        if a[i] == x:
            return i
    return -1
print("element found at index "+str(linearsearch(a,x)))
```

The preceding code is used for a linear search operation. In linear searching, a user will provide a specific element to search in an array and the program will compare the value of the element with each of the values present in the array sequentially.

If you run the preceding code, you will get the output as element found at index 3. This is because indexing in Python starts at 0 and the *a* element is located at the sixth index. The input is the *a* element. You can clearly see in the code that each value present in the array is being compared with the input value provided. This means that the time of execution in this case linearly depends upon the length of the array.

There is another type of very famous algorithm called the divide-and-conquer algorithm, which represents the idea of computational thinking very well. It takes a bigger problem and then divides it into smaller sub-problems, solves each of those sub-problems individually, and then returns the solution, which is usually the solution to the whole problem. The most common example of a divide-and-conquer algorithm is the binary search algorithm, where the array is decomposed into parts and then searching is performed on the individual parts until the element is found.

Let's now learn about the complexity of algorithms and how we can make our algorithm implementations better in the next section.

The calculation of the time and space complexity of algorithms

In this section, we will introduce the concept of the time and space complexity of an algorithm, which helps us to measure the efficiency of an algorithm. This is important to measure because there are ways of optimizing algorithms for specific applications that are time-efficient but take up more memory. The time and space complexity will help us to analyze the performance of various algorithms and determine their use cases accordingly. We will then look at the notations that are used to calculate complexity, and finally, we will analyze and calculate the time and space complexity of a few algorithms.

Time and space complexity

Whenever we deal with algorithms, we are concerned with the speed and memory requirements of a computer program, because certain tasks require immediate real-time outputs. An example might be a self-driving car, where the camera gets real-time data from the road and then the computer processes it in real time to provide numerical outputs, which are fed into the computer controlling the car. The computer sends control signals carrying the information of the numerical outputs to the accelerator and brake sensors. For this reason, it becomes very important to calculate the complexity of any algorithm. Time is a crucial computational resource, and one that is very important to the design and optimization of algorithms.

The two complexities that we are concerned with are **time and space complexity**.

The **time complexity** of an algorithm is defined as the amount of time taken by an algorithm to execute some code in terms of the amount of input to the algorithm. This time is not an actual time in seconds, minutes, or hours; rather, it's the number of times an instruction is run by the computer. **Space complexity** is defined as the amount of memory (usually RAM) taken by the algorithm to execute some code in terms of the amount of input to the algorithm.

Let's dive into the mathematical notation used to calculate the time and space complexity of algorithms.

Notation for time and space complexity

We saw in the previous section the importance of time and space for a computer algorithm, and we saw an example of a linear search operation using Python.

For the calculation of the time and space complexity of algorithms, there are several asymptotic notations that are used to describe various aspects of the complexity of the algorithm. Let's see their definitions now.

- **Big O notation**: For the asymptotic upper bound, we use the O (big O) notation. For a given function $f(n)$, $O(f(n))$ is defined as follows:

  $O(f(n)) = \{g(n)$: There exist positive constants c and n_0 such that

  $0 \leq g(n) \leq c * f(n)$ for all $n \geq n_0\}$.

- **Big Ω notation**: For the asymptotic lower bound, we use the Ω (big Omega) notation. Mathematically, it is defined very similarly to big O notation.

  For a given function $f(n)$, $\Omega(f(n))$ is defined as follows:

  $\Omega(f(n)) = \{g(n)$: There exist positive constants c and n_0 such that
  $0 \leq c * f(n) \leq g(n)$ for all $n \geq n_0\}$.

- **Big Θ notation**: For the asymptotic tight bound, we use the Θ (big Theta) notation. For a given function $f(n)$, $\Theta(f(n))$ is defined as follows:

  $\Theta(f(n)) = \{g(n)$: There exist positive constants c_1, c_2, and n_0 such that

  $0 \leq c_1 * f(n) \leq c_2 * f(n)$ for all $n \geq n_0\}$.

Since now we have covered the essential notations, let's look at the calculation and analysis of a few algorithms to give you an idea of the usage of these notations.

Calculation and analysis of the complexity of algorithms

For the analysis of algorithms, we mostly use big O notation to calculate the worst-case and average-case scenarios of algorithms. The upper bound given by big O notation is a very useful number to analyze the performance of the algorithm. For calculation of big O, we always ignore the lower-order terms and keep only the higher-order terms, because the lower-order terms become insignificant when the input given to a particular program is very high. Big O notation will focus on the number of steps a program took to complete the execution of a program or function.

For example, let's consider the case of linear search, which we discussed earlier. In that, you will observe that the loop will run for the length of the array, which means if there are N elements in the array, then the loop will run till N^{th} element to search for the given input. This means the algorithm will take N steps to complete, and we write this as $O(N)$. There is a possibility that the given input element will be found at the first index of the array itself. In that case, the algorithm took only a single step to find the element, and the complexity then becomes $O(1)$. This means that $O(1)$ is the best-case scenario and $O(N)$ is the worst-case scenario.

However, as we discussed earlier, big O notation will generally be used to describe the worst-case scenarios of algorithms. It is also worth remembering that when the number of steps remains constant, the complexity is $O(1)$, and this is true for reading, inserting, or deleting elements at the end of an array; it does not matter how many elements the array has.

We have described $O(1)$ and $O(N)$; there is another complexity called $O(log\ N)$, and this is used with the binary search algorithm. Since in binary search we keep dividing the array into halves, for an $N = 8$ element array, it would only take $log_2\ N$ steps to find the element, meaning only 3 steps!

Let's now look at some practical code examples in Python 3, where we can calculate the time complexity of the algorithm. The first program we consider is for identifying a prime number:

```python
def prime(n):
    for i in range(2, n):
        if n % i == 0:
            return False
    return True
```

If you consider the preceding code, you can see that the loop will run from 2 to the number that is provided as input by the user. This means that the number of steps taken by the code will be equal to the number given by the user. Therefore, the code has $O(N)$ complexity. Also, an important point to consider is that big O notation throws away the constants, which means that $O(50N)$ is equal to $O(N)$.

This is because for some algorithms, it might be the case that $O(N^2)$ is faster than $O(50N)$ to a certain point, but after that point, $O(50N)$ again becomes faster, so big O notation ignores the constants. This is true, for example, for distinguishing the sorting algorithms bubble sort and selection sort, where they both have $O(N^2)$ complexity, but after a certain number of steps, selection sort becomes $O(N)$ and remains like that no matter the size of the array. It is therefore natural to see that $O(N)$ is faster than $O(N^2)$.

There are a lot of other cases as well where there are different time complexities, such as $O(N*logN)$, $O(N!)$ but they are out of the scope of this book. Computational complexity is a very broad discipline of computer science comprising various data structures and algorithms; proper analysis of all their time and space complexities would be difficult to cover in a short book. There are many good books and online courses on data structures and algorithms out there that discuss these concepts in a lot more detail.

The concepts and calculation of time and space complexity will be extremely useful when we discuss quantum algorithms and compare them with their classical versions in later chapters. For example, Grover's search algorithm will be discussed in *Chapter 9, Quantum Algorithms III – Grover's Search Algorithm and Simon's Algorithm*, where we will see that it takes $O(\sqrt{N})$ time to find an element in an unsorted list!

Summary

In this chapter, we have covered plenty of fundamental concepts related to mathematics and computer science. We also looked at the relevance of mathematical concepts in relation to quantum computing, developing algorithmic thinking to aid us in understanding various quantum algorithms. Finally, you learned about the calculation of the time and space complexity of algorithms, which will allow you to compare the complexities of quantum algorithms with the classical algorithms you see in later chapters.

In the next chapter, we will look at the basics of quantum computing and learn about quantum measurements and single qubit quantum logic gates.

Further reading

- Daniel Andrews, *Big O: How to Calculate Time and Space Complexity*, September 2019. `https://www.inoutcode.com/concepts/big-o/`.

- Dr. Basant Agarwal, Benjamin Baka, *Hands-On Data Structures and Algorithms with Python – Second Edition*, Packt; Second edition, October 2018.

- Dirac, P, (1939), *A new notation for quantum mechanics*. Mathematical Proceedings of the Cambridge Philosophical Society, 35(3), 416–418, doi:10.1017/S0305004100021162.

- P. Kaye, I.Q.C.P. Kaye, P.K.R.L.M. Mosca, R. Laflamme, M. Mosca, and I.Q.C.M.Mosca, *An Introduction to Quantum Computing*, OUP Oxford, 2007

- Paul R. Halmos, *Finite-Dimensional Vector Spaces*, First edition, Undergraduate Texts in Mathematics, Springer Publishing Company, Incorporated, 1993.

- S. Lang, *Algebra*, Third edition, Graduate Texts in Mathematics 211, Springer-Verlag, 2002.

- Grant Sanderson, 3Blue1Brown, `https://www.youtube.com/playlist?list=PLZHQObOWTQDPD3MizzM2xVFitgF8hE_ab`.

2
Quantum Bits, Quantum Measurements, and Quantum Logic Gates

In this chapter, we will learn about the fundamentals of quantum computing, which will be useful in the subsequent chapters when we start coding these aspects. Here, we will be focusing primarily on quantum bits, quantum states, and quantum logic gates. This will give you the mathematical foundations of quantum computing and give you the necessary clarity on the difference between classical and quantum bits, superposition, and the description of quantum logic gates. We will cover the following topics:

- Introduction to single quantum bits – qubits and superposition of qubits
- Illustrating qubits in different bases and the Bloch sphere representation of qubits

- Introducing quantum measurements
- Quantum logic gates

Introducing single quantum bits – qubits and superposition of qubits

In *Chapter 1*, *Essential Mathematics and Algorithmic Thinking*, in the *Vectors* section, you learned about the mathematical representations of **qubits** and we observed that vectors make the computations to be performed onto these qubits a lot easier. In this chapter, you are going to dive deeper into the notion of qubits, not only from a mathematical perspective, and gain a deep understanding of them. This will help you in the next chapter when you program qubits. The qubit is the most fundamental unit of quantum computation and information and can be thought of as the quantum equivalent of a classical bit, which is binary in nature. Classical bits can only be in the states of 0 or 1, which represent the two voltage levels *on* and *off* respectively. This means that classical bits can be only present in either of these two states – 0 or 1 – at any one time. However, qubits can be in a state that is neither 0 nor 1 but a complex linear combination of both!

As you are already aware, qubits are represented mathematically using column vectors, where the dimensions of those vectors represent the number of states a qubit be present in it. It means that when we have one qubit, we can have two states; if we have two qubits, then we can have four possible states; and for N qubits, we can have 2^N states, and these can occur simultaneously. The qubits represent energy states, namely ground and excited states. For our circuit computations and for simplicity we choose the binary values 0 and 1 to represent the ground and excited states respectively. One of the primary properties of quantum computers, in contrast to their classical counterparts, is that they are inherently parallel in nature and all the computations happen in parallel by default. In the next section, we'll take a look at the Bra-Ket notation, which is used to represent qubits.

Learning about the Bra-Ket notation for qubits

In *Chapter 1*, *Essential Mathematics and Algorithmic Thinking*, you learned about the **Bra-Ket** notation or **Dirac notation**, which uses angular brackets, < >, and the vertical bar, |, to represent the qubits.

The 0 qubit can be written as |0 > and 1 can be written as |1 >, which are called ket 0 and ket 1 respectively. Similarly, bra 0 and bra 1 can be written as < 0| and < 1| which denotes the conjugate transpose of the ket 0 and ket 1 respectively.

We can see ket representation of qubits as follows:

$$|0> = \begin{bmatrix} 1 \\ 0 \end{bmatrix} \text{ and } |1> = \begin{bmatrix} 0 \\ 1 \end{bmatrix}$$

The bra notation is as follows:

$$< 0| = \begin{bmatrix} 1 & 0 \end{bmatrix} \text{ and } < 1| = \begin{bmatrix} 0 & 1 \end{bmatrix}$$

If the states contain complex values then the bra will be a complex conjugate of the ket. To illustrate this, let's consider an example. Let's define a ket state to be complex:

$$|a> = \begin{bmatrix} 1 - i \\ 10 + i \end{bmatrix}$$

The bra of a becomes as follows:

$$< a| = \begin{bmatrix} 1 + i & 10 - i \end{bmatrix}$$

The notation <a|b> gives the inner product of the two quantum states, which is a scalar value, and the notation |a><b| gives the outer product of the two quantum states, which is a matrix. The various states of the qubit live in a complex vector space known as the Hilbert space, and it carries a lot of importance in the field of quantum computing.

In a more general sense, a quantum state is usually denoted by $|\psi>$ (pronounced ket psi), which can either represent a qubit or a multidimensional qubit. $|\psi>$ can also represent a superposition quantum state, which we are going to discuss in the next section.

Superposition of qubits

As discussed at the beginning of this section, qubits live simultaneously in multiple states in a complex linear combination. This is what separates them from their classical counterparts. This phenomenon of qubits living in complex linear combinations of quantum states is known as **superposition** and has huge significance in quantum computing. This is one of the fundamental properties of quantum computing that makes it so powerful in carrying out computational tasks that classical computers cannot perform.

The superposition property gives quantum computers the power to perform computations in a parallel manner. It is because of superposition that quantum computers are inherently parallel and don't require separate parallel architecture to achieve parallel computing tasks, as we usually do with **Graphics Processing Units (GPUs)**.

A generic superposition quantum state is defined as follows:

$$|\psi> = \alpha|0> + \beta|1>$$

Where α and β are complex numbers that are known as **probability amplitudes**, and the qubits |0 > and |1 > are said to be in a state of superposition. This is how the qubits actually exist in the realm of quantum computing. Since the qubits are in a state of superposition, it means that there is a certain probability of the |0 > state occurring, just as there is a certain probability of |1 > occurring.

To calculate the probabilities, we take the modulus (absolute value) of the probability amplitude value associated with the qubit and then square it.

Therefore, $|\alpha|^2$ gives us the probability of finding the state |0 > and $|\beta|^2$ gives us the probability of finding the state |1 > when they occur in superposition. Since $|\alpha|^2$ and $|\beta|^2$ gives us the probabilities, they add up to 1:

$$|\alpha|^2 + |\beta|^2 = 1$$

If α and β are complex amplitudes, then we take their modulus value as we normally do for complex numbers.

We will soon see in this chapter that **Hadamard gates** are used to create equal superpositions of qubits, which carries a lot of importance in many quantum algorithms, such as Grover's algorithm. Let's see in the next section how these qubits can be illustrated using different bases.

Illustrating qubits in different bases

We saw in *Chapter 1, Essential Mathematics and Algorithmic Thinking*, that the states |0> and |1> are orthonormal states, which means that they have unit length and are orthogonal to each other. It can also be seen that these states are the most fundamental states that are used to construct other quantum states. Therefore, these states are known as orthonormal **basis states**. These states are linearly independent as well, and any other state can be formed by the linear combination of the states |0> and |1>.

In this section, we will see various illustrations of qubits in different bases, which will help us to understand the physical representation of qubits. We will be discussing the Bloch sphere representation of qubits and then the Z, X, and Y axis basis states. Various illustrations are useful for certain types of quantum algorithms, and they make the mathematics of the algorithms easier to understand. If you learn these different illustrations you will be able to understand some of the quantum computing literature and appreciate the concepts more clearly. Let's start with the Bloch sphere representation of qubits.

Bloch sphere representation of qubits

The Bloch sphere is a 3D geometric representation of a qubit, and it helps us to visualize the quantum states that a qubit can take. It has a unit radius and we can use vector notation to denote the quantum states. The Bloch sphere is only valid for a single qubit because when there is more than one qubit, the dimensions exceed the drawing capacity.

Figure 2.1 depicts the Bloch sphere and the X, Y, and Z basis states, which will be discussed in the upcoming sections. This diagram will help you to visualize the various single-qubit operations that can be performed:

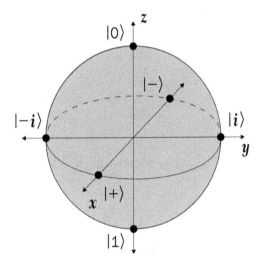

Figure 2.1 – The Bloch sphere representing X, Y, and Z basis states

In a Bloch sphere, the quantum state of a single qubit is represented using the following equation:

$$|\psi> = \alpha|0> + \beta|1> = cos\left(\frac{\theta}{2}\right)|0> + e^{\varphi i}sin\left(\frac{\theta}{2}\right)|1>$$

In *Figure 2.2*, you can see the angles θ and φ clearly, and you can then observe that various quantum states can be formed if these angles are set to certain values:

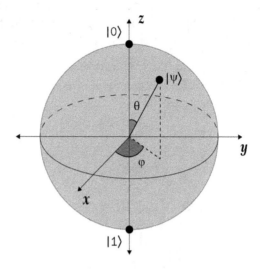

Figure 2.2 – Bloch sphere representing angles θ and φ

Therefore, $\alpha = cos\left(\frac{\theta}{2}\right)$ and $\beta = e^{\varphi i}sin\left(\frac{\theta}{2}\right)$. The angle θ is measured from the positive z axis and has a range $0 \leq \theta \leq \pi$. The angle φ is measured from the positive x axis and has a range $0 \leq \varphi \leq 2\pi$.

With this in mind, if we set $\varphi = 0$ and $\theta = \pi$, then we will achieve the quantum state of $|1>$, and for $\varphi = 0$ and $\theta = 0$, we will achieve the state of $|0>$. So, this process is like moving away from the superposition state that is present in the Bloch sphere towards various points present on the surface of the sphere. It is important to note that since the absolute value (modulus) of a complex amplitude is always 1, so even if a complex valued amplitude is multiplied by a certain quantum state, it doesn't change the state at all.

An interesting fact to note here is that we can write the states $|0>$ and $|1>$ in terms of the other basis state representations. The following equation for $|0>$ demonstrates this:

$$|0> = \frac{|+> +|->}{\sqrt{2}} = \frac{|i> +|-i>}{\sqrt{2}}$$

For state $|1>$, it is as follows:

$$|1> = \frac{|+> -|->}{\sqrt{2}} = \frac{|i> -|-i>}{\sqrt{2}}$$

This provides the useful information that any qubit can be formed by adding or subtracting two or more qubits. So, we saw have seen that the Bloch sphere is a useful visualization technique for single qubits, and is also useful for seeing the mathematical operations that can be performed on them.

With the Bloch sphere covered, let's see the Z basis states in the next section.

The Z basis states — |0> and |1>

You have already seen the orthonormal basis states |0> and |1> multiple times, and these are the most frequently used illustration in quantum computing because of their simple mathematical and physical significance. These states are also known as **computational basis**, **Z basis**, or **standard basis**. As you saw in the *Bloch sphere* section, the |0> state lies on the top of the sphere and the |1> state lies just opposite to the |0> state, which constitutes the z axis of the Bloch sphere.

You are aware that the column vectors |1> and |0> also denote coordinates in the 2D Cartesian plane. It is useful to know that if some other orthonormal basis is chosen for computation purposes, then the states remain the same but their coordinates change. This means that the states |0> and |1> will be the same but their coordinates will no longer be [1   0] and [0   1] respectively. Their coordinates will depend on the particular orthonormal basis state chosen. The Z basis is also known as the **energy basis** because the basis states also correspond to the qubit energy levels.

Let's now move onto the X basis states in the next section and learn about how they are represented.

The X basis states — |+> and |->

The X basis states are also known as **diagonal basis** or **Hadamard basis** states, and they are equal superpositions of the |0> and |1> states. Here is their mathematical description:

$$|+> = \frac{|0> + |1>}{\sqrt{2}} \; and \; |-> = \frac{|0> - |1>}{\sqrt{2}}$$

You can clearly observe that in both states, the probability of finding state $|0>$ is $\left|\frac{1}{\sqrt{2}}\right|^2 = \frac{1}{2}$ and state $|1>$ is $\left|\frac{1}{\sqrt{2}}\right|^2 = \frac{1}{2}$. In this case, $\alpha = \beta = \frac{1}{\sqrt{2}}$ if we compare this with

$|\psi> = \alpha|0> + \beta|1>$.

Next, we move onto our final basis representation of a qubit, which is the Y basis state.

The Y basis states – $|i>$ and $|-i>$

The Y basis states are also known as the **circular basis**, and even they form equal superposition similar to Z basis states but possess complex amplitudes. Let's take a look at their mathematical equations:

$$|i> = \frac{|0> + i|1>}{\sqrt{2}} \; and \; |-i> = \frac{|0> - i|1>}{\sqrt{2}}$$

If you look carefully, you will see that the probability of finding the

$|0>$ and $|1>$ states is $\frac{1}{2}$ and the presence of the complex phase does not create any

effects. Sometimes Y basis states are also denoted by $|\circlearrowright>$ and $|\circlearrowleft>$, which are known as **clockwise** and **counterclockwise** basis states.

You might have seen that we have used the X, Y, and Z notation to explain the various basis illustrations, and these correspond to the axes on the Bloch sphere.

Since we have seen the various representation styles of quantum states, now we need to extract information from them because in the real world, that information will matter. This process is done by taking measurements from the quantum system we possess. Let's look at the measurement aspect of quantum computing in the next section.

Introducing quantum measurements

In quantum computing, whenever we start talking about making measurements, we are referring to the fact that the quantum system is interacting with the environment. Whenever qubits interact with an external environment, the phenomenon of decoherence takes place and they no longer maintain their quantum properties, which severely alters their quantum state. This configuration is what we describe as an **open system**, where the qubits interact with the environment and the time evolution is not inflexible.

The process of measurement can only take place in an open system because the measurement device has to interact with the quantum system and states to extract information from it. After the measurement process, the whole quantum system is severely altered and disturbed.

During the measurement process, a phenomenon known as the **collapse of the wave function** occurs. Prior to measurement of the quantum system, the quantum system lives in the superposition of the basis states but as soon as a measurement is taken, the superposition collapses to a single basis state that corresponds to the result of the measurement. The measurement operation is thus irreversible.

The process of carrying out a measurement involves the selection of a basis state in which we want to perform the measurement and then choosing which measurement to perform. This means that if you choose the Z basis states, then your measurement will either be |0> or |1>. So, if we choose to measure |0> or |1> in the Z basis state, we will get them with 1.0 probability.

The scenario becomes different when we want to measure a |−> in the Z basis state. Since we know that for |−>, states |0> and |1> both occur with 0.5 probability, so after measurement also we get the same results. This means if identical |−> states are prepared 200 times, then around 100 of them will be |0> and the rest will be |1>. Also, if we measure a certain superposition of quantum states and get a particular basis state, then no matter how many times we measure that superposed quantum state, we are going to get that same basis state. This means that if you measure |−> and get |0> after measurement, then if you again measure |−> you will still keep getting |0> as the output.

In these explanations related to measurements, we considered the case known as a **projective measurement**, which is the most fundamental type of measurement system used in quantum computing and quantum mechanics. Let's see in the next section the mathematical component of this kind of measurement.

Mathematics of projective measurements

Projective measurement involves the use of projection operators, which are Hermitian, and their squares are equal to themselves. The process of projective measurement involves taking the eigenvectors of the measurement operator, which are the basis states of that operator, then calculating the projection operators from those eigenvectors using the outer product, and finally, a measurement of a given quantum state is performed using the projection operators obtained earlier.

Let's now see the process mathematically. The example shown here has been adapted from the book *Quantum Computing Explained* by David McMahon, which can be found in the *Further reading* section of this chapter.

Let's assume that you are provided a quantum state:

$$|\psi> = \frac{\sqrt{3}}{2}|0> + \frac{1}{2}|1>$$

Now you would like to take a measurement of this quantum state with respect to the Y operator, which is given by $\begin{bmatrix} 0 & i \\ -i & 0 \end{bmatrix}$. Since you learned how to calculate eigenvalues and eigenvectors in *Chapter 1, Essential Mathematics and Algorithmic Thinking*, you will see that this operator has ± 1 as its eigenvalues and the eigenvectors associated with each eigenvalue are given as follows:

$$|v_1> = \frac{1}{\sqrt{2}} \begin{bmatrix} 1 \\ i \end{bmatrix} \ and \ |v_2> = \frac{1}{\sqrt{2}} \begin{bmatrix} 1 \\ -i \end{bmatrix}$$

The complex conjugates of $|v_1>$ and $|v_2>$ are given as follows:

$$<v_1| = \frac{1}{\sqrt{2}} \begin{bmatrix} 1 & -i \end{bmatrix} \ and \ <v_2| = \frac{1}{\sqrt{2}} \begin{bmatrix} 1 & i \end{bmatrix}$$

Now, using these eigenvectors and their complex conjugates, the projection operators for each eigenvalue can be formed by taking the outer product of these eigenvectors. For the eigenvalue +1, we will get the projection operator as follows:

$$M_{+1} = |v_1><v_1| = \frac{1}{2} \begin{bmatrix} 1 \\ i \end{bmatrix} \begin{bmatrix} 1 & -i \end{bmatrix} = \frac{1}{2} \begin{bmatrix} 1 & -i \\ i & 1 \end{bmatrix}$$

For the eigenvalue -1, we will get the projection operator as follows:

$$M_{-1} = |v_2><v_2| = \frac{1}{2} \begin{bmatrix} 1 \\ -i \end{bmatrix} \begin{bmatrix} 1 & i \end{bmatrix} = \frac{1}{2} \begin{bmatrix} 1 & i \\ -i & 1 \end{bmatrix}$$

You can easily verify that the given state $|\psi>$ is normalized for which $<\psi|\psi> = 1$. We can write the given state $|\psi>$ in the form of a column vector to make the calculations easier:

$$|\psi> = \frac{\sqrt{3}}{2} \begin{bmatrix} 1 \\ 0 \end{bmatrix} - \frac{1}{2} \begin{bmatrix} 0 \\ 1 \end{bmatrix} = \frac{1}{2} \begin{bmatrix} \sqrt{3} \\ -1 \end{bmatrix}$$

Now we can apply the projection operators on to this state $|\psi>$, which is as follows:

$$M_{+1}\,|\psi> = \frac{1}{4}\begin{bmatrix} \sqrt{3}+i \\ -1+i\sqrt{3} \end{bmatrix}$$

$$M_{-1}\,|\psi> = \frac{1}{4}\begin{bmatrix} \sqrt{3}-i \\ -1-i\sqrt{3} \end{bmatrix}$$

Finally, the probability of finding +1 will be given by this:

$$<\psi|M_{+1}|\psi> = \frac{1}{8}\,(3+1) = \frac{1}{2}$$

The probability of finding -1 will be given by this:

$$<\psi|M_{-1}|\psi> = \frac{1}{8}\,(3+1) = \frac{1}{2}$$

This concludes the calculation part of the projective measurement, and you can see that it is a very simple and straightforward method if you want to measure a given quantum state with respect to a particular measurement operator or basis state representation.

With the measurement of qubits covered, we now know how the measurement process happens whenever a quantum operation is carried out. Let's move on to a very important topic, which is the quantum logic gates.

Quantum logic gates

This is one of the most important sections. We discuss all the quantum logic gates that will be later used to construct quantum circuits. We will see the programming aspects of these quantum gates in *Chapter 6, Silq Programming Basics and Features*.

One of the most important properties of quantum logic gates is that they are all unitary, which means they are reversible and there is no loss of information. All the gates preserve the complex vector space transformations, which means if you apply a π rotation in the X axis of the Bloch sphere to reach the state $|1>$ from $|0>$, then the complex conjugate of the gate will help you to reverse the transformation that you did to the Bloch sphere, which means you will return to state $|0>$. This means there is no loss of information, and from the output of the quantum gates you will be able to find out the inputs as well.

Since we now know the fundamental difference between quantum gates and classical gates, let's discuss Pauli gates in the next section.

Pauli gates

Pauli gates are named after the physicist Wolfgang Pauli, who received a Nobel Prize in Physics in 1945. There are three Pauli gates – X, Y, and Z gates – and you will see that they correspond to the different basis representations we saw in the Bloch sphere.

It is important to note that all the Pauli gates are Hermitian. Let's start with the X gate.

The Pauli X gate

The **Pauli X gate** is analogous to the classical NOT gate. Whenever this gate is applied to a qubit, it flips that qubit. If you think about this in terms of the Bloch sphere, then the X gate applies a π (180°) rotation about the x axis, which flips the qubit.

The truth table for the X gate is provided in *Figure 2.3*:

Input	Output
$\vert 0 >$	$\vert 1 >$
$\vert 1 >$	$\vert 0 >$

Figure 2.3 – Truth table of a Pauli X gate

Mathematically, the Pauli X operator is as follows:

$$\sigma_x = X = \begin{bmatrix} 0 & 1 \\ 1 & 0 \end{bmatrix}$$

You can see that the X matrix has the $\vert 0>$ and $\vert 1>$ column vectors stacked together, but the $\vert 1>$ column vector comes first, then the $\vert 0>$, which denotes a flip operation.

Let's calculate the eigenvalues and eigenvectors for the σ_x gate:

1. The characteristic equation for σ_x, which is used for calculating eigenvalues, is as follows:

$$\vert \sigma_x - \lambda I \vert = 0$$

2. We apply the values of σ_x and the identity matrix:

$$\left\vert \begin{bmatrix} 0 & 1 \\ 1 & 0 \end{bmatrix} - \lambda \begin{bmatrix} 1 & 0 \\ 0 & 1 \end{bmatrix} \right\vert = 0$$

3. Simplifying further, we will get the following:

$$\left\| \begin{bmatrix} 0 & 1 \\ 1 & 0 \end{bmatrix} - \begin{bmatrix} \lambda & 0 \\ 0 & \lambda \end{bmatrix} \right\| = 0$$

4. Now subtracting λ from σ_x we have this:

$$\left\| \begin{bmatrix} -\lambda & 1 \\ 1 & -\lambda \end{bmatrix} \right\| = 0$$

5. Now we will use the following relation to gain the characteristic equation of this matrix by calculating the determinant:

$$\lambda^2 - Tr(\sigma_x)\lambda + |\sigma_x| = 0$$

Here, $Tr(\sigma_x) = 0$ and $|\sigma_x| = -1$, so we get the following equation:

$$\lambda^2 - 1 = 0 \ -1 = 0$$

6. If we factorize the preceding characteristic equation, then we will get this:

$$\lambda_1 = 1, \lambda_{2=} -1$$

These are the eigenvalues of the operator σ_x.

7. Now we will move on to calculating the eigenvectors. Let's assume $\lambda_1 = 1$ and put this value into the following equation:

$$(\sigma_x - \lambda_1)X1 = 0$$

$$\begin{bmatrix} -1 & 1 \\ 1 & -1 \end{bmatrix} \begin{bmatrix} x1 \\ x2 \end{bmatrix} = \begin{bmatrix} 0 \\ 0 \end{bmatrix}$$

8. The equations can be formed as follows:

$$-x1 + x2 = 0$$

$$x1 - x2 = 0$$

Since the equations are the same, by simplifying and solving further we will get the following:

$$x2 = x1$$

9. Now we can choose a value for $x1$ to have the eigenvectors. The simplest value is 1. Then we will have the eigenvector $X1 = \begin{bmatrix} 1 \\ 1 \end{bmatrix}$. Normalizing $X1$, we get $|+> = \frac{1}{\sqrt{2}}\begin{bmatrix} 1 \\ 1 \end{bmatrix}$ and in a very similar process, $X2 = \begin{bmatrix} 1 \\ -1 \end{bmatrix}$ and you can verify it yourself. Normalizing $X2$ will give $|-> = \frac{1}{\sqrt{2}}\begin{bmatrix} 1 \\ -1 \end{bmatrix}$.

10. The eigenvalues of the X gate are ± 1 and the eigenvectors are $|+>$ and $|->$ associated with each of the eigenvalues.

For a general superposition state, we have the following:

$$|\psi> = \alpha|0> + \beta|1>$$

By applying an X gate, we will get the following:

$$X|\psi> = \alpha|1> + \beta|0>$$

The X gate is also its own inverse because X X = I.

With the X gate covered, let's now see the Y gate.

The Pauli Y gate

The **Pauli Y gate**, as you might have guessed already, applies a π (180°) rotation around the y axis of the Bloch sphere, which also flips the bit but multiplies a complex amplitude with the output state, which doesn't have an impact on the output state.

The truth table for the Y gate is provided in *Figure 2.4*:

Input	Output
$|0>$	$i|1>$
$|1>$	$-i|0>$

Figure 2.4 – Truth table of a Pauli Y gate

Mathematically, the Pauli Y operator is as follows:

$$\sigma_y = Y = \begin{bmatrix} 0 & -i \\ i & 0 \end{bmatrix}$$

The eigenvalues of the Y gate are ± 1 and the eigenvectors are $\frac{1}{\sqrt{2}}\begin{bmatrix} 1 \\ i \end{bmatrix}$ and $\frac{1}{\sqrt{2}}\begin{bmatrix} 1 \\ -i \end{bmatrix}$, which

is $|i>$ and $|-i>$ associated with each of the eigenvalues. It will be a good exercise for you to prove this statement following the calculations of the X gate we did in the previous section. The calculations are the same as for the X gate, and this exercise will help you to reinforce the ideas of eigenvalues and eigenvectors.

Considering our general superposition state, if we apply a Y gate then we will get the following:

$$Y|\psi> = \alpha i|1> - \beta i|0>$$

You can see the multiplication of complex amplitudes with the states, along with the phase being flipped. Also, the Y gate is its own inverse.

Let's learn about the Z gate now.

The Pauli Z gate

The **Pauli Z gate** applies a π (180°) rotation to the input state around the z axis of the Bloch sphere, which creates a phase shift operation. This gate is also known as the **phase shift gate** or the **phase flip gate** and is used in a lot of quantum algorithms.

The truth table for the Z gate is given in *Figure 2.5*:

Input	Output
$|0>$	$|0>$
$|1>$	$-|1>$

Figure 2.5 – Truth table of a Pauli Z gate

The Pauli Z operator is given as follows:

$$\sigma_z = Z = \begin{bmatrix} 1 & 0 \\ 0 & -1 \end{bmatrix}$$

The eigenvalues of Z gate are ±1 and the eigenvectors are |0> and |1> associated with each of the eigenvalues. It will be a good exercise for you to prove this statement following the calculations of the X gate we did before. The calculations are the same as for the X gate, and this exercise will help you to reinforce the idea of eigenvalues and eigenvectors. Now you can see that the Z gate eigenvectors form the computational basis and, in fact, you can compare all the other Pauli gates with the qubit basis state representation we studied earlier.

Considering our general superposition state, if we apply a Z gate then we will get the following:

$$Z|\psi> = \alpha|0> - \beta|1>$$

You can clearly observe the phase shift for the qubit |1>. Since the sign changes for |1>, the Z gate is also known as the **sign flip gate**.

Let's now take a look at the final Pauli gate, which is the identity gate.

The Pauli I gate

The **Pauli I gate**, which is also known as the **identity gate**, is an operator that's useful for proving the unitary nature of the quantum gates and for the measurement of decoherence in qubits. When it is applied to any qubit, it does not change its state.

The truth table for the I gate is given in *Figure 2.6*:

Input	Output
|0 >	|0 >
|1 >	|1 >

Figure 2.6 – Truth table for the Pauli I gate

The Pauli I operator is given by the following:

$$\sigma_I = I = \begin{bmatrix} 1 & 0 \\ 0 & 1 \end{bmatrix}$$

All the eigenvalues of the I gate are 1, and any vector can be the eigenvector for this gate.

Now we will move onto one of the most important quantum gates, which is the Hadamard gate.

The Hadamard gate – the quantum H gate

The **Hadamard gate** is one of the most important quantum gates you will learn about because it is used in almost all quantum algorithms to create an equal superposition of qubits. This gate is named after Jacques Hadamard and creates a complex linear superposition of two basis states when it is applied to a particular quantum state. The operation of the H gate rotates the input qubit along the z and x axes by $\frac{\pi}{2}$ (90°) each, which causes a total rotation of $180°$.

The truth table for the H gate is given in *Figure 2.7*:

Input	Output
$\lvert 0 >$	$\dfrac{\lvert 0 > +\lvert 1 >}{\sqrt{2}} = \lvert +>$
$\lvert 1 >$	$\dfrac{\lvert 0 > -\lvert 1 >}{\sqrt{2}} = \lvert ->$

Figure 2.7 – Truth table for an H gate

Mathematically, the H gate is defined as follows:

$$H = \frac{1}{\sqrt{2}} \begin{bmatrix} 1 & 1 \\ 1 & -1 \end{bmatrix}$$

It can be observed from that H operator that it consists of the amplitude values of states $\lvert 0>$ and $\lvert 1>$ shown in table output as column vectors stacked together in the matrix. This is true for every other gate that we have studied so far, and for those which we are going to study in the future. You can verify this yourself!

You might be wondering that what happens if we apply the H gate to the $\lvert +>$ and $\lvert ->$ states, and yes you have guessed it right, we will again get back to state $\lvert 0>$ and $\lvert 1>$ because of the reversible nature of the quantum gates.

Like all the Pauli gates, the H gate is also its own inverse, and after applying this to computational basis states we get the Hadamard basis, which is $\{\lvert +>, \lvert ->\}$. The Hadamard gate is Hermitian and unitary as well. As an exercise, prove that the Hadamard gate is Hermitian and unitary, and then show that by applying a Hadamard gate to states $\lvert 0>$ and $\lvert 1>$ gives you the states $\lvert +>$ and $\lvert ->$.

Let's now move onto the S gate.

The S gate

The **S gate** applies a $\frac{\pi}{2}$ (90°) rotation to the input state around the z axis of the Bloch sphere. This means by the operation of the S gate we get a complex amplitude multiplied with the state |1> only.

The truth table for the S gate is shown in *Figure 2.8*:

Input	Output
|0 >	|0 >
|1 >	$e^{i\frac{\pi}{2}}$|1 >

Figure 2.8 – Truth table for the S gate

The S gate operator is defined as follows:

$$S = \begin{bmatrix} 1 & 0 \\ 0 & e^{i\frac{\pi}{2}} \end{bmatrix} = \begin{bmatrix} 1 & 0 \\ 0 & i \end{bmatrix} = e^{\frac{\pi}{4}} \begin{bmatrix} e^{-i\frac{\pi}{4}} & 0 \\ 0 & e^{i\frac{\pi}{4}} \end{bmatrix}$$

The S gate is also known as $\frac{\pi}{4}$ gate.

Let's now take a look at the S dagger gate.

The S† (S dagger) gate

The **S† gate** applies a $-\frac{\pi}{2}$ (−90°) rotation to the input state around the z axis of the Bloch sphere. This gate is similar to the S gate, but everything is negated here.

The truth table for S† is given in *Figure 2.9*:

Input	Output
|0 >	|0 >
|1 >	$e^{-i\frac{\pi}{2}}$|1 >

Figure 2.9 – Truth table for the S† gate

Mathematically, the $S^\dagger$ gate is as follows:

$$S^\dagger = \begin{bmatrix} 1 & 0 \\ 0 & e^{-i\frac{\pi}{2}} \end{bmatrix} = \begin{bmatrix} 1 & 0 \\ 0 & -i \end{bmatrix} = \begin{bmatrix} 1 & 0 \\ 0 & e^{i\frac{3\pi}{2}} \end{bmatrix}$$

This covers the $S^\dagger$ gate, and both S and $S^\dagger$ are variants of the Z gate.

Let's now take a look at the T gate.

The T gate – $\frac{\pi}{8}$ gate

The **T gate** applies a $\frac{\pi}{4}$ $(45°)$ rotation to the input state around the z axis of the Bloch sphere. This gate is very similar to the S gate we studied earlier, except the rotation angle is different.

The truth table for T gate is shown in *Figure 2.10*:

Input	Output
$\lvert 0 >$	$\lvert 0 >$
$\lvert 1 >$	$e^{i\frac{\pi}{4}}\lvert 1 >$

Figure 2.10 – Truth table for the T gate

The T gate operator is provided as follows:

$$T = \begin{bmatrix} 1 & 0 \\ 0 & e^{i\frac{\pi}{4}} \end{bmatrix} = \begin{bmatrix} 1 & 0 \\ 0 & \frac{1}{\sqrt{2}} + i\frac{1}{\sqrt{2}} \end{bmatrix} = e^{\frac{\pi}{8}} \begin{bmatrix} e^{-i\frac{\pi}{8}} & 0 \\ 0 & e^{i\frac{\pi}{8}} \end{bmatrix}$$

The T gate is also known as the $\frac{\pi}{4}$ (45°) gate. The relation between the S and T gate is $S = T \cdot T$ which makes sense because each T gate is a $\frac{\pi}{4}$ (45°) rotation, so 2 times of this rotation gives us rotation $\frac{\pi}{2}$ (90°) which is the S gate.

Let's now move onto the T dagger gate.

The $T^\dagger$ (T dagger) gate

The $T^\dagger$ **gate** applies a $-\frac{\pi}{4}$ $(-45°)$ rotation to the input state around the z axis of the Bloch sphere. This gate is similar to the T gate, but everything is negated here.

The truth table for $T^\dagger$ is given in *Figure 2.11*:

Input	Output
$\lvert 0 >$	$\lvert 0 >$
$\lvert 1 >$	$e^{-i\frac{\pi}{4}}\lvert 1 >$

Figure 2.11 – Truth table for the $T\dagger$ gate

Mathematically, the $T^\dagger$ gate is as follows:

$$T^\dagger = \begin{bmatrix} 1 & 0 \\ 0 & e^{-i\frac{\pi}{4}} \end{bmatrix} = \begin{bmatrix} 1 & 0 \\ 0 & \frac{1}{\sqrt{2}} - i\frac{1}{\sqrt{2}} \end{bmatrix} = \begin{bmatrix} 1 & 0 \\ 0 & e^{i\frac{7\pi}{4}} \end{bmatrix}$$

The relation between the $S^\dagger$ and $T^\dagger$ gate is $S^\dagger = T^\dagger \; T^\dagger$.

Since we have seen the various types of phase gates, let's take a look at the more custom or generalized phase changing gates that can be used to create any kind of rotation on the axis of the Bloch sphere.

The R_φ^Z gate

To make custom/arbitrary rotations around the z axis of the Bloch sphere, we use the R_φ^Z quantum gate.

Mathematically, the rotation matrix is given as follows:

$$R_\varphi^Z = \begin{bmatrix} 1 & 0 \\ 0 & e^{i\varphi} \end{bmatrix} = e^{i\frac{\varphi}{2}} \begin{bmatrix} e^{-i\frac{\varphi}{2}} & 0 \\ 0 & e^{i\frac{\varphi}{2}} \end{bmatrix} = \cos\left(\frac{\varphi}{2}\right)I - i\cos\left(\frac{\varphi}{2}\right)\sigma_z$$

As already discussed, the global phases do not affect the quantum state or output so they can be safely ignored.

The R_φ^X gate

Similar to the arbitrary Z rotations, we can also perform custom X rotations around the *x axis* of the Bloch sphere.

The rotation matrix for X is as follows:

$$R_\varphi^X = \begin{bmatrix} \cos\left(\frac{\varphi}{2}\right) & -i\sin\left(\frac{\varphi}{2}\right) \\ -i\sin\left(\frac{\varphi}{2}\right) & \cos\left(\frac{\varphi}{2}\right) \end{bmatrix} = \cos\left(\frac{\varphi}{2}\right)I - i\cos\left(\frac{\varphi}{2}\right)\sigma_x$$

σ_X is the Pauli X matrix, which we have already studied in detail.

The R_φ^Y gate

To create custom rotation around the Y axis of the Bloch sphere, we use the R_φ^Y quantum gate.

Mathematically, this gate is defined as follows:

$$R_\varphi^Y = \begin{bmatrix} \cos\left(\frac{\varphi}{2}\right) & -\sin\left(\frac{\varphi}{2}\right) \\ \sin\left(\frac{\varphi}{2}\right) & \cos\left(\frac{\varphi}{2}\right) \end{bmatrix} = \cos\left(\frac{\varphi}{2}\right) I - i\cos\left(\frac{\varphi}{2}\right) \sigma_Y$$

σ_Y is the Pauli Y operator, which we discussed in detail at the beginning of this section.

Summary

In this chapter, we discussed the quantum bit and its various basis representations in detail. In addition to that, we learned about the Bloch sphere visualization of a single qubit as well as the various quantum logic gates, which will be extremely useful as we move forward with the coding aspects of quantum computing. This chapter primarily helps us understand the value of knowing the things at work under the hood in various programming platforms.

In all the programming platforms, you will never be required to code these quantum gates from the very beginning, but it is always important to know the functioning and mathematical descriptions of the gates. They will help you to create new quantum algorithms in the near future, and now you have acquired the skills to construct and manipulate these gates using their mathematical descriptions.

With the basics of quantum gates and bits covered, let's move multiple qubit operations and multi qubit quantum logic gates in the next chapter.

Further reading

- Robert Loredo, *Learn Quantum Computing with Python and IBM Quantum Experience A hands-on introduction to quantum computing and writing your own quantum algorithms with Python*, Packt Publishing, 2020

- Dr. Christine Corbett Moran, *Mastering Quantum Computing with IBM QX Explore the world of quantum computing using the Quantum Composer and Qiskit*, Packt Publishing, 2019

- Robert S. Sutor, *Dancing with Qubit How quantum computing works and how it can change the world*, Packt Publishing, 2019

- David McMahon, *Quantum Computing Explained*, Wiley, 2017

3

Multiple Quantum Bits, Entanglement, and Quantum Circuits

In our day-to-day life, we often use multiple attributes of data and situations. For example, a weather forecast system could predict multiple features, such as air pressure in a region, previous rainfall patterns, thunderstorms, and so on. This often requires working with multiple qubits rather than a single qubit to accurately model the scenario. The presence of multiple features is true for many other applications in real life.

In this chapter, you will dive into the basics of multiple qubit quantum computing and learn about entanglement, one of its most useful features. We will also cover the construction of quantum circuits using multiple and single qubit quantum logic gates. Here is a list of topics that we are going to cover in this chapter:

- Introducing multiple quantum bits

- The wonder of quantum entanglement

- Exploring multi-qubit quantum logic gates

- Quantum teleportation
- Quantum superdense coding

We will begin by discussing multiple quantum bits.

Introducing multiple quantum bits

Multiple qubit operations will allow us to implement more complex quantum algorithms in the upcoming chapters. Dealing with multiple qubits is a core requirement in quantum computing because in most cases, the information can only be encoded by the use of many qubits. Multiple qubits also bring flexibility in computation as we can perform quantum operations more conveniently.

You studied some of the basics of tensor products in *Chapter 1, Essential Mathematics and Algorithmic Thinking*, which will now help you to appreciate the nature of multiple qubits in a quantum computing environment. As we know, single qubits are denoted as |0>, |1>, or any generic state $|\psi>$. To denote two qubits, we use the notation |00>, |11>, or any generic state, such as $|\psi\phi>$. We can have two different quantum subsystems, each having their own vector spaces. Their interactions can be denoted by the addition and scalar multiplication of the vector elements, which we usually denote as $\psi\otimes\phi$, which means the tensor product of the quantum systems ψ and ϕ. These two states constitute a larger quantum system.

Now consider if ψ is of a dimensions and ϕ is of b dimensions, then their tensor product has ab dimensions. This also means that the dimensions grow exponentially, and we will see this now through calculations.

We know that, mathematically, qubit |1> is denoted as follows:

$$|1> = \begin{bmatrix} 0 \\ 1 \end{bmatrix}$$

The tensor product of |1> with itself will be the following:

$$|1> \otimes |1> = |11> = \begin{bmatrix} 0 \\ 1 \end{bmatrix} \otimes \begin{bmatrix} 0 \\ 1 \end{bmatrix} = 0\begin{bmatrix} 0 \\ 1 \end{bmatrix} 1\begin{bmatrix} 0 \\ 1 \end{bmatrix} = \begin{bmatrix} 0 \\ 0 \\ 0 \\ 1 \end{bmatrix}$$

If we want to denote a three-qubit system, then we do the following:

$$|1> \otimes |1> \otimes |1> = |111> = \begin{bmatrix} 0 \\ 1 \end{bmatrix} \otimes \begin{bmatrix} 0 \\ 1 \end{bmatrix} \otimes \begin{bmatrix} 0 \\ 1 \end{bmatrix} = \begin{bmatrix} 0 \\ 0 \\ 0 \\ 1 \end{bmatrix} \otimes \begin{bmatrix} 0 \\ 1 \end{bmatrix} = \begin{bmatrix} 0 \\ 0 \\ 0 \\ 0 \\ 0 \\ 0 \\ 0 \\ 1 \end{bmatrix}$$

Now observe carefully that as soon as you start increasing the number of qubits from 1 to 2, then 2 to 3, and so on, the dimension of the vector space also increases.

For the 1-qubit case, we have two dimensions; for the 2-qubit case, we have four dimensions (2x2); for the 3-qubit case, we have eight dimensions (2x2x2); and if you take 4 qubits, then you will have 2x2x2x2 = a sixteen-dimensional column vector. (All the values for the vectors are normalized by applying the absolute square.) This is an exponential increase in the vector space with each addition of a qubit, which means for n qubits, you will have 2^n dimensions!

You can see how the dimension of the vector space grows for multiple qubit systems, and you can store and encode more information into these multiple-qubit systems. With multiple qubits, a phenomenon known as **entanglement** starts happening in the quantum system. Let's have a rundown of it in the next section.

The wonder of quantum entanglement

Entanglement in quantum mechanics and quantum computing is one of the most fascinating phenomena in the world. Even Einstein described it as *spooky action at a distance*. Quantum entanglement is one of the core features of quantum computing, along with superposition and interference, and unleashes the power of quantum computing. The power of quantum computing will be discussed in *Chapter 2, Quantum Bits, Quantum Measurements, and Quantum Logic Gates*.

Consider two quantum systems ψ and ϕ. These two systems are said to be entangled with each other if we cannot measure the systems individually. This means that whenever we measure this entangled system, it always happens together and therefore, the properties of one system can only be explained with reference to the other. This means that to explain the properties of system ψ, we need the help of system ϕ as well. Only then we can fully describe them together, even if they are far apart and not interacting with each other.

To understand entanglement in a more mathematical and quantum computing sense, let's take a look at Bell states and the entanglement phenomenon.

Exploring the Bell states system

The **Bell states**, also known as **Bell basis**, are an example of a **bipartitie system**, which means it only considers two quantum systems. It is a classic example of quantum entanglement and there are a total of 4 states in the Bell basis. Bell states are also called **Einstein-Podolsky-Rosen (EPR) states**.

Before we describe the Bell states, let's first define the two-qubit states, which will later help us to describe the Bell states. We start with the state $|00>$:

$$|0> \otimes |0> = |00> = \begin{bmatrix} 1 \\ 0 \end{bmatrix} \otimes \begin{bmatrix} 1 \\ 0 \end{bmatrix} = \begin{bmatrix} 1 \\ 0 \\ 0 \\ 0 \end{bmatrix}$$

The tensor product state for $|01>$ is as follows:

$$|0> \otimes |1> = |01> = \begin{bmatrix} 1 \\ 0 \end{bmatrix} \otimes \begin{bmatrix} 0 \\ 1 \end{bmatrix} = \begin{bmatrix} 0 \\ 1 \\ 0 \\ 0 \end{bmatrix}$$

For the $|10>$ state, we can write the following:

$$|1> \otimes |0> = |10> = \begin{bmatrix} 0 \\ 1 \end{bmatrix} \otimes \begin{bmatrix} 1 \\ 0 \end{bmatrix} = \begin{bmatrix} 0 \\ 0 \\ 1 \\ 0 \end{bmatrix}$$

Finally, the $|11>$ state is as follows:

$$|1> \otimes |1> = |11> = \begin{bmatrix} 0 \\ 1 \end{bmatrix} \otimes \begin{bmatrix} 0 \\ 1 \end{bmatrix} = \begin{bmatrix} 0 \\ 0 \\ 0 \\ 1 \end{bmatrix}$$

Since we have defined the two-qubit states, it will be easier to define the Bell states as these two-qubit states are used to describe them.

The general description of a Bell state is provided by the following equation:

$$|B_{ab}> = \frac{|0b> + (-1)^a|1b>}{\sqrt{2}}$$

Using this equation, the Bell states are generated as follows:

$$|B_{00}> = \frac{|00> +|11>}{\sqrt{2}}$$

$$|B_{01}> = \frac{|01> +|10>}{\sqrt{2}}$$

$$|B_{10}> = \frac{|00> -|11>}{\sqrt{2}}$$

$$|B_{11}> = \frac{|01> -|10>}{\sqrt{2}}$$

Since we have defined the Bell states to be entangled states, how did we know in advance that the states are entangled? In the next section, we are going to address this exact question of how to verify whether a quantum state is entangled or not.

Verifying entanglement of quantum states

Entanglement of a quantum state exists when that state cannot be written in the form of tensor products. In other words, this state is not separable or cannot be broken into products.

> **Note**
> None of the Bell states can be broken into products.

Let's start with the state $|B_{01}> = \frac{|01> +|10>}{\sqrt{2}}$, which can be simplified and written as follows:

$$|B_{01}> = \frac{1}{\sqrt{2}}\left(\begin{bmatrix} 0 \\ 1 \\ 0 \\ 0 \end{bmatrix} + \begin{bmatrix} 0 \\ 0 \\ 1 \\ 0 \end{bmatrix}\right) = \frac{1}{\sqrt{2}}\begin{bmatrix} 0 \\ 1 \\ 1 \\ 0 \end{bmatrix}$$

Now, if you consider the elements of the vector as $\begin{bmatrix} 0 \\ 1 \\ 1 \\ 0 \end{bmatrix} = \begin{bmatrix} w \\ x \\ y \\ z \end{bmatrix}$, then if $wz = xy$, it means that there is no entanglement. But for $|B_{01}>$, we can see that $wz = 0$ and $xy = \frac{1}{2}$, which means $wx \neq xy$, so it proves that the Bell state is indeed entangled.

The same exercise can be carried out for each of the Bell states described before, and you will find them to be entangled. If you check any other quantum state individually, such as $|00>$ or $|11>$, you will find that $wz = xy$ and they can be broken into tensor products, thereby proving that they are not entangled.

In this section, we have learned about entanglement and how to verify it. This will help you to appreciate the significance of entanglement in quantum teleportation and superdense coding applications discussed later in this chapter.

We will now look into the various multi-qubit quantum logic gates in the next section. Let's go!

Exploring multi-qubit quantum logic gates

In *Chapter 2, Quantum Bits, Quantum Measurements, and Quantum Logic Gates*, you learned about the most important single qubit quantum logic gates used frequently to construct quantum circuits. We will now dive into the multi-qubit quantum logic gates that help to form more complex quantum circuits. These are also used in various quantum algorithms. To begin, we will have a look at the CNOT gate.

The quantum CX or CNOT gate

The **CNOT** or the **CX gate** is one of the most important quantum gates utilized in quantum computing to create entanglement. The C in CNOT is known as **Controlled**. This gate is also known as a **conditional bit flip gate** because, as we will see, it flips the bit when a certain condition is met. This gate acts on two qubits, which can have quantum states ψ and ϕ, where ψ is the **control qubit** and ϕ is the **target qubit**. The target operation performed in this case is the X gate operation, which you learned about in *Chapter 2, Quantum Bits, Quantum Measurements, and Quantum Logic Gates*. It is also worth mentioning that the target operation can be changed by using various other single-qubit quantum gates.

The truth table for the CNOT gate is provided in *Figure 3.1*:

Input	Output
$|00>$	$|00>$
$|01>$	$|01>$
$|10>$	$|11>$
$|11>$	$|10>$

Figure 3.1 – Truth table for the CNOT gate

Since we are now dealing with two qubits, you will see that the matrix for the two-qubit gates are 4x4, therefore for n qubits, you will have a matrix of 2^nx2^n dimensional matrix.

Mathematically, the CNOT matrix is defined as follows:

$$CX = \begin{bmatrix} 1 & 0 & 0 & 0 \\ 0 & 1 & 0 & 0 \\ 0 & 0 & 0 & 1 \\ 0 & 0 & 1 & 0 \end{bmatrix}$$

From the truth table of the *CX* gate, you can clearly observe that the target (second qubit) is flipped whenever the control (first qubit) is in state $|1>$. The *CX* gate is performing an XOR operation on the target qubit and therefore is equivalent to the XOR gate you might know from classical logic gate theory. This means that if you take the control qubit as x and target qubit as y, then essentially a CNOT gate is performing an addition modulo 2 operation on the target qubit as $x \oplus y$, and this is the main reason for the XOR being applied by the CNOT. The advantage we receive here is that the number of inputs and outputs in *CX* is the same, which helps to preserve the reversible nature of quantum gates. On the other hand, classical XOR does not have a reversible nature because the number of inputs and outputs are not the same. Take a look at *Figure 3.2* to better understand how the CNOT gate works:

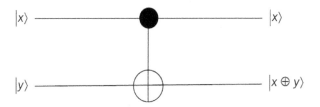

Figure 3.2 – CNOT/CX gate representation

In *Figure 3.2*, the |x> qubit is the control qubit and the |y> qubit is the target. The control is represented as a dot and then you can see the symbol for the XOR operation in the second qubit.

With the CNOT gate covered, we'll move on to looking at another gate, known as the CZ gate.

The quantum CZ or CPHASE gate

The quantum **CZ** gate is the **controlled Z** gate operation similar to the CNOT gate we studied now. This gate is also known as the **CPHASE** gate. Here, the first qubit will control and the second qubit will be the target with a Z operation.

The truth table for CZ will give you a better idea about the working of the CZ gate. The truth table for the CZ gate is provided in *Figure 3.3*:

Input	Output
|00 >	|00 >
|01 >	|01 >
|10 >	|10 >
|11 >	- |11 >

Figure 3.3 – Truth table for the CZ gate

By observing the truth table, you can see that the CZ gate flips the phase of the second qubit, because of which we get the −|11 > state in the end. For all the other states, CZ does nothing because CZ requires the control qubit to be 1 to operate and the target qubit to be 1 as well to reflect the phase changes. In essence, the CZ gate multiplies the phase $(-1)^x$ by the target qubit, where x is the value of the control qubit.

Figure 6.4 shows the CZ gate circuit diagram:

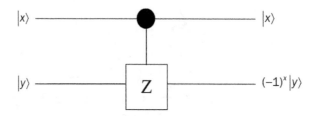

Figure 3.4 – CZ gate circuit

In *Figure 3.4*, the |x> qubit is the control qubit and the |y> qubit is the target. The control is represented as a dot and then you can see the symbol for Z operation in the second qubit and the output we get is $(-1)^x|y>$ in the target qubit.

Mathematically, the *CZ* gate is defined as follows:

$$CZ = \begin{bmatrix} 1 & 0 & 0 & 0 \\ 0 & 1 & 0 & 0 \\ 0 & 0 & 1 & 0 \\ 0 & 0 & 0 & -1 \end{bmatrix}$$

Notice in the *CZ* matrix that the top-left quadrant is a 2x2 identity matrix and the bottom-right quadrant is the matrix for the Pauli Z gate, which you learned about in *Chapter 2, Quantum Bits, Quantum Measurements, and Quantum Logic Gates.*

It will be a good exercise for you to try to derive the truth table and the matrix for controlled Y and controlled H gates, as well as to get a better understanding of the concept. Next, let's take a look at the SWAP gate.

The quantum SWAP gate

As you might have guessed from the name, the **SWAP** gate is used to interchange qubits.

The truth table for the SWAP gate is provided in *Figure 3.5*, which covers the workings of the SWAP gate:

Input	Output
|00 >	|00 >
|01 >	|10 >
|10 >	|01 >
|11 >	|11 >

Figure 3.5 – Truth table for the SWAP gate

If you look at the table carefully, then you will see that the first qubit and the second qubit are interchanged, and this is what SWAP gate does.

Figure 3.6 shows the circuit diagram for the SWAP gate:

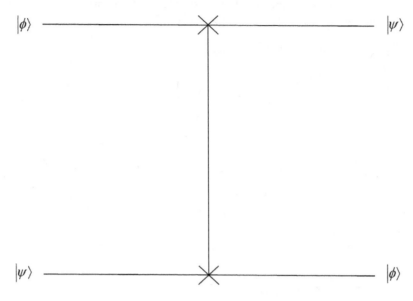

Figure 3.6 – SWAP gate circuit

In *Figure 3.6*, you see that two cross marks have been put into the qubit states $|\phi>$ and $|\psi>$ and they have been interchanged due to the SWAP operation.

Mathematically, the SWAP gate is represented as follows:

$$SWAP = \begin{bmatrix} 1 & 0 & 0 & 0 \\ 0 & 0 & 1 & 0 \\ 0 & 1 & 0 & 0 \\ 0 & 0 & 0 & 1 \end{bmatrix}$$

Let's now move on to three-qubit quantum gates, starting with the CCX gate.

The quantum CCX or CCNOT gate – Toffoli gate

The **CCNOT** gate is a three-qubit quantum gate and is known as the **Controlled-Controlled NOT** gate. The CCX gate is also known as the **Toffoli gate** (named after Tommaso Toffoli). As you might have already guessed from the name, this gate has the first and second qubits as the control and the third qubit as the target. The matrix in the three-qubit case will be 8x8 (2^3x2^3).

The truth table for the CCNOT gate is shown in *Figure 3.7*:

Input	Output
|000 >	|000 >
|001 >	|001 >
|010 >	|010 >
|011 >	|011 >
|100 >	|100 >
|101 >	|101 >
|110 >	|111 >
|111 >	|110 >

Figure 3.7 – Truth table for the CCX gate

From the table, you can see that when the first and second qubits (control qubits) become 1, only then is the X gate operation applied to the third qubit (the target qubit) and the target qubit is flipped. The output on the CCNOT gate can be considered as the AND or the NAND classical logic gate operation.

Figure 3.8 shows the CCNOT gate:

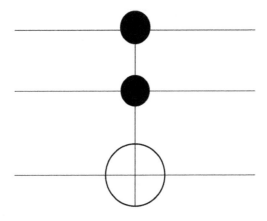

Figure 3.8 – Toffoli gate circuit

From *Figure 3.8*, you can see that the first two qubits are the controls and the third qubit is the target qubit where the operation is applied.

Mathematically, the *CCX* gate is defined as follows:

$$CCX = \begin{bmatrix} 1 & 0 & 0 & 0 & 0 & 0 & 0 & 0 \\ 0 & 1 & 0 & 0 & 0 & 0 & 0 & 0 \\ 0 & 0 & 1 & 0 & 0 & 0 & 0 & 0 \\ 0 & 0 & 0 & 1 & 0 & 0 & 0 & 0 \\ 0 & 0 & 0 & 0 & 1 & 0 & 0 & 0 \\ 0 & 0 & 0 & 0 & 0 & 1 & 0 & 0 \\ 0 & 0 & 0 & 0 & 0 & 0 & 0 & 1 \\ 0 & 0 & 0 & 0 & 0 & 0 & 1 & 0 \end{bmatrix}$$

From the preceding matrix, you can see that the upper-left quadrant of 4x4 is the identity operation and the lower-right quadrant of 4x4 is the controlled NOT operation, which verifies that this is the CCX gate matrix.

With the Toffoli gate covered, let's learn about the Fredkin gate.

The quantum CSWAP gate – Fredkin gate

The **CSWAP** or **Fredkin** gate, as you might have guessed, is a controlled version of the SWAP gate that we have already covered. This gate acts on three qubits. The first qubit is the control and the other two qubits are swapped whenever the control qubit is set to state $|1>$.

The truth table for the Fredkin gate is provided in *Figure 3.9*:

Input	Output
$|000>$	$|000>$
$|001>$	$|001>$
$|010>$	$|010>$
$|011>$	$|011>$
$|100>$	$|100>$
$|101>$	$|110>$
$|110>$	$|101>$
$|111>$	$|111>$

Figure 3.9 – Truth table for the Fredkin gate

From the preceding truth table, you can see that when the first qubit (the control qubit) is 1 then the second qubit and the third qubit are swapped.

Figure 3.10 shows the Fredkin gate circuit:

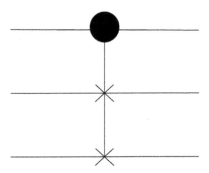

Figure 3.10 – CSWAP gate circuit

From *Figure 3.10*, you can see that the first qubit is held as control and the second and third qubits are being swapped. Since you have already studied the SWAP gate operation, this gate should be easy to understand.

Mathematically, the Fredkin is defined by the following matrix:

$$CSWAP = \begin{bmatrix} 1 & 0 & 0 & 0 & 0 & 0 & 0 & 0 \\ 0 & 1 & 0 & 0 & 0 & 0 & 0 & 0 \\ 0 & 0 & 1 & 0 & 0 & 0 & 0 & 0 \\ 0 & 0 & 0 & 1 & 0 & 0 & 0 & 0 \\ 0 & 0 & 0 & 0 & 1 & 0 & 0 & 0 \\ 0 & 0 & 0 & 0 & 0 & 0 & 1 & 0 \\ 0 & 0 & 0 & 0 & 0 & 1 & 0 & 0 \\ 0 & 0 & 0 & 0 & 0 & 0 & 0 & 1 \end{bmatrix}$$

Since now we have covered all the essential multi-qubit gates, you will be able to read standard quantum computing literature that uses these gates frequently. It will also help you to understand various quantum algorithms.

An interesting fact to note is that the Bell states that we covered in the previous section is made by putting a Hadamard in the first qubit and then a CX gate with first qubit as control and second qubit as target.

Let's now move on to a very interesting topic, quantum teleportation.

Quantum teleportation

Quantum teleportation is a truly fascinating phenomenon in quantum computing. It is used to transfer a quantum state from one place to another place without the need to travel the space between the source and destination. Although this may sound magical, it happens with the help of entanglement.

To make things easier, let's look at an example. Suppose Alice wants to send some information using a quantum state to Bob. She could send it by copying the quantum state she has, but due to the **no-cloning theorem** she is unable to copy her state (the no-cloning theorem states that quantum states cannot be copied).

To begin the teleportation process, consider that Alice and Bob both share a Bell state, which is an example of an entangled state.

There are a total of four kinds of operations that Bob can perform on his qubit to find out the state that Alice has sent to him:

- If measured value of a and b is 00, then Bob does nothing.

- If measured value a and b is 01, then Bob applies an X gate to his qubit (c qubit).

- If measured value a and b is 10, then Bob applies a Z gate to his qubit (c qubit).

- If measured a and b is 11, then Bob applies a Z gate and an X gate to his qubit (c qubit).

Figure 3.14 shows the teleportation circuit that will be implemented using the Silq programming language:

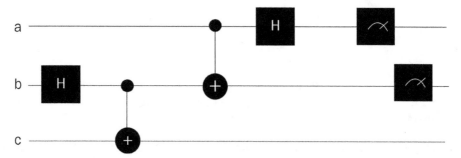

Figure 3.14 – Teleportation circuit

From *Figure 3.14*, we can see that Alice generates an entangled state between the qubits **b** and **c**. After this, Bob undoes the operation of Alice by applying a CNOT and Hadamard gate between qubit **a** and **b**. Then Bob makes a measurement and, based on that, applies the operations that have been described before.

The phenomenon of quantum teleportation is extremely important in research related to quantum communications. Quantum teleportation paves the way to transmit quantum information over great distances without suffering any decoherence. With the quantum teleportation covered, we are now ready to move on to superdense coding.

Quantum superdense coding

In quantum teleportation, we saw that two classical bits are used to transfer a quantum state from Alice to Bob. In **superdense coding**, we use a single quantum state to send two classical bits.

There are two classical bits, which means a total of 4 combinations. Now, depending on Alice and what she wants to send to Bob, she will apply one of the following gate operations:

- If Alice wants to send 00, then nothing is done.
- If Alice wants to send 01, then a Z gate is applied.
- If Alice wants to send 10, then an X gate is applied.
- If Alice wants to send 11, then ZX is applied.

Figure 3.15 shows the circuit for the superdense coding:

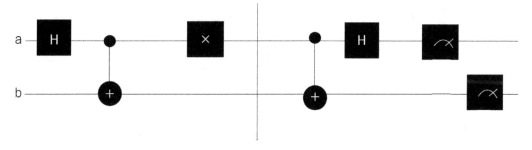

Figure 3.15 – Superdense coding circuit

From *Figure 3.15*, you can see that Alice generates a shared entanglement between qubits **a** and **b** and, to encode her secret message, she uses the X gate, which means she is sending value with 10 as information to Bob. Bob then undoes the operation applied by Alice by applying CNOT and Hadamard operations.

The expected output after the measurement can be summarized as follows:

- If the classical bits sent are 00, then the output of the measurement will be |00>.

- If the classical bits sent are 01, then the output of the measurement will be |10>.

- If the classical bits sent are 10, then the output of the measurement will be |01>.

- If the classical bits sent are 11, then the output of the measurement will be –|11>.

The superdense coding technique that you have learned has immense significance in transmitting or encrypting messages between two parties, and it cannot be intercepted by any other third party. Superdense coding is therefore like a quantum encrypted coding scheme.

Summary

We have covered a lot of important concepts in this chapter, ranging from multi-qubit gates to constructing quantum circuits to teleportation and superdense coding. By now, you have gained a thorough understanding of entanglement and the thought process behind making complex circuits, such as teleportation and superdense coding. The important applications learned in this chapter – teleportation and superdense coding – are heavily used for quantum communications. This will help you to appreciate the ongoing research and work happening in the field of quantum communication and cryptography.

In the next chapter, we will discuss the physical or hardware realization of a quantum computer and compare some of the popular hardware technologies used to build a quantum computer.

4
Physical Realization of a Quantum Computer

For many years, quantum computing has only been a theoretical area of research because the principles of quantum mechanics were very difficult to create in a physical lab environment. We know that theoretical studies alone are not enough until and unless we make it practical and apply those techniques in our daily lives. With the advancement of technology and physics devices of course, quantum computers came to be physically realizable. The challenges of quantum programming that we discussed in the previous chapter are related to physical quantum computers because, ultimately, the code is going to run on the hardware, and the problems in quantum programming arise also due to the challenges currently present in physical quantum computers today.

In this chapter, we will see the physical realization of quantum computers using various techniques based on quantum physics. The devices that we will discuss here work on the principles of quantum mechanics. We will cover the following topics:

- Criteria for quantum computation existence
- Superconducting qubit-based quantum computers
- Quantum annealing-based quantum computers

- Ion-trap quantum computers
- Nuclear magnetic resonance and optical photonic-based quantum computers

Criteria for quantum computation existence

In this section, we will be looking at the conditions which are necessary for making quantum computing a reality. All the current quantum computers are affected by quantum noise, which is also known as **decoherence**. Decoherence creates loss of quantum information and is therefore considered as a type of noise, and happens when the qubits interact with the environment over a long duration of time. A high accuracy of the computations performed by quantum computers is achieved when there is less interaction of qubits with the environment. Decoherence destroys the unitary operations that are a very important aspect of quantum computation, as we discussed in *Chapter 1, Essential Mathematics and Algorithmic Thinking*.

There are primarily four conditions that are required to make quantum computing happen. They are as follows:

- Quantum information depiction
- Unitary transformation capability
- Making the reference initial quantum states ready
- Output measurement

Let's discuss each of these conditions briefly, starting with quantum information depiction in the next section.

Depicting quantum information

As you are aware, quantum computing is all about unitary transformations happening between different quantum states and therefore the way we depict our quantum information plays an important role. Whenever we want to represent a certain state, we should always consider the number of qubits and the number of possible finite states that can be realized using those qubits. For example, when we have one qubit, then the possible finite states are two. If we have two qubits, then we can have four possible states. If we have n qubits, then we can have 2^n states. The symmetry of these quantum states is very useful for minimizing the decoherence of the quantum states. This symmetry arises because quantum operations happen inside the complex **Hilbert space**, which is a type of vector space where inner product as well as calculus operations are allowed. A proper characterization of qubits will help us to create scalable quantum computers in the near future with arbitrary numbers of qubits.

Unitary transformation capability

Unitary transformations can be easily constructed using single qubit gate operations and CX gates, therefore, to have a proper unitary system the gates should be properly realized by the quantum hardware. If there are systematic errors or imperfections present in the qubit operations, then it leads to decoherence.

Reference initial quantum states preparation

The proper and repeated initialization of quantum states is a crucial requirement for the unitary evolution of quantum systems. In the ideal scenario, the input state prepared must be a pure state and it should have a zero entropy, then only that state is a perfect state. A *pure state* means that there should be no interaction between the environment and the qubits, which will help the qubits to evolve and transform their states unitarily.

We will now see the final condition, which is output measurement after the quantum circuit or operations have been executed.

Output measurement capability

The output measurement capability of quantum computing is a very important concept because by measuring the state of the qubit we are able to know the output of a particular quantum algorithm. The output of quantum algorithm works on the principle of wave function collapse in which a particular quantum state comes with a certain probability after we measure the output of the quantum algorithm. Since the output of a quantum algorithm is in a superposition of qubits, the output is the probability of a certain qubit coming as we measure the output of the algorithm.

Since we have now seen the conditions necessary for the purpose of quantum computation, you now have an idea about the various conditions that are important for the physical realization of quantum computing. Let's now start discussing the various technologies that help us to realize quantum computer hardware. We will start by discussing superconducting qubits.

Superconducting qubit-based quantum computers

In this section, let's learn about the technology of **superconducting qubits**, which is used by tech giants such as Google, IBM, and Rigetti to make their own quantum computers. This section will aid you in appreciating the practical implementation of qubits about which you have read so far. Let's dive into superconducting qubits in the next section.

Superconducting qubits

Superconducting qubits work on the phenomenon of superconductivity. **Superconductors** are those materials that possess a critical temperature point below which their resistance vanishes and they conduct electricity freely. Unlike normal conductors where single electrons are responsible for the conduction of electricity, superconductors conduct by electron pairs also known as **Cooper pairs**. The Cooper pairs form a superfluid and flow without any loss of energy, which also indicates that the viscosity becomes zero. Another important characteristic to note is that since Cooper pairs are flows like superfluid, there is no interaction with the environment, which is important for unitary evolution and to maintain coherence. *Figure 4.1* shows four qubits of IBM's quantum computer:

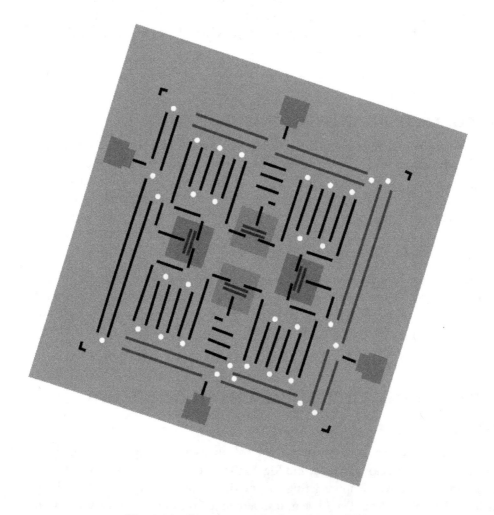

Figure 4.1 – Four superconducting qubits by IBM

Superconducting qubits are usually made up of aluminum, which is easily able to maintain the coherence of the qubits for longer, and helps the Cooper pairs to stay intact. Since these Cooper pairs represent the qubits, each of them is associated with a **wave function**. Wave functions are complex valued functions that mathematically describe a quantum state. The main characteristics of a wave are its amplitude and phase, and the wave function is no exception to this. In the case of the Cooper pairs, the number of pairs together represent the amplitude, and the magnetic field represents the phase of the wave function.

An important component that is very significant in superconducting qubits is a circuit called the **Josephson junction**. The Josephson junction consists of two or more superconductors, each of which is linked weakly by a thin insulator layer in between. In fact, this layer is so thin that, when superconductive temperature is reached, the Cooper pairs are able to tunnel through the layer, helping the superconductors to couple together. This system is achieved at very low temperatures, such as 10 mK (milli-Kelvin) in the dilution refrigerator. Most of the qubits that have been constructed use the Josephson junction mechanism with some capacitors having superconducting contacts. The circuit thus formed is an LC circuit (Inductor-Capacitor) where L is the Josephson junction and C is the capacitor. When this LC circuit is tuned properly, it behaves like a qubit. Superconducting quibts are popular because they provide huge controllability over the quantum states and have the lowest noise level, making them a favorable candidate for large-scale quantum computers. To know more about the superconducting qubit technology, refer to the paper in the *Further reading* section titled *A Quantum Engineer's Guide to Superconducting Qubits*.

Even though superconducting qubits have a low noise level when making a qubit or a quantum gate, that level is still currently beyond 0.1%, which is too high. Due to this, an extremely large number of quantum gate operations cannot be performed as the results will not be accurate. So, we are currently in the era of **NISQ (Noisy Intermediate-Scale Quantum)** where achieving accurate quantum computations with 50-100 qubits is quite significant. Let's discuss more about the NISQ era in the next section.

NISQ era

The quantum computing era that we are living in today is known as the **NISQ** era, as mentioned in the previous section. Today's quantum computers with 50-100 qubits are not powerful enough for many applications, because for those applications we would require thousands of qubits. But even with 50-100 qubit quantum computers, they can still be utilized for many-body physics problems, quantum chemistry simulations, quantum cryptography, and much more. In *Figure 4.2*, you can clearly observe the differences between fault-tolerant and NISQ quantum computers:

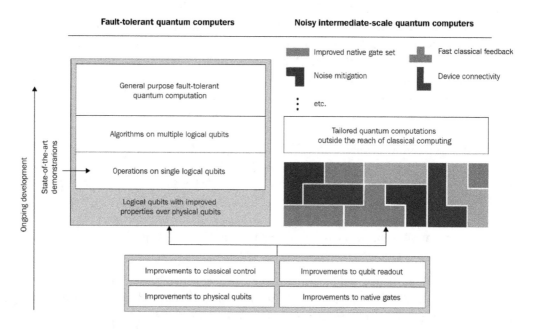

Figure 4.2 – Fault-tolerant versus NISQ quantum computers

The word *NISQ* was coined by John Preskill to describe the quantum computers we have today and that will be available in the coming few years. He mentioned that *intermediate-scale* in the NISQ acronym refers to the quantum computers with 50-100 qubits that will be available over the next few years. In the NISQ acronym, the word *noisy* refers to the fact that we currently have limited control over the qubits created through various technologies that are dependent on the principles of physics and are mostly affected by noise due to decoherence. Due to the presence of noise in qubits, thousands of qubits with gate operations cannot be performed well because they will get overwhelmed by the noise present in the system. Quantum error correction techniques can be used to overcome the effects of noise, but scaling this for thousands of qubits is very challenging.

Google and IBM have already released 72-qubit and 50-qubit superconducting circuits for quantum computers respectively and IBM is promising to bring a 1,000-qubit quantum computer by the year 2023. To gain more of an idea about this, check the articles in the *Further reading* section titled *Quantum Supremacy using a Programmable Superconducting Processor* and *IBM's Roadmap for Scaling Quantum Technology*.

With the NISQ era covered, you are now aware that it will take some years yet to truly reach fault-tolerant quantum computing, where all fabricated qubits are noise-free and we do not require error correction at every stage as we do now. Let's now move on to another technology known as quantum annealing in the next section.

Quantum annealing-based quantum computers

Quantum annealing is a technique used to find the global minimum or optimal solution to a problem that can have a large number of solutions. Essentially it is used for optimization problems such as the **Traveling Salesman Problem (TSP)**, which seeks to find the shortest path for a traveling salesman to visit every city on the route only once and then return back to their starting city. The TSP sounds very simple in description but is a very hard problem to solve because as the number of cities increase, thousands, millions, or even billions of paths emerge as well, which makes this a combinatorial optimization problem. For this kind of problem, quantum computers are the best because the TSP cannot be solved even by today's fastest computers.

D-Wave, a Canadian company, uses the quantum annealing technology to solve combinatorial optimization problems and their computers have been purchased by Google, Microsoft, and NASA for research on quantum computing. *Figure 4.3* shows the functioning of the D-Wave quantum annealing system:

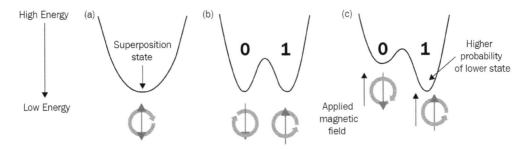

Figure 4.3 – D-Wave quantum annealing

In the D-Wave system, the qubits are formed using circulating currents that have a magnetic field associated with them and can form superposition states as well. The quantum annealing process is run to form the states 0 and 1. If a magnetic field is now applied to this configuration, then the energy level can be controlled, as shown in *Figure 4.3*. The probability of getting the 0 and 1 states can be adjusted using the strength of the magnetic field. Quantum annealing is less flexible in nature and cannot solve Shor's algorithm, which is an integer factorization algorithm, whereas the superconducting-qubit circuit models are very flexible and can run Shor's algorithm easily. Another point to note here is that in quantum annealing, constructing qubits is much easier, but for superconducting qubits it is very difficult as it requires the usage of dilution refrigerators to prevent decoherence.

Some of the potential applications of the quantum annealing technique can be found in portfolio optimization, optimizing telecommunication networks, optimizing medical treatment for cancers, optimization of machine learning and deep learning models, and much more.

Let's now explore ion-trap-based quantum computers in the next section.

Ion-trap quantum computers

Ion-trap-based quantum computers are completely dependent on electron spins and through these spins are able to represent the qubits. Atomic spins are very subtle in nature and difficult to observe, due to which they are also difficult to control too. Therefore, to have control over these particles, it is necessary to isolate them from the environment. This process is done by trapping a minimal number of atoms with the help of an electromagnetic field, and immediately cooling them so that they lose their kinetic energy. As soon as this process is completed the atomic spin can be controlled to construct qubits. *Figure 4.4* shows the ion-trap-based quantum computer:

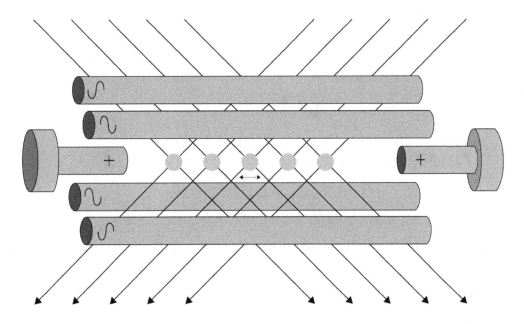

Figure 4.4 – Trapped ions

From *Figure 4.4*, we can observe that the ions are trapped between the cylindrical electrodes and this apparatus is usually kept in a high-vacuum container. The arrows shown are modulated laser light beams, which are placed incident to the ions so that their states can be perceived. For quantum computation to take place using these trapped atoms, any kind of unitary transform needs to be present in the atomic states. For single-qubit operations, we usually apply an electromagnetic field tuned to a particular frequency, and then the duration of this field as well as the phase both help to perform rotations on the qubits, which can exhibit various operations.

The initial quantum states in the trapped ions can be created by cooling the atoms, helping us to do various qubit calculations. It should be noted that ion-trap-based quantum computers are subjected to decoherence, so to overcome this, let's now move onto the next section, which describes nuclear magnetic resonance.

Nuclear magnetic resonance

In the **Nuclear Magnetic Resonance (NMR)** technique, electromagnetic waves are used to control and detect the spin of the nucleus of the atom. You must have heard about the NMR technique being used for spectroscopy and in chemistry as well. In chemistry, it is used to determine the structure of various molecules. In *Figure 4.5* you can see the physical apparatus used to build an NMR quantum computer:

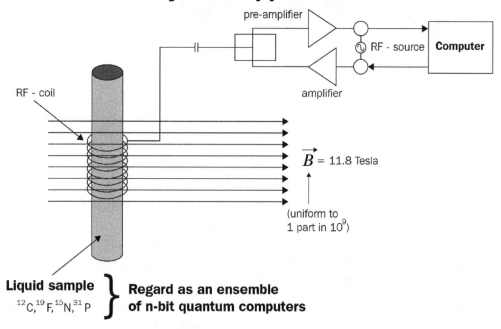

Figure 4.5 – An NMR quantum computer

The NMR apparatus consists of a liquid sample containing either carbon, fluorine, nitrogen, or phosphorus, which can be regarded as an ensemble of *n*-bit quantum computers. The molecules of the liquid emit NMR signals of a frequency of 500 MHz when the magnetic field around them is 11.8 tesla and are commonly mixed in a solvent to prevent inter-molecular interactions. The bore of a large superconducting magnet holds the liquid sample, which is connected to the RF circuit containing amplifiers. For a more detailed introduction to NMR equipment and its workings, refer to the book titled *Quantum Computation and Quantum Information* in the *Further reading* section.

For NMR quantum computer operations, firstly the nuclei of the liquid are allowed to reach thermal equilibrium and then, using a classical computer, RF signals are applied to create the desired nuclei states. Finally, to measure the state of the spins, the pre-amplifier is enabled and the other amplifier is switched off completely. The initial state in this system is created by polarizing the nuclei spins using a strong magnetic field. To perform quantum computations, refocusing pulses are utilized for single-qubit operations by reversing the time evolution in such a way that a particular frequency spins starting from a given point to come back to the same point. The only disadvantage of NMR is that during the initial state preparation, it reduces the signal exponentially with the number of qubits if the initial polarization is not very high.

Let's now move onto another physics-based technology called optical photonics in the next section.

Optical photonics-based quantum computers

Optical photonics is a fascinating branch of physics that deals with optical photons, which are chargeless particles responsible for the phenomenon of light. It is because of optical photons that we are able to see the world around us. As well as this, these photons have been used in optical fibers for many years to enable high-speed internet connections and better network connectivity. It turns out that these same photons can be used to perform quantum computations as well!

Figure 4.6 shows a quantum operation using optical equipment for quantum computation. **BS** refers to the **beam splitter**, which is used to split a light beam into two parts. The **phase shifter** used is non-linear in nature and introduces delays or advances in the phase of the laser signal used here:

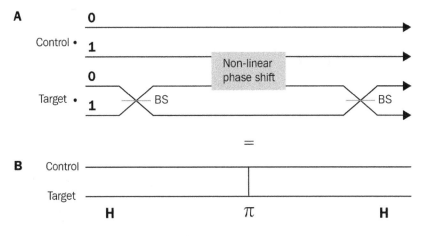

Figure 4.6 – Optical quantum computer operation

In the preceding figure, you can see that the beam splitter is used to create the Hadamard gates and a controlled pi gate is created using the non-linear phase shifter. Consequently, all quantum operations can be performed using these optical devices on single qubits. Each photon can represent a single qubit, or they can be in superposition in the form of $c_0 \left|0\right> + c_0 \left|1\right>$, which is known as dual-rail representation.

A Toronto-based quantum computing company called Xanadu uses optical photonics-based quantum computers and have released their own quantum computer in the cloud for commercial access. This is the world's first optical-based quantum computer in the cloud, along with the superconducting examples currently provided by IBM and Google.

Apart from the techniques covered in this chapter for quantum hardware realization, there exist other technologies as well for the physical realization of a quantum computer. Some of these techniques include topological quantum computing, cavity QED, quantum dot, nitrogen vacancy center, and neutral atom technologies. If you want to dig deeper into these fields, then there are references available in the *Further reading* section.

Summary

In this chapter, we explored the various technologies currently being used by industries and researchers to realize the hardware of a quantum computer on which you can run your quantum operations. You will now be able to analyze the challenges involved in the making of a real quantum computer and understand how hard it is to make the quantum states coherent for an extended duration without any interaction from the environment.

Upon completion of this chapter, we also conclude *Part 1* of this book, which enabled you to gain some background knowledge and motivation to aid you in studying the further chapters in the upcoming parts. In the next chapter, we will start diving into the challenges faced by quantum communities in quantum computer programming.

Further reading

- Michael A. Nielsen, Issac L. Chuang, *Quantum Computation and Quantum Information*, Cambridge University Press, 2010

- John Preskill, *Quantum Computing in the NISQ era and beyond*, arXiv, July 2018

- Philip Krantz, Morten Kjaergaard, Fei Yan, Terry P. Orlando, Simon Gustavsson, William D. Oliver, *A Quantum Engineer's Guide to Superconducting Qubits*, arXiv:1904.06560, April 2019

- Jay Gambetta, *IBM's Roadmap for Scaling Quantum Technology*, IBM Research Blog, September 2020

- John Martinis, Sergio Boixo, *Quantum Supremacy using a Programmable Superconducting Processor*, Google AI Blog, October 2019

- Ville Lahtinen, Jiannis K. Pachos., A Short Introduction to Topological Quantum Computation, arXiv:1705.04103, September 2017

- Mirhosseini, M., Kim, E., Zhang, X. et al. *Cavity quantum electrodynamics with atom-like mirrors*. Nature 569, 692–697 (2019), available at `https://doi.org/10.1038/s41586-019-1196-1`

- Tyler Maxwell, Maria Gabriela Nogueira Campos, Stephen Smith, Mitsushita Doomra, Zon Thwin, Swadeshmukul Santra, *Chapter 15*, *Quantum Dots*, Micro and Nano Technologies, Nanoparticles for Biomedical Applications, Elsevier, 2020

- Liu Gang-Qin, Pan Xin-Yu. *Quantum information processing with nitrogen–vacancy centers in diamond*. Chinese Physics B, 2018, 27(2): 020304

- Loic Henriet, Lucas Beguin, Adrien Signoles, Thierry Lahaye, Antoine Browaeys, Georges-Olivier Reymond, Christophe Jurczak, *Quantum computing with neutral atoms*, arXiv:2006.12326, September 2020

Section 2: Challenges in Quantum Programming and Silq Programming

From this part onward and the next part, you will dive deep into the basics of quantum computation and its implementation using the Silq programming language. Various significant quantum circuits and quantum gates will be discussed and implemented together. After completing this part, you will feel confident in your ability to understand the math and implementation of various quantum circuits using Silq programming.

This section comprises the following chapters:

5
Challenges in Quantum Computer Programming

Early computers were originally as large as a room and required a lot of power in order to operate. Today, quantum computers are also the size of a room and require heavy electricity to operate. We currently face various challenges when developing quantum programming languages, which are mostly low level and circuit based.

This chapter will introduce you to the challenges faced by researchers in programming quantum computers. This will encourage you to think about the shortcomings of the programming languages, and therefore ways to solve these challenges. We will cover the following topics in particular:

- A brief history of classical computers
- The challenges of today's classical computers
- Understanding the assembly language
- HLLs for classical computers

- Low-level circuit programming of quantum computers

- Introducing quantum programming languages such as IBM Qiskit, Microsoft Q#, and Google Cirq

- The challenges of quantum computer programming

A brief history of classical computers

Charles Babbage, also known as *the father of the computer*, was the first person to develop a mechanical classical computer, called the **difference engine**. In this computer, the parts were entirely made by hand and punched cards were used to provide inputs to the computer. Then, **electromechanical computers** were developed during World War II and these were much more efficient than the mechanical difference engine developed by Babbage, using electrical switches to operate the mechanical relays in order to perform calculations. With the advent of vacuum tubes, this changed completely. This was because vacuum tubes are able to control the flow of electric current through the tube whenever an electric potential is applied at the tube ends.

Electronic Numerical Integrator and Computer (**ENIAC**) was the first programmable and digital computer made for a wider audience. This was constructed in 1945 and consisted of a variety of electronic and electrical components, such as vacuum tubes, diodes, resistors, capacitors, and crystal rectifiers.

The way in which vacuum tubes work gave birth to the idea of the transistor, which can be perceived as a miniaturized version of vacuum tubes. *Figure 5.1* shows the very first transistor, referred to as a point-contact transistor, which was developed by William Shockley, John Bardeen, and Walter Brattain in 1947 (they are also credited with the invention of the bipolar junction transistor in 1948):

First commercially available point-contact transistor

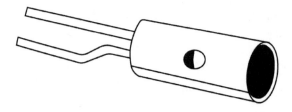

Figure 5.1 – Replica of the point-contact transistor

The development of integrated circuits by Jack Kilby in 1958 revolutionized classical computing and is the main foundation for today's classical computers. Today, you can find electronic chips and circuits that consist of extremely small transistors almost everywhere. The classical computers that we use have billions of transistors in a small electronic chip. Via this discussion of history, you can understand the challenges of quantum computers in a better manner with regards to the fact that they face challenges in computation, which is today done in computers as large in size as rooms. An excessive amount of research is done today to miniaturize quantum computers because of their sophisticated technology that exceeds classical computers.

Let's now focus on these challenges and limitations that today's classical computers are facing, as well as looking at the reasons for moving toward quantum computers.

The challenges of today's classical computers

The previous section demonstrated that researchers have always wanted computing capabilities to be as energy-efficient and portable as possible, which we can see through microprocessor companies such as Intel who keep shrinking the size of the processor and try to squeeze in as many transistors as possible in a small area of a chip with less heat dissipation. However, this brings a challenge: with a small scale of transistors, the phenomenon of quantum mechanics starts to dominate!

Because of the phenomenon of quantum mechanics, the classical computation process starts to give inaccurate results, as well as the fabrication of silicon chips being hindered.

According to Moore's law, originating in 1965, it is predicted that the number of transistors in new electronic chips would double every 2 years.

The semiconductor chip fabrication is certainly facing a physical limit when it comes to building more miniaturized microchips because of the quantum mechanical effects that happen during the fabrication process.

There are a few other challenges as well that today's classical computers are facing and these include searching for values in an unstructured database and factorization of very large integers. These problems require huge computational power and if tried in a classical computer today, it would take years to find solutions to these kinds of problems. It is important to find solutions related to the problem of factorization because factorization problems are an essential part of our modern cryptographic systems. It is natural to think that quantum computers will be able to break any classical cryptographic systems because of the inherent parallelism present in their computation system. It is for this reason that today there is a lot of research being conducted in the field of quantum cryptography that cannot be broken and is most secure.

Some of the other limits or challenges that are faced by today's classical computing devices include **processing speed** and **communication delays**. Classical computers are sequential devices and they perform calculations one at a time. To make it parallel, **Graphics Processing Units (GPUs)** were introduced, which possess a huge number of classical processors connected in parallel, so that the information processing is faster. GPUs are used for gaming, graphics design, space research, and much more. However, GPUs are also classical devices and there is a certain limit of chip size we can approach for its manufacturing of the parallel cores required for computation. Classical computers also face communication delays because of the slow memory speed, which takes up a lot of energy in every computation. A lot of research is being carried out to make energy-efficient classical computing devices so as to increase the communication speed.

We now understand the challenges that are faced by classical computers today, which will help you take notice of the sophisticated challenges involved in the construction of quantum computers and their programming capabilities. This will also help you to make an analogy between the classical challenge and quantum challenges. Now let's focus on the programming aspects of these classical computers. In the next section, we will briefly discuss the assembly language, which was used to program early microprocessors.

Understanding the assembly language

The development of **High-Level Languages (HLLs)** was carried out during the twentieth century. Before these HLLs came into existence, some architecture-specific languages were developed to program the early microprocessors that carried out various operations. Programming is giving certain instructions to the computer to achieve a particular task and to let the computer handle repetitive tasks.

During the early development of classical computers, researchers were gaining more knowledge about the hardware and architecture details of the computer, and consequently, they created languages that were more architecture-specific or low-level. They are called *low-level* because the level of abstraction between these languages and the machine language (binary representation) is low. One of the early languages developed was the **assembly language**, which was based on the architecture of microprocessors. Before the assembly language, the machine code was used, which represented the operations using binary digits (0 and 1). Let's see an example of the assembly language code of an 8086 microprocessor:

```
MOV CX, 0000
MOV AX, [3000]
MOV BX, [3002]
Add AX, BX
```

```
JNC MEMORY
INC CX
MOV [3004], AX
MOV [3006], CX
END
```

You might have guessed from the program that it performs the addition of two numbers with or without a carry function. Let's see line by line how the program works. This will help you to understand the equivalent low-level circuit programming of quantum computers, which we will discuss later in this chapter.

In the program, the values 3000, 3001, 3004, and 3006 are memory location addresses. AX, BX, and CX are registers that are present in the 8086 microprocessor. First, the CX register is initialized with the 0000 number, which acts as a counter. Then, the AX and BX numbers are moved to locations 3000 and 3002 and an addition operation is carried out between them and stored in the AX register. If there is no carry generated from the addition process, then the MOV [3004], AX and MOV [3006], CX lines are executed; otherwise, the counter is incremented by the INC CX line.

In the preceding program, you can see that it is compulsory to be familiar with the instruction set of the 8086 microprocessor in order to carry out any operation using the processor. As well as, the programmer should be familiar with the low-level architecture of the processor, which means that the process of writing code here is like circuit-level programming. The preceding code was only for simple addition; if you now want to write code for a more complex task, then the programming task becomes very tedious and the program becomes larger, making it difficult to understand. Some of the other disadvantages of the assembly language are that it suffers from non-portability because the code is customized to a certain architecture and therefore is optimized for that certain architecture. Assembly languages are difficult to understand by a wider audience because of the circuit level and architecture familiarity that is required.

Even though the assembly language has disadvantages, the execution speed of this programming language is very fast because of the close connection between the low-level circuit details of the processor. However, to reach a wider audience and to make the language simpler, researchers started looking toward higher-level programming languages that use English words as keywords to perform the operations.

In the next section, let's dive into the evolution of these HLLs for classical computing. This will serve as the background to study high-level programming for quantum computing as well.

HLLs for classical computers

We have now seen the evolution of classical computers and the very first low-level programming languages, which were developed to provide instructions to the computer to achieve some tasks. Similar tasks can also be achieved using HLLs whose programming syntax is much easier to comprehend by a wider audience as well.

In HLLs, there are certain advantages, which are as follows:

- The amount of abstraction present is stronger than that of low-level circuit programming languages.

- HLLs provide an interface between the low-level circuit elements, such as registers and memory, and the users who would like to use simple expressions and statements to perform programming operations.

- HLLs also help to perform better memory management and can automate processes significantly faster than lower-level languages.

The IBM 704 mainframe computer used the Fortran HLL for its programming and was later used by other organizations and individuals as well. During the 1960s and 70s, lots of significant development took place in the area of HLLs to make them available to a wider audience with better abstraction and unique features.

Some of the notable languages that were developed during the 1970s include the **C language**, **Prolog**, and the **Structured Query Language** (**SQL**). The C language was developed for general-purpose computing and can be used by anyone to learn programming, as well as developing interesting applications such as games and software. Due to the automation the HLLs were able to bring, the field of **Artificial Intelligence** (**AI**) was also gaining recognition and because of this, the **Prolog** language was introduced, which was able to define simple logic operations, and the programs were expressed in the form of facts and rules. When the surge of data came, it was essential to develop a structure to store the data in a systematic manner, because of which SQL came into the picture.

Let's explore all of these languages briefly and learn how they compare. This will enhance our thinking and understanding of the evolution of the HLLs for classical computers and how the same process of HLL development can be done with quantum computers too as is being done at present by various researchers. One of the results of that research is the Silq language.

Here is a sample C program that shows the C program's ability to add two numbers:

```
#include<stdio.h>
int main() {
```

```
    int a, b, sum;
    printf("\nEnter two numbers: ");
    scanf("%d %d", &a, &b);
    sum = a + b;
    printf("Sum : %d", sum);
    return(0);
}
```

Here, you can see that the program starts with `#include<stdio.h>`, which is a standard library used to get input from the keyboard and display output on the monitor. Then, from `int main()`, the `main` function is called, inside which all the operations take place. The a, b, and sum integers are defined, which are stored in **Random Access Memory (RAM)** at a particular memory address. The `printf()` statement prints statements on the monitor and `scanf()` is used to gain input from the user through the keyboard. The required operation of addition is performed and then the result is displayed on the monitor. To let the operating system know that the program has run successfully, it is required to use a `return()` statement. In this way, the `main()` function returns a 0 value if the program execution is successful, otherwise returning a non-zero value.

When comparing the C program with the assembly language program, the most notable difference that you can see is the ease and elegancy of the C language. You can see the syntax of the programming language is very intuitive and straightforward and we do not require the knowledge of the architecture of the Intel Core i9 processor to run this program.

The main software that connects the HLL with the machine-level or low-level architecture language is known as the compiler. The compiler is software that will take your C program or any other high-level program and convert it into a low-level program so that the machine can understand the operations. This is because machines only understand voltage values and not the English words used in the C language. The compiler takes the whole program and converts it into machine code, and if there is an error, it is informed after the conversion.

There is another software called the **interpreter** that does a similar job to the compiler but reads the code line by line. If any line has an error, it will not proceed further until the error has been rectified.

Let's look at Prolog programming briefly, which is used to program AI systems. Nowadays, Python programming is used for AI-related tasks:

```
bigger(elephant, horse)
bigger(horse, donkey)
```

```
bigger (donkey, dog)
bigger (donkey, monkey)
```

The preceding code shows a very simple Prolog program and you can easily identify the results of the statements written as they are logical. If you query the Prolog language about whether the statements are true or false, then it will give the answers as follows:

```
?- bigger (donkey, dog)
Yes
?- bigger (monkey, elephant)
No
```

Prolog is very different from the C language and completely works on first-order logic, where we can define the logic with proper facts. The syntax of Prolog is quite simple and it is a compiled language in the same way as the C language.

Finally, let's take a look at SQL; you will see how it is entirely different from C and Prolog:

```
CREATE TABLE Persons (
    PersonID int,
    LastName varchar(255),
    FirstName varchar(255),
    Address varchar(255),
    City varchar(255)
);
```

You might have already guessed by looking at the code that it creates a table. The name of the table is Persons, and the information provided inside the brackets are the column names that the table is supposed to have. It also provides information about the type of data, such as integer or character type. This is important information because the type of data decides the amount of memory each type will occupy in RAM.

We have now seen three different HLLs and their writing style, which is very elegant, simple, and intuitive. During the 1980s, more features were developed and added to all of these languages to make them easier to use, understand, and apply to real-world applications.

For example, C++ was introduced, which provided the features of object-oriented programming not present in the C language. With the dawn of the internet in the 1990s, the focus of programming languages shifted toward scripting-based languages, which are helpful in designing websites and various other networking services. Today, the most common trend is to develop applications and software and make them open source so that they are available to the general public free of charge.

In this section, we discussed the evolution of the HLLs of classical computers. You can observe that in not much time (think 30 years or so), the features of HLLs became extremely user-friendly, now easily used by any industry or for research purposes. We hope to have the same kind of evolution for quantum computers as well and **Silq programming** will prove to be one of the notable steps toward making this happen. This will help current and future researchers develop quantum software and applications rather than worrying about the low-level circuit programming of quantum computers.

In the next section, we are going to discuss the low-level circuit programming of quantum computers, which is done today by various researchers and companies. You will find this analogous to the classical computing assembly language discussed before.

Low-level circuit programming of quantum computers

In the previous section, we saw the usefulness of HLLs for classical computers, which use a compiler or interpreter to take care of the translation of high-level code into machine code. We also saw that larger programs, such as software or computer applications, will be very difficult to write in low-level languages as the code becomes very complex and harder to understand.

As you know, quantum computing is currently in its early stages of development and the process that the field of quantum computing is going through is very similar to that of classical computing. Today, thanks to the HLLs of classical computing, we have software development kits available in classical HLLs that help us to program basic operations on quantum computers. Some of the prominent examples of these kits are **Microsoft Q#**, **IBM Qiskit**, and **Google Cirq**, which will be discussed in the next section.

Most of the programming for quantum computing is done at the circuit level, which means low-level. We manually code the circuit operations ourselves to achieve a specific task or operation that can be run on a quantum simulator or a real quantum computer:

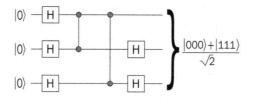

Figure 5.2 – An example of a quantum circuit

In *Figure 5.2*, you can see that some quantum gates have been applied to the |0> qubit. These gates are known as **Hadamard gates** and you learned about them in *Chapter 2, Quantum Bits, Quantum Measurements, and Quantum Logic Gates*. They are used to create an equal superposition of the qubits. This circuit makes a state of $\frac{|000> + |111>}{\sqrt{2}}$, which is known as a **GHZ state**, named after Greenberger, Horne, and Zeilinger, who first studied it.

If you want to code such a circuit, there are methods available in software kits such as Qiskit, but now you can see a similar situation to what we encountered when we started with classical computing, which was the assembly language relying on low-level architecture details of classical circuits. We are used to dealing with gates, registers, and memory addresses to perform a particular task. The circuit shown in *Figure 5.3* can also be constructed using different gates:

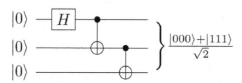

Figure 5.3 – The equivalent of a GHZ circuit

In *Figure 5.3*, you can see that the same GHZ state is generated but this time a new type of gate operation is applied called a **CNOT** or **CX gate**; you have learned about this in *Chapter 3, Multiple Quantum Bits, Entanglement, and Quantum Circuits*. So, one question that arises here is the optimality of the quantum circuit, because each quantum circuit is associated with a circuit cost. The lower the cost of the circuit, the better it becomes, and this is one of the fundamental ways to calculate the efficiency of the quantum program. Some of the common ways to evaluate the efficiency of a quantum program are measuring the number of quantum bits, the number of instructions, the runtime, and the circuit depth.

In today's quantum computers, we face the problem of environmental noise and it is very difficult to isolate the quantum particles to create a qubit state, which is why noise is always present in the qubits. These quantum devices which are noisy are called **Noisy Intermediate-Scale Quantum** (**NISQ**) devices, it was discussed in *Chapter 4, Physical Realization of a Quantum Computer*. From the preceding circuit of GHZ, you can now guess that it will be difficult to make a quantum operating system or software or any quantum-based web application if we only rely on low-level circuit programming where the level of abstraction is very low. If the circuit size for a particular application becomes large, then it becomes subjected to errors too. To develop more sophisticated applications for quantum computers, quantum HLLs are a huge necessity and the Silq programming language is a major step in this direction.

In this section, we saw the low-level circuits for quantum computers and in *Chapter 6, Silq Programming Basics and Features*, onward, you will see high level quantum programming language - Silq, which will look like C language for quantum computers. NISQ devices face 10 times more noise for CX gates than other single-qubit gates and that is why during the cost calculation, the number of CX gates is multiplied by 10. It can be seen that the fewer gates there are, the better the cost of the quantum circuit is.

In the next section, we will discuss some of the classical HLL software development kits that are currently used for quantum programming.

Introducing quantum programming languages

In this section, our goal is to introduce you to the classical HLL software development kits that are currently being used by researchers and industry for the programming of quantum computers. The goal here will be to briefly discuss these languages and some simple programs so that you can understand the low-level quantum programming we are doing currently by utilizing the classical HLLs. Let's start with IBM's Qiskit programming language.

The IBM Qiskit quantum programming language

IBM launched their Qiskit (`https://qiskit.org/`) programming toolkit in March 2017 to spread more and more awareness and they have done an excellent job in providing valuable resources on various important quantum algorithms as well as their real-life practical implementations. IBM has created quantum simulators, as well as unveiling their quantum computer hardware in the cloud in 2016 so as to make it commercially available to a larger audience.

Qiskit is primarily divided into four major components, each having its own significance and applications:

- **Qiskit Terra**: This provides tools for creating low-level quantum circuit programming and is used heavily by various researchers and industry people.

- **Qiskit Ignis**: This provides tools for quantum error correction and mitigation.

- **Qiskit Aqua**: This supports various applications of quantum algorithms, such as optimization, AI, and finance.

- **Qiskit Aer**: This has been developed for the simulation of noise models and the performance assessment of quantum circuits.

Let's now go through a simple Qiskit quantum program and you will see the circuit programming being done using the tools. We will be looking at the code of the GHZ state quantum circuit described in the previous section:

```
import numpy as np
from qiskit import *
from qiskit import Aer
```

The preceding statements import all the libraries, such as `numpy` for numerical computations and `qiskit` for creating and executing the quantum circuit. `Aer` is the library that has the quantum simulators and can run on classical computers. Next, let's start making the circuit for the GHZ state:

```
circ = QuantumCircuit(3)
circ.h(0)
circ.cx(0, 1)
circ.cx(0, 2)
```

Here, a quantum circuit of three qubits is created, then Hadamard is applied to the first qubit. Next, a CX gate is applied with the first qubit as the control and the second as the target. Similarly, a second CX gate is applied. In the next code block, let's see the simulation of the circuit:

```
backend = Aer.get_backend("qasm_simulator")
job_sim = execute(circ, backend)
sim_result = job_sim.result()
print(sim_result.get_counts(circ))
```

In the preceding chunk of code, the QASM simulator from the IBM Aer library is called and the quantum circuit is executed by the simulator multiple times. Here, with each run of the circuit, it generates either the 000 or 111 state. The output of this code is { '000' : 541, '111': 483}.

With this simple example, you can see the nature of quantum circuit programming; it becomes more complex when the problem is much more complex to solve. It will be beneficial for you to check IBM's resources on quantum computing (https://qiskit. org/textbook/preface.html), where you will be able to find more complex circuits for various applications that are difficult to understand.

Next, let's take a look at the Q# programming language developed by Microsoft and see some sample code to understand this language.

The Microsoft Q# quantum programming language

Microsoft released the Q# (https://docs.microsoft.com/en-us/quantum/) programming language in December 2017 to gain pace with quantum computing and to make useful contributions to this field. Q# is also very similar to IBM Qiskit and provides all the low-level quantum circuit programming features for development.

Let's see some code from the Microsoft tutorials that is based on creating a Bell state, $\frac{|00> +|11>}{\sqrt{2}}$, and we have studied these states in *Chapter 3, Multiple Quantum Bits,*

Entanglement, and Quantum Circuits:

```
operation TestBellState(count : Int, initial : Result) : (Int,
Int)    {
        mutable numOnes = 0;
        using ((q0, q1) = (Qubit(), Qubit())) {
            for (test in 1..count) {
                SetQubitState(initial, q0);
                SetQubitState(Zero, q1);
                H(q0);
                CNOT(q0,q1);
                let res = M(q0);
                // Count the number of ones we saw:
                if (res == One) {
                    set numOnes += 1;
                }
```

```
            }
            SetQubitState(Zero, q0);
            SetQubitState(Zero, q1);
        }
        // Return number of times we saw a |0> and number of
        // times we saw a |1>
        return (count-numOnes, numOnes);
    }
```

You can observe in the code that a quantum circuit operation is being defined and a variable called numOnes acts as a counter to count the number of times a particular state is produced by Microsoft's quantum circuit simulator. ((q0, q1) = (Qubit(), Qubit())) is used to define the qubits and then inside the for loop, each of the qubits is initialized. A Hadamard gate is applied to the first qubit and a CX gate is applied with the first qubit as the control and the second as the target. After these operations, a measurement is carried out on the first qubit and finally, the count of the number of zeros and ones is printed.

From the preceding code, you can observe that Microsoft Q# code is quite complex and larger in size than IBM Qiskit. Let's now discuss our final quantum programming kit – Google Cirq.

The Google Cirq quantum programming language

Cirq (https://quantumai.google/cirq/tutorials) was announced by Google in July 2018 at an international quantum machine learning conference and since then, they have developed it to give the quantum community ease with their platform. Google is very active in the field of quantum computing and in March 2020, they also released **TensorFlow Quantum** (TFQ) to develop the field of quantum machine learning. We will be focusing on some important aspects of quantum machine learning in *Chapter 13, Quantum Machine Learning*.

For now, let's take a look at some sample Cirq code for creating the GHZ state. The code is provided in Python 3:

```
import cirq
```

The preceding line imports the Cirq library and will be used to carry out the quantum operations and the making of the quantum circuit. Next, we will define the qubits:

```
qbit = cirq.LineQubit.range ( 3 )
qc = cirq.Circuit ()
```

We defined the three qubits that will be required to make the GHZ state and the quantum circuit, with the help of which we will be able to apply different quantum gates to the qubits. Now we will append these operations:

```
qc.append (cirq.H(qbit[0]))
```

We apply the Hadamard gate to the first qubit and append it to the quantum circuit. Now we are going to apply the CNOT gate:

```
for i in range (2):
    qc.append ( cirq.CNOT ( qbit [i] , qbit [i+1]) )
```

Here, the CX gate is being applied with the first qubit as the control and the second as the target. Similarly, again a CX is applied as the loop runs two times. The circuit construction is complete; next, let's measure the circuit:

```
qc.append (cirq.measure (* qbit , key ='x') )
```

The measurement operation is applied in order to take the measurements of the states generated by the quantum circuit. To visualize the circuit, we will perform a `print` operation:

```
print (qc)
```

The `print` statement prints the quantum circuit that is being created here. In the last stage, we will simulate the circuit using the Cirq simulator:

```
simulator = cirq.Simulator ()
results = simulator.run ( qc , repetitions = 500)
counts = cirq.plot_state_histogram (results)
```

As we saw in IBM Qiskit, Google also uses its own quantum simulator to simulate the quantum circuit many times to collect measurements for each of the 000 or 111 states generated by the quantum circuit and returns the number of times the states were being produced by the circuit.

Comparing Cirq with Qiskit, you can find many similarities and the code structure is compact and easy to understand, in contrast to Q#, where the code is much larger and it is complex to create even simple programs.

By comparing various quantum programming tools using classical software development kits, you will have got an idea of the low-level circuit programming that we are currently focusing on and is used widely by everyone in the industry, research, and academia. But as discussed before, to develop bigger applications and to truly unleash the potential of quantum computers, HLLs specifically for quantum are an extreme necessity.

In the final section of this chapter, let's now understand the challenges of quantum programming.

The challenges of quantum programming

Throughout this chapter, we have aimed to show you the progress of classical computing hardware and software and contrast it with the developments we are currently seeing with quantum computers and quantum programming. This was important to do because the improvements of the later technologies are dependent upon the previous ones as they give us a coherent thought process and intuition to use our common sense to think about the natural extension of technology and help us to develop a wider perspective of looking at things from a different angle.

In this section, let's discuss the challenges currently faced by researchers of quantum computing and quantum programming. Let's see the challenges one by one briefly:

- **Quantum programming difficulty**: If we want to contrast classical programing with quantum programming, then we are in a better position to compare the classical programming with quantum programming because classical computing languages are already mature and we can use them to build efficient quantum programming languages. The reason is that in classical computing, we deal only with two bits – 0 and 1. Therefore, the machine code becomes easier to write. But in quantum computing, as you know from *Chapter 1*, *Essential Mathematics and Algorithmic Thinking*, quantum states can remain in the superposition of qubits as well. Now, you can imagine the difficulty we would have if were to write machine code for quantum computers. There would be many possibilities for representing qubits and not just two!

- **The audience not being familiar with low-level languages**: With the help of classical HLLs, we have developed software development kits for quantum programming that have improved our life for quantum computing. However, low-level circuit programming has its own limitations and creates a hindrance in the progress of technology because the wider audience is not able to understand the complex aspects.

- **Knowledge of low-level architecture for quantum computing**: Today, if we want to program a quantum computer using the existing software tools, we must have an idea of the architecture and quantum gates and circuit-level knowledge so that we can create and simulate the quantum circuits using a classical simulator or on real quantum hardware. These languages work on individual qubits and this is very similar to other hardware description languages, such as VHDL, which are used for describing digital electronic circuits.

- **Uncomputation challenge**: Another fundamental challenge that today's classical HLLs do not possess is that of **uncomputation**. Uncomputation is an integral part of quantum programming that helps to undo the computation that was performed and helps to clear the quantum memory. This is important because the uncomputation step helps to preserve the unitary nature of quantum circuits and is in line with the laws of quantum mechanics. Today, we have to perform the step of uncomputation manually after the creation of our quantum circuit, which is a tedious and time-consuming process.

- **Cost of the quantum circuit**: For the low-level circuit programming of quantum computers, we saw that the GHZ state can be represented by two different kinds of circuits and then the challenge becomes to have a circuit that has better efficiency. Currently, we are calculating the cost of the quantum circuit but we want the quantum HLLs to take care of these low-level details and we should not worry about these circuit models.

For all the problems discussed here, Silq programming paves the way to success. Silq combines the features of the latest developments happening in the field of classical HLLs as well as the quantum programming necessities to address these issues successfully. This language will prove to be a boon to scientists and engineers who are working on various applications and require quantum computers for their work. This will also enable us in the future to construct quantum operating systems, software, and applications for quantum computers. You can consider Silq as the C language of quantum computing. We will discuss the Silq programming language in *Chapter 6, Silq Programming Basics and Features*.

Summary

This chapter introduced you to the developments that happened when classical computing was first developed and the challenges that were overcome. In a very similar manner, quantum computing and programming are now facing challenges that can also be overcome in time. You can now appreciate the various challenges that are faced in the low-level circuit programming for quantum computers, which are similar to the ones faced while programming classical computers. This will help you to explore more in this direction and find novel ways of solving challenges related to quantum programming.

It is also very important to note that software is just one part of quantum computing. The main challenges lie in the quantum hardware, because of which the programming of quantum computers becomes a difficult task. In the next chapter, we will discuss the Silq programming language, its features and use it to make simple quantum logic gates.

Further reading

Frederic Lardinois, *Silq is a new high level programming language for quantum computers*, `https://techcrunch.com/2020/06/15/silq-is-a-new-high-level-programming-language-for-quantum-computers/`, June 2020

6
Silq Programming Basics and Features

To provide a better understanding and commercial value for technical as well as non-technical audiences, programming languages have evolved a lot from being low-level to high-level, which hides the abstract details. In the case of quantum computing, we are now moving toward making high-level languages that can abstract out the low-level details that are not useful for many users. The Silq programming language is the first step in this direction.

In this chapter, you will learn about the basics of the Silq programming language and its various constructs, which will help you to do high-level quantum programming. You will get into the features of the Silq language that make it unique from other programming languages. We will cover the following topics:

- Introducing the Silq programming language and its special features
- Silq programming language installation
- Introducing Silq data types
- Defining variables in the Silq programming language

- Control flow in the Silq programming language
- Functions and iterations in the Silq programming language
- Introducing Silq annotations
- Simple example programs using the Silq programming language

Technical requirements

You can download the code samples for this chapter from this book's official GitHub repository at `https://github.com/PacktPublishing/Quantum-Computing-with-Silq-Programming`.

Introducing Silq and its special features

In *Chapter 5, Challenges in Quantum Computer Programming*, you saw the significance of a high-level programming language for a classical case and we discussed the problems we face with today's quantum programming languages, which rely on a low-level circuit programming-based model. To tackle all the disadvantages that we discussed, the **Silq programming language** was introduced, which solves most of the problems that today's low-level quantum programmers face. This section will give you an introduction to the Silq language and its various features. Let's now dive into the cutting-edge, high-level programming language for quantum computing – Silq – in the next section.

Introducing Silq

The Silq programming language for quantum programming was introduced at the **Programming Language and Design Implementation** (**PLDI**) conference in London in June 2020. Silq is a high-level programming language for quantum computing that has a **strong static type** system similar to that of Java and was developed at ETH Zurich by Benjamin Bichsel, Timon Gehr, Maximilian Baader, and Martin Vechev. Since this language is strongly static-typed, this means that the type of the variable is known at the compile time of the program and the variables defined in the program can only be of a specific data type, which means string data cannot be added with integer data types and so on. As discussed in *Chapter 5, Challenges in Quantum Computer Programming*, Silq tackles the issue of uncomputation and the difficult circuit-level syntax that is required by other quantum programming languages.

The Silq programming language offers some exciting features that make it different from other programming languages such as Q#. In most of the discussions regarding comparison, we will be comparing it mainly with the Q# language because it is similar to the high-level programming for quantum computing but the code is still tedious to write. In the following subsections, we will look at some of these features. Let's start with uncomputation.

Safe automatic uncomputation

Whenever we work on our classical computers, all the programming that creates temporary values in memory needs to be removed. Similarly, in quantum computation, we need to take care of the temporary values that are generated during the computation process, but as we learned in *Chapter 2*, *Quantum Bits, Quantum Measurements, and Quantum Logic Gates*, if we interfere with the quantum system, it collapses to a certain basis state termed **measurement**. This means that to clear the temporary values, we create an implicit measurement effect that destroys our quantum superposition state and entanglement.

In today's quantum programming languages, to remove the temporary values from memory, the uncomputation part is carried out explicitly, which is a very tedious process for large quantum circuits and computations. If you compare this with the classical computing process, then you will see that the uncomputation process is done automatically by the classical compiler. To address this loophole in quantum computing, Silq provides the safe, automatic uncomputation of the temporary values in the backend.

Intuitive semantics

In the Silq programming language, the semantics that compose the language are very easy to understand when compared to other quantum programming languages, such as Q#. This is because Q# has much more complex semantics and code becomes difficult to write because of the semantics. The programs written in Silq are type checking-enabled, so it automatically checks the data types to see whether they are defined in the correct manner or not. Due to fairly easy semantics, Silq programs are supported by **Quantum Random Access Memory** (**QRAM**), which is a quantum counterpart of classical RAM and, therefore, the programs are termed **physical** in nature. To find out more about the concept of QRAM, refer to the *Quantum random access memory* paper in the *Further reading* section. This also means that Silq will also be supported by modern quantum computing hardware easily.

Reduces and simplifies code

This point follows on naturally from the previous point, which means that when the semantics are simplified and easy, then there is a huge reduction in the code, and when the code is not large in size, then it becomes much simpler to read and understand the code. You will see soon that Silq code is much more compact and intuitive than other quantum programming languages we have considered before and very simple to work upon. Simplified code is less subjected to various programmatic errors, as we will see next.

Prevents errors

Simplified code and smaller code prevent a lot of errors. The most important characteristic feature of Silq is that it does not accept those kinds of semantics that cannot be realized on a physical quantum computer. As described before, Silq prevents implicit measurements so that the programs we write only consider variables that can be safely uncomputed.

Now that you know about the interesting features of Silq and the benefits of programming with Silq, let's start with the installation of the Silq language in the next section.

Installing Silq

In this section, we will go through the steps that will get the code editor and the Silq programming language installed on your computer. Let's start by installing Microsoft **Visual Studio** (**VS**) Code in the next section.

Installing Microsoft Visual Studio Code

Please follow these steps in sequence to install **Microsoft VS Code** on your computer. The steps are as follows:

1. Go to the `https://silq.ethz.ch/install` page and select an operating system according to your needs. In our case, we will be using the Microsoft Windows installation procedure. *Figure 6.1* shows the Silq installation page:

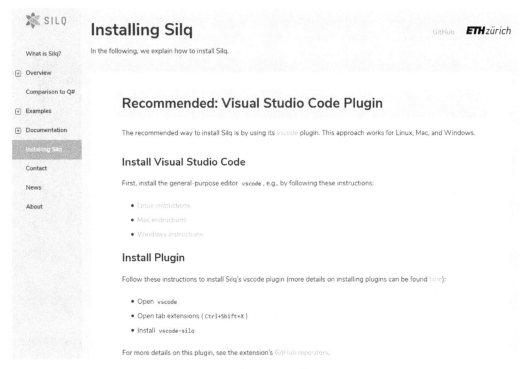

Figure 6.1 – The Silq installation page

2. For our Microsoft installation of VS Code, we land on the page shown in *Figure 6.2*, which shows you the installation link. Click on the link that says **Download the Visual Studio Code installer for Windows**:

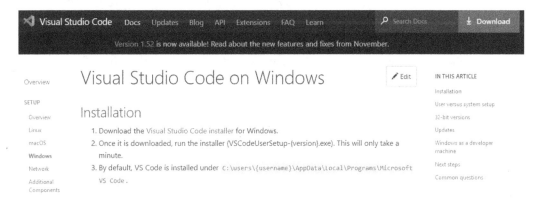

Figure 6.2 – VS Code installation page

3. After clicking the link, a dialog box will open. Click on **Save file** and install the installer. VS Code will start installing on your computer.

4. As soon as the installer opens, accept the agreement and choose the desired folder location of the install. You can let it remain as the default as well. Some additional tasks will be asked by the installer for you to select. Choose the options shown in *Figure 6.3*:

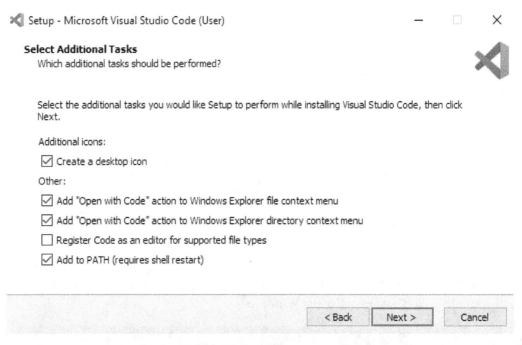

Figure 6.3 – Additional tasks VS Code installer window

5. After selecting the appropriate additional tasks, click **Next** and then **Install**. You will see the installation finished window. Click on **Finish**. VS Code is successfully installed on your computer!

6. After the installation, launch the VS Code editor.

We have now successfully installed VS Code, so let's now move on to installing the Silq programming language plugin in the next section.

Installing the Silq plugin

Now, we will start installing the Silq plugin into the VS Code studio we installed. The steps are as follows:

1. On the keyboard, press *Ctrl + Shift + X* to open the **Extensions** tab or click on the **Extensions** tab on the left-hand side just after the **Run** tab. *Figure 6.4* shows how your window will look after opening the **Extensions** tab:

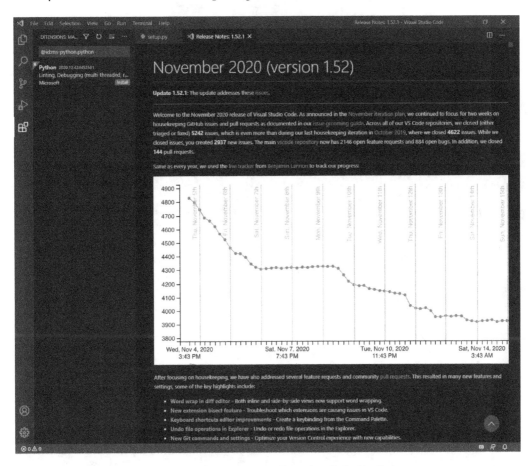

Figure 6.4 – The Extensions tab in the VS Code editor

2. Now, in the search bar of the **Extensions** tab, type `vscode-silq`, and you will see the plugin as shown in *Figure 6.5*:

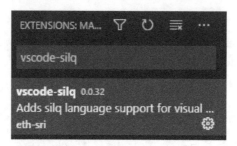

Figure 6.5 – Silq plugin in VS Code

3. Click on the **vscode-silq** plugin and install it.

4. To install the Silq Unicode plugin, press *Ctrl + P* and you will see a search window appear as shown in *Figure 6.6*:

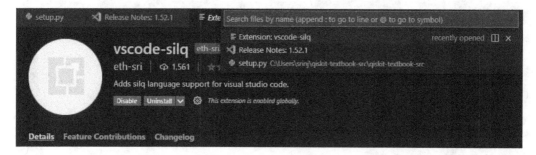

Figure 6.6 – Search bar in the VS Code editor

5. In the search bar, type `ext install freebroccolo.input-assist` and hit the *Enter* key to install the extension. *Figure 6.7* shows the window that will appear after you press *Enter*. You will be able to see the window in the **Extensions** tab:

Figure 6.7 – The Input Assist plugin in the VS Code editor

6. After installing Input Assist, press *Ctrl +* , or go to the bottom-left corner of the VS Code editor and click on the gears symbol to access the **Settings** option.

7. Once you are in **Settings**, search for `input-assist.languages` in the **Settings** search bar. Then, click on **Edit in settings.json**.

8. Now, an editor window will open. Add the line `"input-assist.languages"`: `["plaintext", "silq"]`, as shown in *Figure 6.8*, and press *Ctrl + S* to save:

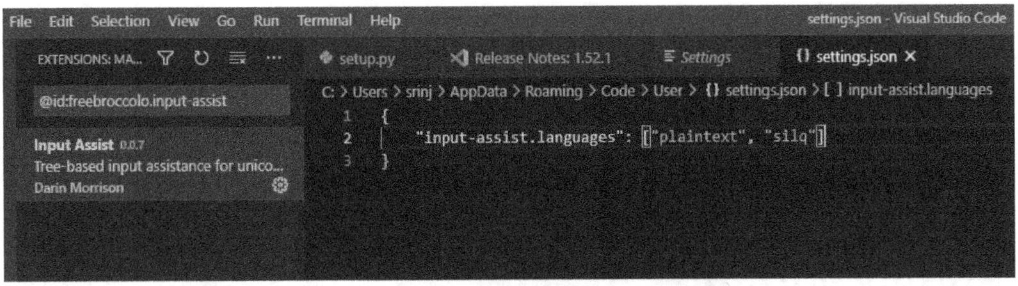

Figure 6.8 – The JSON file in the VS Code editor

After following all the steps, you have now successfully installed Silq with Unicode input on your computer. An important point to note here is that Silq is currently only supported by the Visual Code IDE. To start programming, you need to open a new file and set the extension of that file to `.slq` so that it runs Silq code. To type Unicode characters (`https://silq.ethz.ch/documentation#/documentation/7_symbols`), use \ and start typing the name of that character. For example, if you want the Greek letter *tau* (τ), then type `\tau` and hit the *Enter* key.

Now, in the next section, let's get started with the Silq data types.

Introducing Silq data types

In this section, let's learn about the various common data types that the Silq language offers. We will define both the Unicode symbols and the normal alphabet:

- **B** or $\mathbb{B}$: Boolean data type used to denote 0 and 1 binary digits

- **N** or $\mathbb{N}$: The classical natural numbers set, starting with 0,1,…

- **Z** or $\mathbb{Z}$: The classical integers set, starting with …,-1,0,1,…

- **Q** or $\mathbb{Q}$: The classical rational numbers set

- **R** or $\mathbb{R}$: The classical real numbers

1 or **𝟙**: The singleton type, which contains a single element

uint[n]: *n*-bit unsigned integers, where *n* belong to classical natural numbers

int[n]: *n*-bit signed integers in two's complement form, where *n* belongs to the classical natural numbers

𝜏^n: Vector of length *n*

𝜏[]: Dynamic length arrays

To learn more about various other Silq data types, visit Silq's documentation at `https://silq.ethz.ch/documentation`, where many of the functionalities of Silq are provided.

In the next section, let's get started with defining variables in Silq.

Defining variables in Silq

Let's see how to assign data to a variable in the Silq language. **Variable assignment** is one of the fundamental techniques used in programming to store data in memory and then access it as and when required in a particular program.

The symbols that are used to do variable assignment are : = (colon and equals symbol) and : (colon symbol), which are used to assign a particular data type to the variable. Let's see an example of this in the following code:

```
x:=H(x);
```

In the preceding code, you can see that H(x) is assigned to the x variable, which is a qubit, and H(x) is the Hadamard gate applied to the x qubit.

Now, if you want to make x a qubit, then you have to assign it the Boolean data type. This is shown in the next code block:

```
x:=0:𝔹;
```

This means that you have defined x as the 0 qubit and have made it of the quantum Boolean type. To make x of the classical type, you have to use the ! Silq annotation to distinguish quantum and classical types. For example, !𝔹 is classical Boolean. We will discuss Silq annotations later, in the section titled *Introducing Silq annotations*.

> **Note**
> Please note that ; (semicolon) is used to end a statement.

We have looked at variable assignment and the distinction between the classical and quantum data types defining method, so now let's look at conditionals in the next section.

Control flow in Silq

Similar to other programming languages, Silq provides **control flow** statements, which decide the order of execution of the code we write in Silq. Control flow is also known as **conditionals**, where a condition is provided and executed when some criteria are fulfilled. The statements are executed whenever a certain condition is satisfied.

In the following code, we see an example of a CH gate, which is a two-qubit gate and was discussed in in *Chapter 3, Multiple Quantum Bits, Entanglement, and Quantum Circuits*. The conditionals are applied using `if` and `else` statements. Curly brackets, { }, are used to begin and end a chunk of code. The syntax is given as follows:

```
if x {      // controlled on x,
  y:=H(y); // apply H to y
}
```

The code shows that if x qubit is true (meaning it is 1), then a Hadamard operation will be applied to the y qubit, which is the controlled Hadamard operation.

Let's look at **classical control flow** statements. An example using both `if` and `else` statements is shown in the following code:

```
if b{
    x := H(x);
    return measure(x);
  }else{
    return measure(x);
  }
```

This code says that if b is true, then the statements written inside the `if` condition will be executed; otherwise (`else`) the statements written inside `else` will be executed.

With the variables and control flow covered, we are now moving on to the exciting part, where you will be executing the statements in your VS Code editor and see them running on your PC!

In the next section, let's move on to functions and looping in Silq.

Functions and iterations in Silq

Functions are blocks of reusable code that are organized in a way such that it brings modularity to your code and makes your code clear and legible to read. Just as with any other programming language, Silq offers some built-in functions to use and lets us define our custom functions according to our requirements. For example, you have already seen H() in the preceding code blocks, which is a Hadamard function and a built-in function.

Iterations in computer programming are the repeated execution of code statements until they meet a certain condition. These are also known as **loops** in computer programming. Silq offers two different kinds of iteration statements, namely while and for loops.

Let's now see some example code where iterations are being implemented inside a function. Please note that to run Silq programs, it is important that you always define a function called main() and then execute your code inside that function. You can create custom functions later, but main() is compulsory:

```
def geometric():!ℕ{
    count := 0;
    ok := true;
    while ok{
        count += 1;
        ok = measure(H(false));
    }
    return count;
}
```

In the preceding code, the def keyword is used to define a function named geometric(), which is of the classical natural numbers type, as denoted by !ℕ. This means that all the operations happening inside the function are completely classical, but quantum operations are also supported. As we know from *Chapter 2, Quantum Bits, Quantum Measurements, and Quantum Logic Gates*, a measure operation is a classical operation. The return statement returns the value of the count variable and the while loop runs until the value of ok becomes false, which it will become eventually as soon as the measurement is 0.

If you have noticed, the `geometric()` function is a custom function and can be run inside the `main()` function. The `geometric()` function returns a sample from the geometric distribution. Let's see the running of this function. The complete code written in Silq is shown in the following code block. It is good practice to press *Ctrl* + *S* to save your code and then run it:

```
def main() {
    return geometric();
}


def geometric():!N{
    count := 0;
    ok := true;
    while ok{
        count += 1;
        ok = measure(H(false));
    }
    return count;
}
```

The output of the code is provided in *Figure 6.9* and if you run the code multiple times by pressing *F5*, then you will get various values of the `count` variable:

Figure 6.9 – The geometric() function output

The preceding output is 1, which means that the `while` loop converged after the first count itself. If you run the code repeatedly, you will receive random values such as 4 and 8.

We have seen an example of a `while` loop, so let's now see an example of a `for` loop, where we will create an equal superposition of qubits using the Hadamard gate. The complete code is as follows:

```
def main() {
    return UniformSuperposition[1]();
}
```

```
def UniformSuperposition[n:!N]():B^n{
  qubits := vector(n,0:B); // vector of length n filled
                          // with zeros
  for i in [0..n){
      qubits[i] := H(qubits[i]);
  }
  return qubits;
}
```

The UniformSuperposition[n: !N] (): B^n function takes n (classical) as input, which defines the number of qubits that you want to make a superposition for. B^n defines the function of the quantum type and is of n qubits. The in-built vector (n, 0: B) function is used to create a vector of n qubits initialized to 0, onto which the Hadamard gate is applied using the for loop to each qubit. The brackets, [and), in the for loop denote inclusive 0 and exclusive n, respectively. Finally, the qubits are returned. The // characters are used to add comments that are not executed by the program. From the code, you can see that n=1 is called from the main () function. The output of the one-qubit superposition can be seen in *Figure 6.10*:

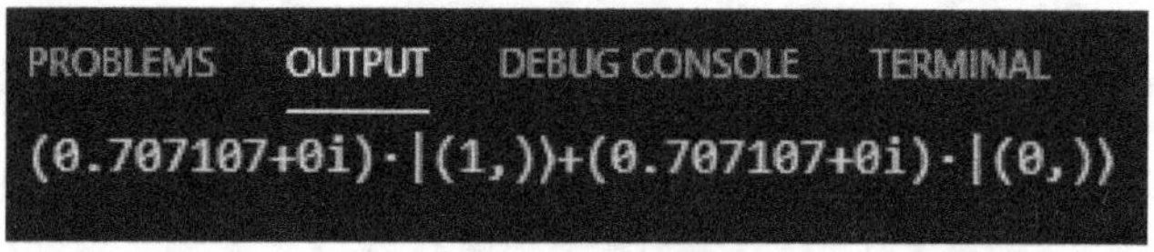

PROBLEMS   **OUTPUT**   DEBUG CONSOLE   TERMINAL

(0.707107+0i)·|(1,))+(0.707107+0i)·|(0,))

Figure 6.10 – Equal superposition of one qubit

In *Figure 6.11*, you can see the superposition of n=2 qubits and you can try different values of n to create more superposition:

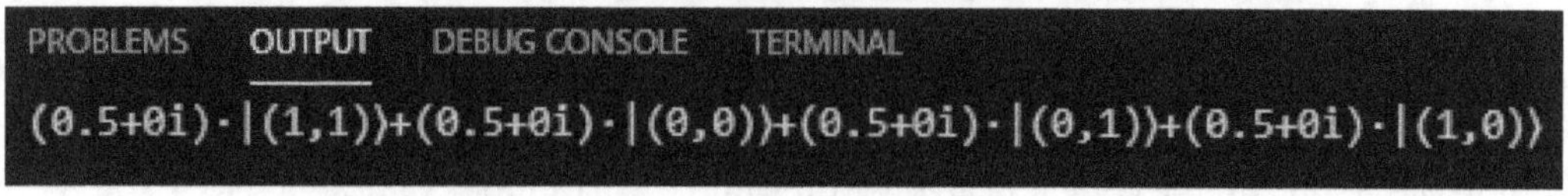

PROBLEMS   **OUTPUT**   DEBUG CONSOLE   TERMINAL

(0.5+0i)·|(1,1))+(0.5+0i)·|(0,0))+(0.5+0i)·|(0,1))+(0.5+0i)·|(1,0))

Figure 6.11 – Equal superposition of two qubits

Since you have now learned about functions and their workings, you can run the CNOT code we defined before, which is an example of **quantum control flow**. Let's see the code next:

```
def main() {
  return CX(1:B,0:B);
}
```

```
def CX(const x:B,y:B):B{
  if x{
    y := X(y);
  }
  return y;
}
```

In the preceding code, you can observe that you will get an output of 1 because the CNOT gate returns an output of 1 when the first qubit is 1. Here, the first qubit is x and the second qubit is y, which is 0 and is flipped by the operation of the CX gate.

Notice also that while calling the CX() function inside the main() function, we need to explicitly define the numbers 1 and 0 of the Boolean type, B, to signify that they are quantum bits; otherwise, the program throws errors.

Some of the notable features that quantum control offers are as follows:

- The branches of if and else are mfree. We will be discussing mfree annotation in the next section.

- Implicit uncomputation happens at the end of the two branches, which means that the condition is lifted and all the variables that were present inside the if and else branches are left constant after the uncomputation.

- Both the if and else branches cannot perform classical operations such as defining variables, arrays, or functions of the classical type. This is to prevent accidental superposition of classical variables, arrays, or functions.

Since now you know about the construction of Silq programs using functions, iterations, and control flow, let's see in the next section some common Silq annotations that help us to define quantum computing operations more smoothly.

Introducing Silq annotations

The Silq language provides various kinds of annotations that help to perform quantum computation and classical operations in an intuitive manner. There are a total of five Silq annotations; let's see them one by one.

Introducing classical type annotations – !

We have discussed this annotation type when differentiating quantum variables or operations from classical ones. As soon as you put ! before a variable or a function, it becomes classical in nature.

A few properties of classical types that are worth mentioning are as follows:

- If we use two ! symbols before a variable or a function, it means the same as putting one, for example, ! !N = !N.

- Classical types can commute with tuples in Silq, for example, $!(\tau \times \tau) \equiv !\tau \times !\tau$, and therefore we have

$$!(\tau \times \tau) \equiv !(\tau \times !\tau) \equiv !(!\tau \times \tau) \equiv !(!\tau \times !\tau).$$

- Classical types can commute with dynamic length arrays, such as $!\tau[] \equiv (!\tau)[] \equiv !(\tau[])$.

- Classical types can also commute with fixed-length arrays, for example, $!\tau^\wedge n \equiv (!\tau)^\wedge n \equiv !(\tau^\wedge n)$.

An important thing to note about classical types is that they can be re-interpreted as quantum values, such as $!\tau <: \tau$, and this is useful for computation.

Let's now move on to the next annotation, namely qfree.

The qfree annotation

The qfree annotation is used to denote the evaluation of functions or expressions that do not create or destroy superpositions. This annotation helps with automatic uncomputation and it ensures that if qfree is being evaluated on classical expressions, then it should only yield classical outputs.

For example, the Hadamard operation is not a qfree operation because it creates superposition, but all the Pauli gates we learned about in *Chapter 2, Quantum Bits, Quantum Measurements, and Quantum Logic Gates*, are qfree because they never create or destroy any superposition.

An example of the qfree function is provided as follows:

```
def Eval(f:𝔹  qfree 𝔹)qfree{
    return f(false); //  myEval is qfree
}
```

Here, in this `Eval` function, `f` is another function that is defined as `qfree` and the evaluation happens on `f(false)`, so the whole function becomes `qfree` itself. An important point to note is that Silq only supports uncomputation for `qfree` functions.

Let's now move on to the `mfree` annotation provided by the Silq programming language.

The mfree annotation

The `mfree` annotation is used to denote that a function can be evaluated without using any measurement operator. Again, taking our same example of `qfree`, we can make it `mfree`, as follows:

```
def Evalm(f:B  mfree B)mfree{
    return f(false); //   ^ myEval is mfree
}
```

In this function, you can see that `f` is `mfree` and the evaluation takes place on `false`, which means that the whole function, `Evalm()`, is `mfree` itself.

Let's see another example of `mfree` to reinforce our understanding, which is as follows:

```
def f(x:B) mfree:B{
    return H(x);
}
```

`mfree` can be used as long as the function does not contain any measurement operations.

Now, let's look at the `const` annotation in Silq in the next section.

The const annotation

The `const` annotation, as you might have guessed, is used to define the variables that need to be constant in a given scope. Concretely, each parameter of a function and each variable in the context may be annotated as `const`.

Let's look at the following function to see how `const` is defined:

```
def Evalcon(const x:B,f:const B!  B){
    return f(x);
}
```

You can see the const keyword is used for the x variable and the f function to make them constant throughout the Evalcon() function scope.

Let's look at the last annotation offered by Silq, which is lifted.

The lifted annotation

The qfree functions with constant arguments are known as lifted functions. In Silq, classical arguments are inherently treated as constants. The following example demonstrates lifted:

```
def Or(x:𝔹, y:!𝔹)lifted{ // x and y are implicitly const
    return x||y;  //  Or is lifted
}
```

The Or function defined in the previous code is lifted and x and y variables are implicitly constant by Silq convention. For more information on lifted functions, you can visit the *Functions* section of the Silq documentation at https://silq.ethz.ch/documentation, which lists the commonly lifted functions used by Silq. You will find that all the mathematical operations are lifted functions.

With the basics of Silq programming covered, you are now ready to start making simple circuits using Silq by employing single-qubit operations. It will be good to show some of the basic quantum logic gates and how they are programmed in Silq. Let's dive into this in the next section.

Simple example programs using Silq

In this section, let's see some simple quantum circuits that can be implemented in Silq; mostly, we will be focusing our discussion on the quantum logic gates that we learned about in *Chapter 2, Quantum Bits, Quantum Measurements, and Quantum Logic Gates*.

Let's start with the Pauli X gate, which looks as follows in the Silq language:

```
def main() {
    return PauliX();
}


def PauliX() {
    x:=0:𝔹;
    return X(x);
}
```

The preceding program is fairly easy to understand and implement. You can see that the x qubit is initialized to 0, so the expected output should be 1. *Figure 6.12* shows the output of this program:

Figure 6.12 – Pauli X output

Now, let's see the Pauli Y gate. The code for the Y gate is as follows:

```
def main() {
    return PauliY();
}


def PauliY() {
    y:=1:𝔹;
    return Y(y);
}
```

For the Pauli Y gate, we have initialized the y qubit from state $|1>$ and the expected output is $-i|0>$. In *Figure 6.13*, you can see the output of the Pauli Y gate:

Figure 6.13 – Pauli Y output

Now, let's take a look at the Pauli Z gate, the code for which is as follows:

```
def main() {
    return PauliZ();
}


def PauliZ() {
    z:=1:𝔹;
    return Z(z);
}
```

We have applied Pauli Z to the |1 > qubit, for which the output should be −|1 >. This is shown clearly in *Figure 6.14*:

Figure 6.14 – Pauli Z output

Let's take a look at the Hadamard gate operation, the code for which is as follows:

```
def main() {
    return Hadamard();
}


def Hadamard() {
    x:=0:𝔹;
    return H(x);
}
```

Hadamard is being applied to the |0 > qubit and we get a superposition state of |0 > and |1 > as output, which is shown in *Figure 6.15*:

Figure 6.15 – Hadamard gate output

In the preceding output, it is to be noted that the number 0.707107 is $\frac{1}{\sqrt{2}}$. The rest of the gates can be implemented in a similar fashion and we recommend you try it for yourself as it will be a nice exercise and will help you to understand the programming constructs involved in implementing various quantum gates in Silq. Additionally, it will help you to appreciate the workings of quantum gates.

Summary

This chapter has taught you some of the basics of Silq programming, such as its various features and constructs. With the completion of this chapter, you have now developed hands-on experience with the Silq programming language and can now utilize it to do quantum programming tasks. You will appreciate the simple and intuitive nature of the Silq programming language. With the completion of this chapter, you have now developed an understanding of the practical implementation of various quantum operations and constructing simple single-qubit quantum circuits.

In the next chapter, we are going to dive deeper into programming multiple qubits and various multi-qubit quantum circuits using Silq.

Further reading

- Benjamin Bichsel, Timon Gehr, Maximilian Baader, and Martin Vechev, *Silq: A High-Level Quantum Language with Safe Uncomputation and Intuitive Semantics*, PLDI, June 15-20, 2020

- Vittorio Giovannetti, Seth Lloyd, and Lorenzo Maccone, *Quantum random access memory*, arXiv:0708.1879, March 2008

7

Programming Multiple-Qubit Quantum Circuits with Silq

Tackling multiple qubits in quantum computing is a very useful skill because in most real-world applications and quantum algorithms, multiple qubits are utilized to encode information. Silq provides an easy syntax and the flexibility needed to work with multiple qubits with ease.

In this chapter, you will dive into the programming aspects of multiple-qubit quantum systems and use Silq to construct quantum circuits using multiple- and single-qubit quantum logic gates. Here is a list of the topics that we are going to cover in this chapter:

- Exploring multi-qubit quantum logic gates in Silq
- Constructing quantum circuits using quantum logic gates with Silq
- Quantum teleportation with Silq
- Quantum superdense coding with Silq

Technical requirements

You can download the code samples for this chapter from this book's official GitHub repository at `https://github.com/PacktPublishing/Quantum-Computing-with-Silq-Programming/tree/main/Chapter07`.

Exploring multi-qubit quantum logic gates in Silq

In *Chapter 3*, *Multiple Quantum Bits, Entanglement, and Quantum Circuits*, you looked at the most important multi-qubit quantum logic gates, which are used frequently to construct quantum circuits. As discussed in that chapter, having multiple qubits gives us an advantage in that we can encode more information in an efficient way. So, we will now dive into multi-qubit quantum logic gates in Silq. Let's start our discussion with the CNOT gate.

The quantum CX or CNOT gate

In Silq, the CX gate is usually created using an `if` condition because when the condition becomes true, only then is the target qubit flipped.

Let's see the Silq implementation of the CX gate:

```
def main() {
   return CX(1:𝔹,0:𝔹);
}


def CX(const x:𝔹,y:𝔹):𝔹{
   if x{
      y := X(y);
   }
   return y;
}
```

In the preceding code, you can see the function of the CX gate, where the x qubit (the first qubit) is the control and y (the second qubit) is the target qubit. The code signifies that whenever the x qubit is true (Boolean value 1), the X gate operation will be applied to the y qubit. Notice that in the main function, you need to explicitly provide the arguments as CX(1:𝔹,0:𝔹);. Otherwise, you will get errors.

The output of the CX gate from the preceding code is provided in *Figure 7.1*:

Figure 7.1 – CX gate output

As expected, the output of the code is |1> (y qubit) because the control qubit was set to |1> and the target was initially |0>. As soon as the control qubit is applied, the y bit is flipped by the X gate and the output becomes |1>.

Let's now take a look at the CZ gate.

The quantum CZ or CPHASE gate

In Silq, a CZ gate is usually created using an if condition because when the condition becomes true, only then is the phase of the target qubit flipped.

Let's look at the Silq implementation of the CZ gate:

```
def main() {
    return CZ(1:𝔹,1:𝔹);
}


def CZ(const x:𝔹,y:𝔹):𝔹{
    if x{
        y := Z(y);
    }
    return y;
}
```

The preceding code is the same as the CX gate code; the only difference is the X operation is being replaced by the Z gate operation. The x qubit (the first qubit) is the control and y (the second qubit) is the target qubit. The code signifies that whenever the x qubit is true (Boolean value 1), the Z gate operation will be applied to the y qubit. Notice again that in the main function, you need to explicitly provide the arguments as CZ(1:B,0:B);. Otherwise, you will get errors. The output of this code is displayed in *Figure 7.2*:

Figure 7.2 – CZ gate output

From the output, you can clearly see that the second qubit (the target) returned is −|1 > because the input provided was |11>. This means that the CZ gate only takes action when the input is |11>, and for all the other inputs, it remains the same as the input.

It would be a good exercise for you to try controlled Y and controlled H gates to understand the phenomena in a better way. Next, let's take a look at the SWAP gate.

The quantum SWAP gate

A quantum **SWAP** gate is used to interchange two qubits. There are no control qubits present in this gate and we usually depict the gate using cross marks on the qubits that we want to swap. In Silq, we perform the swapping operation with the help of another reference variable.

The following is a Silq implementation of the SWAP gate:

```
def main() {
    return SWAP(1:B,0:B);
}


def SWAP(x:B, y:B) {
    a:=y;
    y:=x;
    x:=a;
    return (x,y);
}
```

If you observe the previous code, it performs a SWAP operation using a third temporary variable, a, and then returns both the values of x and y. The input provided here is |10 > and the output should be |01 >, which is shown in *Figure 7.3*:

Figure 7.3 – SWAP gate output

As expected, the output of the SWAP gate is |01>, and similarly, you can try it for other values as well, following the truth table and verifying your results.

Let's now move on to 3-qubit quantum gates, starting with the CCX gate.

The quantum CCX or CCNOT gate – the Toffoli gate

In Silq, the CCX gate is created using an if condition on the first and second qubits because when the condition becomes true, only then is the target qubit (third qubit) flipped.

The Silq implementation of the CCX gate is as follows:

```
def main() {
    return CCX(1:B,1:B,1:B);
}


def CCX(const x:B,const y:B,z:B):B{
    if x && y{
        z := X(z);
    }
    return (z);
}
```

In the preceding code, you can see that both x and y (the first and second qubits) are controlled with the target as the z qubit.

The output of the code is given in *Figure 7.4*:

| PROBLEMS | **OUTPUT** | DEBUG CONSOLE | TERMINAL |

(1+0i)·|0⟩

Figure 7.4 – CCX gate output

As we can see, for the x and y qubits to both be 1, the X operation is applied to the z qubit, which is then flipped from 0 to 1.

The quantum CSWAP gate – the Fredkin gate

The **CSWAP** or **Fredkin** gate, as you might have guessed, is a controlled version of the SWAP gate that you just learned about. There are no control qubits present in this gate, and we usually depict the gate using controlled cross marks on the qubits that we want to swap. In Silq, we perform the swapping operation with the help of another reference variable.

The Silq implementation of the Fredkin gate is as follows:

```
def main() {
  return CSWAP(1:𝔹,0:𝔹,1:𝔹);
}


def CSWAP(x:𝔹, y:𝔹, z:𝔹) {
  if x{
    a:=z;
    z:=y;
    y:=a;
  }
  return (x,y,z);
}
```

In the preceding code, you can see the control operation being applied to the x qubit, and the y and z qubits are the ones that are being swapped inside the if condition.

Figure 7.5 shows the output of the Fredkin gate:

Figure 7.5 – Fredkin gate output

The input provided to the CSWAP gate was |101> and the output that we receive is |110>, which suggests that the CSWAP operation is working perfectly.

Since now we have covered all the essential multi-qubit gates, you will find it a lot easier to navigate chapters on quantum algorithms, and you will also be able to understand various research literature on quantum computing. We'll now move on to constructing quantum circuits in the next section.

Constructing quantum circuits with quantum logic gates using Silq

In this section, we will discuss some basic quantum circuits that can be created using quantum logic gates. All the quantum gates that you studied in this chapter and in *Chapter 2, Quantum Bits, Quantum Measurements, and Quantum Logic Gates*, are the primary gates that are required to create various quantum circuits.

You have seen the basic implementation aspects of multiple-qubit quantum logic gates using Silq, and now you are ready to utilize those multiple-qubit gates to construct interesting quantum circuits. Let's start with Bell states.

Implementing Bell states in Silq

Bell states are among the fundamental quantum circuits you will encounter in quantum computing and are utilized in quantum teleportation and superdense coding protocols, as you will see in this chapter.

You can see the quantum circuit for Bell state creation in the following figure:

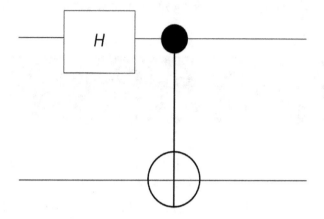

Figure 7.6 – Bell state circuit

The Silq implementation of the Bell state is defined in the following code:

```
def main() {
   b:=1:𝔹;
   b:=H(b);

   c:=1:𝔹;
   if b{
      c := X(c);
   }

   return (b,c);
}
```

Observe the previous code very carefully. You can see that first, a Hadamard operation is applied to the b qubit. It is important to apply the Hadamard operation in order to bring the qubits into a state of superposition, which helps us to take advantage of the quantum mechanical properties in quantum computing. Then, with the b qubit (the first qubit) as the control, the CX gate is applied, where the target is the c qubit (the second qubit). The answer is returned as (b,c).

The output of the circuit is as follows:

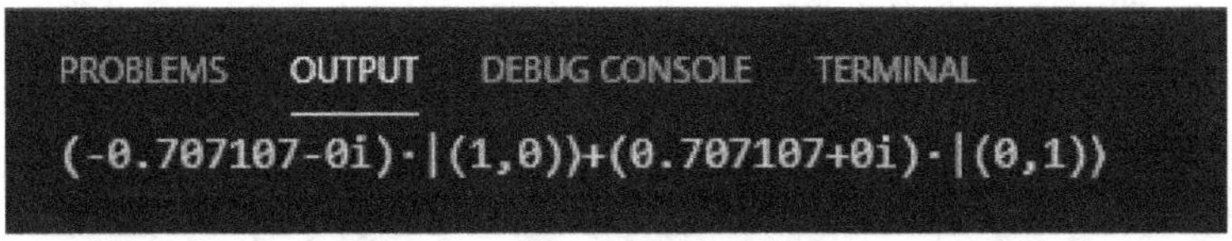

```
PROBLEMS    OUTPUT    DEBUG CONSOLE    TERMINAL

(-0.707107-0i)·|(1,0))+(0.707107+0i)·|(0,1))
```

Figure 7.7 – The Bell state $|B_{11}>$

If you look at the input, you can see that both the b and c qubits have been initialized as $|11>$ and the output that you are getting is the state $|B_{11}> = \dfrac{|01> - |10>}{\sqrt{2}}$.

Let's now learn about another implementation of the CX gate that only uses CZ and Hadamard gates.

Decomposing the CX gate

The concept that we will look at in this section is known as **gate decomposition** and consists of breaking a quantum gate into multiple single-qubit and CX gates. We are going to look at the CX gate and study its decomposition through Hadamard operations and the CZ gate.

The Silq code for the decomposed CX gate is as follows:

```
def main() {
    return DecomposedCX();
}


def DecomposedCX(){
    b:=1:B;
    b:=H(b);

    a:=1:B;
    if a{
        b := Z(b);
    }

    b:=H(b);

    return b;
}
```

If you take a look at the preceding code, you will find that the a qubit is the first qubit and b is the second qubit where the Hadamard operation and the CZ gate are applied. When we set b and a as |1>, we get the output shown in *Figure 7.8*:

Figure 7.8 – Decomposed CX gate output

Since both the qubits are 1, we get the output as 0 because of the CX operation being implemented by this decomposed quantum circuit. Now it will be a good exercise for you to verify that $HZH = X$ and $HXH = Z$, both using Silq and using matrix multiplication.

Implementing the GHZ state using Silq

If you remember from *Chapter 5, Challenges in Quantum Computer Programming*, we discussed a circuit known as the **GHZ state**, which represents the entangled version of 3 qubits, just as Bell states do for 2 qubits. Now, since we know about the construction of quantum circuits, we can make the GHZ state as well using Silq:

```
def main() {
    return GHZ();
}


def GHZ(){
    a:=0:B;
    b:=0:B;
    c:=0:B;


    a:=H(a);


    if a{
        b := X(b);
    }


    if b{
        c := X(c);
```

```
        }

    return (a,b,c);

}
```

In the preceding code, you can see that the Hadamard operation is being applied to the first qubit and then CX operations are being applied to the second and third qubits.

The output of the circuit is shown in *Figure 7.9*, and it will be a good exercise to try the other equivalent GHZ circuit by yourself!

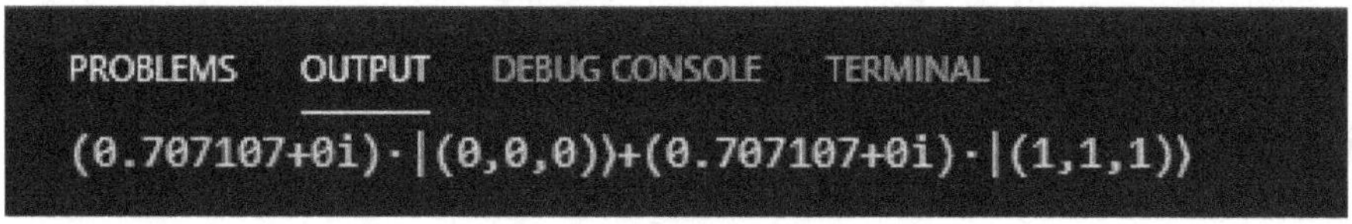

PROBLEMS   OUTPUT   DEBUG CONSOLE   TERMINAL

(0.707107+0i)·|(0,0,0))+(0.707107+0i)·|(1,1,1))

Figure 7.9 – GHZ state output

The state that we achieve here is $\frac{|000> + |111>}{\sqrt{2}}$, and it is a three-qubit entangled state.

You are now encouraged to verify the entanglement of this state by performing the calculations that we learned about for the Bell state in this chapter.

Let's look at the implementation of a classical half adder circuit using Silq next.

Implementing a classical half adder circuit in Silq

In this section, we will see an interesting implementation of the classical half adder circuit using quantum gates, and you will learn about the quantum implementation of classical logic gates as well.

To start with, let's see the truth table of the half adder circuit in *Figure 7.10*:

A (Input)	B (Input)	S (Sum Output)	C (Carry Output)
0	0	0	0
0	1	1	0
1	0	1	0
1	1	0	1

Figure 7.10 – Truth table for the half adder

From the truth table, we understand that the sum column is the output of an XOR gate and the carry column is the output of an AND classical gate, and the AND gate output is equal to the output generated by the CCX gate. (You can verify this yourself as an exercise.) This means a half adder circuit can be implemented by the combination of both of these gates.

The circuit diagram for the half adder is shown in *Figure 7.11*:

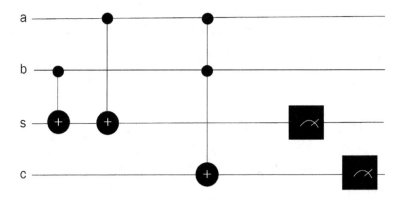

Figure 7.11 – Half adder circuit

From *Figure 7.11*, you can see that for the sum (the s qubit), we utilize two CNOT gates to implement the sum operation, and we use a Toffoli gate to implement the carry (c qubit) operation. In essence, you can see that we have just implemented a quantum circuit based on the truth table we obtained.

The Silq implementation is now shown in the following code block:

```
def main() {
  return HalfAdder();
```

```
}
def HalfAdder(){
  // Define 4 Qubits - a & b inputs, s & c are sum and carry -
  // outputs
  a:=1:𝔹;
  b:=1:𝔹;
  s:=0:𝔹;
  c:=0:𝔹;
  // XOR Gate Operation

  // CX operation on b and s qubit
  if b{
    s := X(s);
  }
  // CX operation on a and s
  if a{
    s := X(s);
  }
  // AND Gate Operation
  if a && b{
    c := X(c);
  }
  return (s,c);
}
```

In the preceding code, observe carefully that the XOR gate consists of two CX gates that are acting on the sum qubit to execute the sum operation of the adder, and the AND gate operation is nothing but the Toffoli gate that you saw earlier!

The output of the circuit is given in *Figure 7.12*:

Figure 7.12 – Half adder output

The output of the circuit is |01> when the input provided is |11>, and you can verify this from the truth table given in *Figure 7.11*.

As you can see, when the input is |11>, which is the A and B qubits, then we get the output |01>, which is the S and C qubits.

Through these examples, you will now be able to implement simple and larger quantum circuits, and you should now understand the various combination of single- and multi-qubit quantum gates that are possible.

Let's now move on to a very interesting topic in the next section called quantum teleportation!

Quantum teleportation

Quantum teleportation is a truly fascinating phenomenon that happens in quantum computing and by the help of which we are able to transfer a quantum state from one place to another without having to traverse the space in between. For quantum teleportation, we consider two communicating parties, Alice and Bob. Alice sends a qubit to Bob to communicate a message. This is the essence of quantum teleportation.

Let's take a look at the Silq code for teleportation to gain a better understanding of the process:

```
def main() {
    return Teleportation();
}
def Teleportation(){
    // Initialize Qubits - 'a' qubit is to be teleported by Alice
    // to Bob
    a:=0:𝔹;
    b:=0:𝔹;
    c:=0:𝔹;
    // Alice's Operations
    // Creating the Bell State
    b:=H(b);

    if b{
        c := X(c);
    }
```

```
// Alice applies CX and H to 'a' qubit
if a{
    b := X(b);
}

a:=H(a);
// Alice measures her qubits 'a' and 'b'
ma1:=measure(a);
ma2:=measure(b);
print(ma1);
print(ma2);
// Bob's measurement
//c:=Z(c);
//c:=X(c);
return (c);
}
```

The previous code is for the teleportation protocol. To understand the quantum teleportation protocol, we need to start with three qubits, as shown in the code: a, b, and c. Suppose a is the qubit that Alice wants to send to Bob, and c is the qubit where Bob is supposed to apply some operations to know about Alice's state. In the code, we have started with a being at the 0 state, which means we want to send the 0 state to Bob.

First of all, the Bell state is prepared between the b and c qubits, which shows that both Alice and Bob have an entangled state. Then, Alice applies some operations to her a and b qubits, which involves applying a CX gate and a Hadamard gate. After this, she measures her a and b qubits. The output of the measurement is shown in *Figure 7.13*:

Figure 7.13 – Teleportation output when a and b are 01

Now, if you run the code repeatedly by pressing *F5*, you will see different values for a and b, and accordingly, you will find that the operations mentioned earlier for Bob always work without any problems. To illustrate this fact, let's have a look at another result in *Figure 7.14*:

Figure 7.14 – Teleportation output when a and b are 11

Observe now that the measured a and b values are 11 and Bob's state is |1>, which means if Bob applies a Z gate and then an X gate, he will get |0>, which was sent by Alice!

To reinforce this fact, take a look at *Figure 7.15*, where a and b are 10 now:

Figure 7.15 – Teleportation output when a and b are 10

Observe that since a and b are 10, Bob needs to apply a Z gate to the c qubit that is at |0>, and when he applies the Z gate, the state remains at |0>, so he gets to know that the state sent by Alice was |0>.

You can try this same experiment with Alice's state as |1> and you will find that it works out!

With quantum teleportation covered, you have now learned about the transmission of qubits with the help of shared entanglement between two communicating parties. We are now ready to move on to superdense coding in the next section.

Quantum superdense coding

In the *Quantum teleportation* section, we saw that two classical bits are used to transfer a quantum state from Alice to Bob. In **superdense coding**, we use a single quantum state to send two classical bits.

Let's look at the Silq implementation of superdense coding to understand this protocol better:

```
def main() {
   return SuperDenseCoding();
}
def SuperDenseCoding(){
   a:=0:𝔹;
   b:=0:𝔹;

   // Bell State Preparation
   a:=H(a);
   if a{
      b := X(b);
   }

   // Alice's Operation - 11 is sent
   a:=Z(a);
   a:=X(a);

   // Bob's Operation
   if a{
      b := X(b);
   }

   a:=H(a);

   return(a,b);
}
```

Observe in the preceding code that the classical bits `11` are sent by Alice because she applies a ZX operation. The output of the code is shown in *Figure 7.16*:

PROBLEMS	**OUTPUT**	DEBUG CONSOLE	TERMINAL

`(-1+0i)·|(1,1))`

Figure 7.16 – Superdense coding ouput for 11

Just to show another example, take a look at *Figure 7.17*:

PROBLEMS	**OUTPUT**	DEBUG CONSOLE	TERMINAL

`(1+0i)·|(0,1))`

Figure 7.17 – Superdense coding output for 10

Observe that we received |01> because `10` was sent by applying the X operation. Similarly, you can try the other remaining operations to verify the workings of superdense coding. The main value of superdense coding lies in the fact that we can provide quantum information at an earlier stage independent of any future quantum operation to be applied to that quantum information. This is helpful for security purposes, so that even if an eavesdropper breaks in, they won't be able to decipher the information sent by Alice to Bob.

Summary

We have covered multi-qubit gates and used them to construct quantum circuits, and then we moved on to teleportation and superdense coding using the Silq language. By now, you will have gained a thorough understanding of the practical implementation of entanglement and the thinking process behind making complex circuits such as ones for the teleportation protocol. The Silq-based circuit implementation skills that you gained here will be helpful in the upcoming chapters where you will be implementing various basic and advanced quantum algorithms.

From the next chapter, we will start discussing useful quantum algorithms that have been utilized for various applications, such as cryptography and finance.

Section 3: Quantum Algorithms Using Silq Programming

In this part, you will dive deep into the basics of quantum algorithms and its implementation using the Silq programming language. Various significant quantum algorithms will be discussed and implemented together. After completing this part, you will feel confident in your ability to implement various quantum algorithms using Silq.

This section comprises the following chapters:

- *Chapter 8, Quantum Algorithms I – Deutsch-Jozsa and Bernstein-Vazirani*
- *Chapter 9, Quantum Algorithms II – Grover's Search Algorithm and Simon's Algorithm*
- *Chapter 10, Quantum Algorithms III – Quantum Fourier Transform and Phase Estimation*

8

Quantum Algorithms I – Deutsch-Jozsa and Bernstein-Vazirani

The Deutsch-Jozsa and Bernstein-Vazirani algorithms are two long-established examples that illustrate that quantum algorithms can be exponentially faster than classical ones in certain kinds of problems. In this chapter, we will use these algorithms to showcase basic features of Silq implementation, such as variable assignment, state superposition, controlled application and measurement, as well as safe uncomputation: one of the key concepts of the Silq language.

In this chapter, we are going to cover the following main topics:

- Quantum parallelism and interference
- The Deutsch-Jozsa algorithm – classical and quantum solutions along with the Silq implementation
- The Bernstein-Vazirani algorithm – classical and quantum solutions along with the Silq implementation

You will learn how to implement two basic algorithms in Silq and this will help you to gain intuition on how to use Silq core concepts to your advantage when designing more complex algorithms in future chapters.

Technical requirements

In order to run the algorithms presented in this chapter, you need to have Silq installed. Please refer to the Silq website to see how to download it: `https://silq.ethz.ch/`.

The code for the algorithms as well as examples can be found on our GitHub repository: `https://github.com/PacktPublishing/Quantum-Computing-with-Silq-Programming/tree/main/Chapter08`.

Introducing quantum parallelism and interference

In this section, we will look at **quantum parallelism** and **quantum interference**: two mechanisms that are often used in combination in quantum algorithms to reduce the number of computation steps compared to classical ones. Thanks to this, you will be able to understand how to take advantage of quantum computing to design algorithms.

Quantum parallelism

In a classical computer, information is kept in memory registers consisting of bits with values equal to either 0 or 1. Quantum memory registers differ because each of their constituting qubits can be in a superposition of the $|0\rangle$ and $|1\rangle$ basis states, leading the quantum memory register itself to potentially be in a superposition of states. From this ability to represent several states, which can be viewed as inputs to a function into one single state, arises a quantum phenomenon known as **quantum parallelism**. Applying a function to a state in superposition produces the superposition of the outputs, therefore effectively performing an exponential amount of computation with the same cost as applying the function to a single input.

Typically, a uniform superposition of states can be obtained by applying a Hadamard transform to each qubit of the memory register. Suppose you have n qubits initialized to $|0\rangle^{\otimes n}$ and you apply a Hadamard transform to each one of them. As $H(|0\rangle) = |+\rangle$, any given qubit will become the superposition $\frac{|0\rangle + |1\rangle}{\sqrt{2}}$, leading the whole state to be as follows:

$$\frac{|0\rangle + |1\rangle}{\sqrt{2}} \otimes \frac{|0\rangle + |1\rangle}{\sqrt{2}} \otimes \cdots \otimes \frac{|0\rangle + |1\rangle}{\sqrt{2}}$$

This last state is the uniform superposition on 2^n integers and can be written as follows:

$$\frac{1}{\sqrt{2^n}} \sum_{x=0}^{2^n-1} |x\rangle$$

Let's take a simple example to show how being able to prepare a state that is the superposition of all the inputs to a function allows us to compute the superposition of all the outputs by evaluating the function only once.

We take a function, $f:\{0,1\}^2 \to \{0,1\}$, which takes as input a two-bit integer and returns a single bit as output. Classically, computing the outputs corresponding to the four different inputs for f would require evaluating the function individually on each one of the possibilities: $f(0,0), f(0,1), f(1,0), f(1,1)$. Quantum parallelism, however, gives us the ability to explore an exponential number of computational paths at once by taking advantage of the quantum superposition of states. To compute an input state, $|\varphi\rangle$, corresponding to the uniform superposition of the four inputs to the function, we saw that we need to apply the Hadamard transform to both qubits of state $|00\rangle$:

$$H^{\otimes 2}|00\rangle = H|0\rangle \otimes H|0\rangle = \frac{|0\rangle + |1\rangle}{\sqrt{2}} \otimes \frac{|0\rangle + |1\rangle}{\sqrt{2}}$$

Our state, $|\varphi\rangle$, is, therefore, the superposition of the four possible states on two qubits, each existing with an equal ¼ probability:

$$|\varphi\rangle = \frac{|00\rangle + |01\rangle + |10\rangle + |11\rangle}{2}$$

Now, we cannot simply evaluate function f on state $|\varphi\rangle$ because it is not a reversible function, and we need to **lift** it to a version where all operations on the qubits may be reversed. In order to do that, we define the unitary operation:

$$U_f|a\rangle|b\rangle \mapsto |a\rangle|b \oplus f(a)\rangle$$

We see that U_f is reversible with $U_f^{-1} = U_f$:

$$U_f U_f|a\rangle|b\rangle = U_f|a\rangle|b \oplus f(a)\rangle = |a\rangle|b \oplus f(a) \oplus f(a)\rangle = |a\rangle|b\rangle$$

To compute f on a qubit state, we simply apply U_f on state $|x\rangle|0\rangle$ because the following applies:

$$U_f |x\rangle |0\rangle = |x\rangle |f(x)\rangle$$

Let's now look at what happens when applying this operation to the superposition of the inputs $|\varphi\rangle$:

$$U_f|\varphi\rangle|0\rangle = \frac{1}{2}U_f(|00\rangle + |01\rangle + |10\rangle + |11\rangle)|0\rangle$$

$$= \frac{1}{2}(U_f|00\rangle|0\rangle + U_f|01\rangle|0\rangle + U_f|10\rangle|0\rangle + U_f|11\rangle|0\rangle)$$

$$= \frac{1}{2}(|00\rangle|f(00)\rangle + |01\rangle|f(01)\rangle + |10\rangle|f(10)\rangle + |11\rangle|f(11)\rangle)$$

We see that in this computation, the second register is the superposition of the four different outputs of f on the different possible inputs. Thus, a single query to the function was enough to obtain the evaluation of the function on the entirety of the input state.

However strong the mechanism of quantum parallelism is to follow an exponential number of computational paths at once, it is not yet powerful enough to be taken advantage of. Having the superposition of the outputs is useful but trying to measure the state directly would result in its collapse to a single value, thus losing all benefits of the quantum mechanism. Therefore, this approach needs to be coupled with other techniques to enhance the probability of measuring an interesting and useful value. One of these techniques is to use quantum interference to modify to our advantage the probabilities of getting a given output on a measurement, reducing the odds of undesired outcomes to the smallest value possible.

Quantum interference

Measuring a state that is in superposition will provoke its collapse to a single state, thus potentially losing useful information if the measured state is not the desired one. **Quantum interference** is a phenomenon that intervenes before the measurement is made in order to increase the probability of a favorable outcome, where the idea is to reduce the *randomness* of the measurement as much as possible by tweaking the probability amplitudes to our advantage.

Consider the basic superposition of states $|\phi\rangle = \frac{1}{\sqrt{2}}(|0\rangle + |1\rangle)$, where measuring will lead to the states $|0\rangle$ or $|1\rangle$ with an equal probability of $\frac{1}{2}$. Here, a simple measurement is totally random: you get either state with the same probability. Let's look at what happens when applying the Hadamard transform to this state. You may recall that we have the following:

$$H|0\rangle = \frac{1}{\sqrt{2}}(|0\rangle + |1\rangle)$$

$$H|1\rangle = \frac{1}{\sqrt{2}}(|0\rangle - |1\rangle)$$

Thus, by linearity, we have the following:

$$H|\phi\rangle = \frac{1}{\sqrt{2}}(H|0\rangle + H|1\rangle))$$

$$= \frac{1}{\sqrt{2}}\left(\frac{1}{\sqrt{2}}(|0\rangle + |1\rangle) + \frac{1}{\sqrt{2}}(|0\rangle - |1\rangle)\right)$$

$$= \frac{1}{2}(|0\rangle + |1\rangle + |0\rangle - |1\rangle)$$

$$= |0\rangle$$

Applying the Hadamard transform to state $|\phi\rangle$ outputs state $|0\rangle$ with a probability of 1. We were able to remove the randomness by increasing the probability of measuring state $|0\rangle$ from 0.5 to 1 and decreasing the probability of measuring state $|1\rangle$ from 0.5 to 0. This happens because there are two paths that lead to state $|0\rangle$ that have the same probability amplitude and therefore interfere *constructively*, and two paths that lead to state $|1\rangle$ that have opposite amplitude and therefore interfere *destructively*.

Quantum interference stems from the fact that even though probabilities cannot be negative, a quantum state may have a negative probability amplitude. It is therefore possible to provoke constructive or destructive interference in order to add or destroy probability amplitudes for a given quantum state.

Combining quantum interference and parallelism is a powerful tool that can be found at the heart of many quantum algorithms. Starting from a uniform superposition of states, you can apply a function to it only once and retrieve the superposition of the outputs. Then, using quantum interference, you can manipulate this state in superposition in order to tweak the probabilities of the different outcomes on a measurement, even annihilating the odds of getting an undesired result in the best cases. This possibility to run through an exponential number of computational paths at once is a great advantage of quantum algorithms over classical ones. In the next section, we are going to implement the Deutsch-Jozsa algorithm, one of the first quantum algorithms to rely on these mechanisms.

Implementing the Deutsch-Jozsa algorithm

The **Deutsch-Jozsa algorithm** refers to a quantum algorithm designed by Richard Cleve, Artur Ekert, Chiara Macchiavello, and Michele Mosca in 1998, improving on the 1992 version from David Deutsch and Richard Jozsa. It was created with the idea of showing that the power of state superposition in a quantum algorithm could significantly reduce the number of computation steps needed compared to its classical counterpart.

In this section, you will learn how to solve a Deutsch-Jozsa problem theoretically both in a classical and in a quantum way. You will then practically implement a quantum algorithm solving that problem while gaining intuition of some of Silq's core features.

Problem statement

Let's start by defining a problem that can be solved by the Deutsch-Jozsa algorithm. The objective is to determine the nature of a function, $f:\{0,1\}^n \rightarrow \{0,1\}$, which takes as input an n-bit integer and returns either 0 or 1. We are guaranteed that this function is either **constant** (returning either 0 or 1 on all inputs) or perfectly **balanced** (returning 0 on half of the inputs and 1 on the other half). The goal is to determine which one it is with the minimum number of queries possible.

Classical solution

Before using quantum computation to solve the Deutsch-Jozsa problem, let's take a quick look into the classical way to solve it. In the worst case, you'll need to evaluate the function on strictly more than half of the inputs. Indeed, if the function is balanced, you could theoretically fall on the same value every time if you evaluate it on half of the inputs. Thus, one last query is necessary to make a choice with probability 1, which makes the total number of queries equal to $2^{n-1} + 1$, where 2^n is the size of the input space.

Quantum solution

The key idea behind the quantum solution to the Deutsch-Jozsa problem is to generate a particular state such that a single query to the function is enough to decide whether the function is balanced or constant. Taking advantage of the quantum state superposition allows us to considerably reduce the computation time as the number of function calls needed drops down from more than half of the inputs to one. In the following steps, we detail how to reach the desired quantum state:

1. We begin with n qubits initialized to $|0\rangle$ and one qubit initialized to $|1\rangle$ so that we have the initial $(n+1)$-qubit state:

$$|\psi_0\rangle = |0\rangle^{\otimes n} \otimes |1\rangle$$

2. Then, a Hadamard transform is applied to each one of the qubits, modifying the state to the following:

$$|\psi_1\rangle = \frac{1}{\sqrt{2^{n+1}}} \sum_{x=0}^{2^n-1} |x\rangle(|0\rangle - |1\rangle)$$

3. We reached that state because $H(|0\rangle^{\otimes n})$ is the uniform superposition on n qubits and $H(|1\rangle) = |-\rangle$. Applying a phase on the last qubit conditionally on the evaluation of the function (denoted by f) on the superposition of the n others transforms the state to the following:

$$|\psi_2\rangle = \frac{1}{\sqrt{2^{n+1}}} \sum_{x=0}^{2^n-1} (-1)^{f(x)}|x\rangle(|0\rangle - |1\rangle)$$

4. Finally, the last qubit is set aside by a measure and, once again, we apply the Hadamard transform on the remaining ones, yielding the final state:

$$|\psi_3\rangle = \frac{1}{2^n} \sum_{y=0}^{2^n-1} \left[\sum_{x=0}^{2^n-1} (-1)^{f(x)}(-1)^{x \cdot y} \right] |y\rangle$$

In the preceding equation, $x \cdot y = x_0 y_0 + x_1 y_1 + \ldots + x_{n-1} y_{n-1} \bmod 2$ is the sum of the bitwise multiplication of x by y.

Now that we have generated this state using one single query, recall that our goal is to determine whether function f is balanced or constant. In order to do that, we consider the probability of measuring state $|0\rangle^{\otimes n}$, which is equal to $|\frac{1}{2^n} \sum_{x=0}^{2^n-1} (-1)^{f(x)}|^2$. Suppose that f is balanced. Then, the previous sum contains as many +1s as −1s, resulting in destructive interference and the probability amplitude being equal to 0. If, on the contrary, f is constant, the terms in the sum interfere constructively, leading the probability amplitude to evaluate to 1.

In the quantum solution of the Deutsch-Jozsa problem, we take advantage of state superposition to detect the pattern of the function by applying it to all the inputs at once. Thus, one unique query is necessary to generate a state such that a simple measure will give away whether the function is balanced or constant.

Two-qubit example

Before looking at the Silq implementation, let's illustrate the Deutsch-Jozsa quantum solution on a two-qubit example. Suppose that the function $f: \{0,1\}^2 \rightarrow \{0,1\}$ is defined as a balanced function with $f(00) = f(01) = 0$ and $f(10) = f(11) = 1$. The steps of the Deutsch-Jozsa algorithm described in the previous section are as follows:

1. The state is initialized to the following:

$$|\psi_0\rangle = |00\rangle \otimes |1\rangle$$

2. Then, a Hadamard transform is applied to each of the qubits:

$$|\psi_1\rangle = \frac{1}{2}(|00\rangle + |01\rangle + |10\rangle + |11\rangle) \otimes \frac{|0\rangle - |1\rangle}{\sqrt{2}}$$

3. A phase is applied conditionally on the evaluation of f on the first two qubits:

$$|\psi_2\rangle = \frac{1}{2}(|00\rangle + |01\rangle - |10\rangle - |11\rangle) \otimes \frac{|0\rangle - |1\rangle}{\sqrt{2}}$$

$$= \frac{|0\rangle - |1\rangle}{\sqrt{2}} \otimes \frac{|0\rangle + |1\rangle}{\sqrt{2}} \otimes \frac{|0\rangle - |1\rangle}{\sqrt{2}}$$

4. Finally, the last qubit is measured and the first two qubits go through another Hadamard transform, resulting in the state $|\psi_3\rangle = |10\rangle$.

We know that the function f is balanced because measuring the final state gives 2 instead of 0. Let's now implement the Deutsch-Jozsa algorithm in Silq.

Silq implementation

Now that we have seen how quantum computing is useful to solve the Deutsch-Jozsa problem, we will implement the algorithm in Silq. We will make a function, deutsch_jozsa, that takes as input a function, $f: \{0,1\}^n \rightarrow \{0,1\}$, for an integer, $n \in \mathbb{N}$, and returns 1 if f is constant and 0 if f is balanced.

To begin with, we want our initial state to be the combination of the superposition of all the input states and the Hadamard transform of a qubit in state $|1\rangle$. As assigning a new variable transforms the current state in its tensor product with the added qubit(s), we can linearly construct our initial state in three steps. First, we assign state $|0\rangle^{\otimes n}$ to a variable, cand, which is equivalent to having an array of n qubits initialized to state $|0\rangle$. Then, we want to transform the state of this variable into the superposition of all input states, which can be done by applying the Hadamard transform to each of the qubits in the array. Finally, the $(n+1)^{th}$ qubit used to introduce a phase in our state, which will later create the

destructive or constructive interference, is initialized in the target variable directly to the state $H(|1\rangle) = |-\rangle = \dfrac{(|0\rangle - |1\rangle)}{\sqrt{2}}$. As seen when studying the quantum solution, we want to generate the following state:

$$|\psi\rangle = \frac{1}{\sqrt{2^{n+1}}} \sum_{x=0}^{2^n-1} |x\rangle(|0\rangle - |1\rangle)$$

The following snippet of code illustrates the creation of this initial state:

```
cand := 0:int[n];
for k in [0..n) {
  cand[k] := H(cand[k]);
}
target := H(1: B);
```

As required, the cand variable is initialized to the superposition of all input states thanks to the application of the Hadamard transform to each qubit in state $|0\rangle$ during the for loop and the target variable is initialized to $H(|1\rangle) = |-\rangle$.

It is time to move on to the key part of the Deutsch-Jozsa algorithm: the conditional phase-flipping based on the function's application to the superposition of the inputs. In Silq, you obtain the desired state with a simple if loop and the X bit-flip gate, which maps $\sum \gamma_x|x\rangle$ to $\sum \gamma_x|1-x\rangle$. Because function f does not introduce or destroy superposition, it can be flagged as qfree. Besides, the cand variable is not modified during the loop and can be viewed as a temporarily const so that function f is lifted, which means f(cand) can safely be uncomputed from the current state. Without this uncomputation, the state would have been equal to the following:

$$|\psi\rangle = \frac{1}{\sqrt{2^{n+1}}} \left[\sum_{x=0}^{2^n-1} (-1)^{f(x)}|x\rangle(|0\rangle - |1\rangle)|0\rangle - \sum_{x=0}^{2^n-1} (-1)^{f(x)}|x\rangle(|0\rangle - |1\rangle)|1\rangle \right]$$

We see here that a new qubit, corresponding to f(cand), would have been entangled with our state and that the automatic uncomputation prevented this undesired effect from occurring. Finally, the measurement of the target ancillary qubit and the second round of application of the Hadamard transform to the remaining qubits ensure that the initial state is modified into the following state:

$$|\psi\rangle = \frac{1}{2^n} \sum_{y=0}^{2^n-1} \left[\sum_{x=0}^{2^n-1} (-1)^{f(x)} (-1)^{x \cdot y} \right] |y\rangle$$

This transition to the state that we were trying to reach is detailed in the following snippet of code:

```
if f(cand) {
    target := X(target);
}
measure(target);
for k in [0..n) {
    cand[k] := H(cand[k]);
}
```

We see here that the phase-flip of the target ancillary qubit is applied conditionally on the value of f(cand), taking advantage of the automatic uncomputation in Silq. Then, the measurement of target and the application of Hadamard transforms to each qubit of cand give us the required state.

All that is left to do is to measure the current state and store the value in a result variable. As we established, the probability of measuring 0 is 1 if f is constant and 0 if f is balanced so that when returning the (result == 0) Boolean, as in the following code, the deutsch_jozsa function will output 1 for a constant input and 0 for a balanced one:

```
result := measure(cand);
return result==0;
```

To test our implementation, we define a constant function as a **lifted** lambda function that returns 1 on all inputs and assert that the output of the deutsch_jozsa function is 1 as planned:

```
constant := λ(x:int[2]) lifted:B{return 1:B};
x := measure(deutsch_jozsa(constant));
assert(x == 1);
```

In the same way, we define a balanced function as a **lifted** function that returns 1 on half of the inputs (when the least significant bit of the input is 1) and 0 on the other half, and assert that the output of the deutsch_jozsa function is 0 as planned:

```
def balanced(x:int[2])lifted:B{
    if (x[0]==1) {
        return 1:B;
    }
    else {
        return 0:B;
    }
}
x := deutsch_jozsa(balanced);
assert(x == 0);
```

The balanced function defined here returns 1 when the least significant bit of the input is 1 and 0 when the least significant bit of the input is 0. As required, it returns 1 on half of the input space and 0 on the other half because a random input has a ½ probability of having 1 as its least significant bit.

Designing a more concise version of the algorithm

Thanks to the properties of Silq, the Deutsch-Jozsa algorithm can be rewritten without the target ancillary qubit because a simple if loop allows flipping the state conditionally by using the built-in phase(π) instruction, which corresponds to the Pauli-Z gate. We can therefore present the Deutsch-Jozsa algorithm in a very concise way:

```
def deutsch_jozsa[n:!N](f: const int[n] !→ lifted B):!B{
    cand := 0:int[n];
    for k in [0..n) { cand[k] := H(cand[k]); }

    if f(cand) {
```

```
    phase(π);
}
```

```
for k in [0..n) { cand[k] := H(cand[k]); }
```

```
result := measure(cand);
return result==0;
}
```

In this version of the implementation, the phase-flipping X gate is replaced by the Silq built-in `phase` function, which applies a global phase corresponding to its input to the whole quantum state. This lets us get rid of the ancillary qubit and we can do the entire state computation on the n-qubits `cand` register.

Now that you have learned how to implement the Deutsch-Jozsa algorithm in Silq, we will look at another useful example, the Bernstein-Vazirani algorithm, and see how to implement it.

Implementing the Bernstein-Vazirani algorithm

The **Bernstein-Vazirani algorithm** refers to a quantum algorithm designed by Ethan Bernstein and Umesh Vazirani in 1992. In the same way as the Deutsch-Jozsa algorithm, its goal is to demonstrate that with some categories of problems, quantum algorithms provide an advantage over classical ones.

In this section, you will learn how to solve the Bernstein-Vazirani problem theoretically both in a classical and in a quantum way. You will then practically implement a quantum algorithm solving that problem while gaining intuition on some of Silq's core features.

Problem statement

Let's start with the definition of the problem solved by the Bernstein-Vazirani algorithm. The objective is to determine the value of a secret string encoded within a function, $f: \{0,1\}^n \rightarrow \{0,1\}$, passed as input. We know that f is a function taking as input an n-bit integer and returning its dot product (modulo 2) with some unknown string, $s \in \{0,1\}^n$. In other words, we have $f(x) = x_0 s_0 + x_1 s_1 + \cdots + x_{n-1} s_{n-1} \bmod 2$ for $x \in \{0,1\}^n$ and the goal is to find the value of $s \in \{0,1\}^n$ with the minimum number of queries possible.

Classical solution

Before using quantum computation to solve the Bernstein-Vazirani problem, let's take a quick look into the classical way to solve it. In the classical version of the Bernstein-Vazirani problem, one query to the provided function will deliver at best one bit of information. Thus, if you evaluate it on all the powers of 2, you will find the secret string in n queries:

$$f(100\ldots00) = s_0$$
$$f(010\ldots00) = s_1$$
$$\blacksquare\ \blacksquare\ \blacksquare$$
$$f(000\ldots01) = s_{n-1}$$

Each query provides one bit of the secret string, which means n queries are needed to reconstruct it classically.

Quantum solution

The Bernstein-Vazirani problem is designed so that the quantum solution requires only one query to the function to retrieve the secret string instead of n in the classical solution. What needs to be done is to use this query to generate a particular quantum state in which a measurement will give the string with a probability of 1. In the next steps, we detail how to reach the desired quantum state:

1. We begin with n qubits initialized to $|0\rangle$ and apply a Hadamard transform to each one of them to obtain the uniform superposition on n qubits:

$$|\psi_0\rangle = \frac{1}{\sqrt{2^n}} \sum_{x=0}^{2^n-1} |x\rangle$$

2. Then, we apply a phase on the state conditionally on its evaluation by function f (the one and only query):

$$|\psi_1\rangle = \frac{1}{\sqrt{2^n}} \sum_{x=0}^{2^n-1} (-1)^{f(x)} |x\rangle = \frac{1}{\sqrt{2^n}} \sum_{x=0}^{2^n-1} (-1)^{s \cdot x} |x\rangle$$

3. Here, we see that a phase is picked up for the ith qubit if and only if $f(x_i) = s_i \cdot x_i = 1$, which leads to $s_i = x_i = 1$. The current state is therefore equivalent to the following:

$$|\psi_2\rangle = \frac{|0\rangle + (-1)^{s_0}|1\rangle}{\sqrt{2}} \otimes \cdots \otimes \frac{|0\rangle + (-1)^{s_{n-1}}|1\rangle}{\sqrt{2}}$$

4. Now, recall that $H(|+\rangle) = |0\rangle$ and $H(|-\rangle) = |1\rangle$ and look at what happens when applying a Hadamard transform to each of the qubits of the state. Those that picked up a phase and got changed to $|-\rangle$ are the ones for which $s_i = 1$ and those that stayed as $|+\rangle$ are the ones for which $s_i = 0$. Thus, applying a Hadamard transform to the qubits will change our state to $|\psi_3\rangle = |s\rangle$ and a simple measure of the state in the standard basis will give us the string, s:

$$|s_0, s_1, \ldots, s_{n-1}\rangle \overset{H}{\leftrightarrow} \frac{|0\rangle + (-1)^{s_0}|1\rangle}{\sqrt{2}} \otimes \cdots \otimes \frac{|0\rangle + (-1)^{s_{n-1}}|1\rangle}{\sqrt{2}}$$

Because of its design, the quantum solution to the Bernstein-Vazirani problem takes advantage of the quantum superposition of states to retrieve the secret string using only one unique query to the function. It also exploits quantum interference when applying the Hadamard transform a second time to ensure the measurement of the sought secret string.

Two-qubit example

Before looking at the Silq implementation of the Bernstein-Vazirani algorithm, let's take an example with function $f:\{0,1\}^2 \to \{0,1\}$ associated with the two-bit secret string, $s = 01$. The steps of the algorithm are as follows:

1. We initialize the state to the uniform superposition on two qubits by applying the Hadamard transform on both qubits of state $|00\rangle$:

$$|\psi_0\rangle = \frac{1}{2}(|00\rangle + |01\rangle + |10\rangle + |11\rangle)$$

2. We apply a phase conditionally on the evaluation of f:

$$|\psi_1\rangle = \frac{1}{2}((-1)^{01\cdot00}|00\rangle + (-1)^{01\cdot01}|01\rangle + (-1)^{01\cdot10}|10\rangle + (-1)^{01\cdot11}|11\rangle)$$

$$|\psi_1\rangle = \frac{1}{2}(|00\rangle - |01\rangle + |10\rangle - |11\rangle)$$

3.   This state is equivalent to the following:

$$|\psi_2\rangle = \frac{|0\rangle + |1\rangle}{\sqrt{2}} \otimes \frac{|0\rangle - |1\rangle}{\sqrt{2}}$$

4.   Applying a last Hadamard transform to both qubits thus gives us the state $|\psi_3\rangle = |01\rangle$.

Now, we only have to measure this final state to obtain the secret string, s, with a probability of 1. Let's now implement the Bernstein-Vazirani algorithm in Silq.

Silq implementation

Now that we have seen how quantum computing is useful to solve the Bernstein-Vazirani problem, we will implement the algorithm in Silq. We will make a function, `bernstein_vazirani`, that takes as input a function, $f:\{0,1\}^n \rightarrow \{0,1\}$, for an integer, $n \in \mathbb{N}$, where $f(x) = s \cdot x \bmod 2$ for a secret string, $s \in \{0,1\}^n$, and returns this secret string.

The initial state of our quantum algorithm is the uniform superposition on n qubits, which can be obtained by preparing state $|0\rangle^{\otimes n}$ and applying the Hadamard transform to each of the qubits. The following formula illustrates how to generate this state:

$$\frac{1}{\sqrt{2^n}} \sum_{x=0}^{2^n-1} |x\rangle$$

The following snippet of code illustrates the creation of this initial state:

```
cand := 0:uint[n];
for k in [0..n) {
  cand[k] := H(cand[k]);
}
```

In the same way as in the Deutsch-Jozsa algorithm, the key part of the Bernstein-Vazirani algorithm is the conditional application of a phase in the state based on the function's application to the superposition of the inputs. The `phase` (π) instruction inside the `if` loop in the following snippet of code flips the phase of the state if the condition is met. The safe uncomputation of the ancillary qubit produced by this `f(cand)` condition is ensured by the fact that function *f* does not introduce or destroy superposition and can be flagged as qfree, and the `cand` variable is temporarily viewed as const. The following snippet of code shows this conditional phase-flip:

```
if f(cand) {
    phase(π);
}
```

Finally, we apply the Hadamard transform to all the qubits, where we start with the following state:

$$\frac{|0\rangle + (-1)^{s_0}|1\rangle}{\sqrt{2}} \otimes \cdots \otimes \frac{|0\rangle + (-1)^{s_{n-1}}|1\rangle}{\sqrt{2}}$$

And we change it into $|s\rangle$, such that a measure of the current state is enough to retrieve the secret string, *s*, and return it, as in the following snippet of code:

```
for k in [0..n) {
    cand[k] := H(cand[k]);
}

s := measure(cand);
return s;
```

To test the implementation, we first define the `scal` function as the number of bits equal to 1 when applying a bitwise AND on the two inputs, as shown in this code:

```
def scal[n:!N](const x:uint[n], const y:uint[n])qfree:uint[n]
{
    count := 0:uint[n];
    for k in [0..n) {
        count += x[k] && y[k];
    }
    return count;
}
```

Then, we define function f as the dot product modulo 2 of a secret string, s, and parameter x:

```
def f[n:!ℕ](s:!uint[n])(x:uint[n])lifted:𝔹{
  y := scal(s, x)%2;
  return y==1;
}
```

Finally, we check that for different values of s (for example, every three-bit permutation in the following example), the algorithm correctly finds the secret string:

```
for i in [0..8) {
  s := i coerce !uint[4];
  s₀ := bernstein_vazirani(f(s));
  assert(s==s₀);
}
```

Here, secret string s is used to compute the $f(s): x \rightarrow scal(s, x)\%2$ function and we assert that the s_0 string returned by the Bernstein-Vazirani algorithm is effectively equal to s. In the second line, the `coerce` keyword forces the secret string to be a classical unsigned integer on four qubits.

To verify the two-qubit example defined in the previous section with $s = 01$, you can use the following code and verify that the returned value is effectively 1:

```
s := 1 coerce !uint[2];
s₀ := bernstein_vazirani(f(s));
return s₀;
```

In this section, you learned how to implement the Bernstein-Vazirani algorithm in Silq by taking advantage of quantum parallelism and interference to generate a state in which a measurement outputs the desired string.

Summary

Over the course of this chapter, we have seen two famous problems: Deutsch-Jozsa and Bernstein-Vazirani, designed to demonstrate that quantum algorithms can use the properties of quantum computing, such as the superposition of states or quantum interference, to gain an advantage over their classical counterparts.

After studying how to solve the problems theoretically with quantum techniques and looking at what the speedup was compared to the classical solution, we then practically implemented the algorithms in Silq and tested them on some examples.

We familiarized ourselves with Silq programming by implementing basic quantum algorithms using concepts such as the uniform superposition of states for a given number of qubits, which will be used in the next sections when designing more complex algorithms. It was also useful to showcase safe uncomputation, which is one of the key features of the Silq language.

In the next chapter, we will build on what we learned in this chapter to implement the famous quantum search algorithm known as Grover's algorithm.

9

Quantum Algorithms II – Grover's Search Algorithm and Simon's Algorithm

In the classical computing system, the problem of searching for an element in a particular database or array is a significant one. The complexity of searching for an element in an unstructured database in the classical computing case leads to taking time. However, in the case of quantum computing, the complexity of searching for an element in an unstructured database can be done in less time than that of the classical case.

In this chapter, you will dive into Grover's search algorithm, which is primarily an algorithm to search for elements in an unstructured database with a search speed better than that of classical search. We will cover the following topics:

- Introducing search algorithms

- Getting started with Grover's search algorithm

- Grover's search for one solution using Silq programming

- Grover's search for multiple solutions using Silq programming

- Grover's search for an unknown number of solutions using Silq programming

- Introducing Simon's algorithm

Technical requirements

You can download the code samples and the output results for this chapter from this book's official GitHub repository at `https://github.com/PacktPublishing/Quantum-Computing-with-Silq-Programming/tree/main/Chapter09`.

Introducing search algorithms

In *Chapter 8, Quantum Algorithms I – Deutsch-Jozsa and Bernstein-Vazirani*, you saw and implemented function checking algorithms that helped you to identify whether a particular function is constant or balanced. Now, in this chapter, we will be building upon the foundations of function checking and will implement the famous quantum searching algorithm known as **Grover's search algorithm**.

Before we begin our discussion on quantum search algorithms, let's first understand the **search algorithms** classically available to us. The two most prominent search algorithms are **linear search** and **binary search**, which are used widely to search for an element in a database or array. In linear search, each element of the array is traversed and is compared with the marked element that we are trying to search. Since each element is being compared, if the desired element is present at the very end of the array, then it will take N searches to find the desired element provided we have N number of elements in our array. This is the worst-case scenario and consumes a lot of time when the database or array is very large in size.

In the case of binary search, we assume that our array or database is sorted in either ascending order or descending order and this algorithm works on the idea of divide and conquer. In binary search, we select a search key (a marked item value that we desire to find) and then break the array into two parts from the middle element of the array depending upon the value of the search key. For example, if the search key value is less than the middle element, then the array is broken into two parts – the lower half and the upper half. If the search key is less than the middle element value, we continue our search only on the lower half; otherwise, we continue our search on the upper half. For a linear case, the time complexity is $O(N)$ because in the worst case, we have to search the whole array or database. But in the case of binary search, the time complexity is $O(\log N)$ and is a good improvement over that of the linear search algorithm. In this chapter, you will see that Grover's algorithm provides a quadratic speedup of $O(\sqrt{N})$, which is better than both the classical algorithms we discussed here!

In the next section, let's get started with Grover's search algorithm.

Getting started with Grover's search algorithm

Grover's search algorithm is a quantum version of the searching algorithm that helps to accomplish an unordered search, which means finding an element or multiple elements in a database or array. This algorithm shows the power of quantum computing in the sense that it minimizes the number of operations to carry out the searching process compared to its classical search versions. Grover's algorithm provides a speedup in the searching process and utilizes the technique of **amplitude amplification** for the marked item that we are trying to search.

As you already saw in *Chapter 8, Quantum Algorithms I – Deutsch-Jozsa and Bernstein-Vazirani,* how the algorithms required an oracle in order to run, in a very similar manner, Grover's algorithm also requires an oracle that encodes the marked item (the element that we want to search) in a list of several items. This oracle is known as **Grover's oracle** and can be thought of as a black box. Another, and the most important, part of Grover's algorithm is the **Grover diffusion operator**, which is responsible for the process of amplitude amplification, where the amplitude of a marked item is increased and the amplitude of other elements is decreased. The process of amplitude amplification can be thought of as increasing the amplitude of the marked element, thereby making it have a higher probability so that during measurement, it becomes easy to find the marked element.

Let's now go through the various steps involved in Grover's search with a pictorial as well as mathematical description to have a clear understanding of the process of Grover's search mechanism. To make the explanation simple, we will consider searching only one solution (marked element) using Grover's search.

To start with, let's consider that you have a function, $f: \{1, ..., N\} \rightarrow \{0,1\}$, that can be encoded by Grover's oracle and we want to search for a marked element, say, x^*, such that $f(x^*) = 1$, and then we want to find the value of that x^* as well.

Let's start with the superposition of all the qubits that are initialized to |0> already. This is achieved by applying the Hadamard gate to all the qubits. This also makes the amplitude of all the elements equal. Assume $N = 2^n$, where n is the number of qubits:

$$|00 ... 0 > \rightarrow |\psi > = \frac{1}{\sqrt{N}} \sum_{x=1}^{N-1} |x >$$

From *Figure 9.1*, you can see the marked element, x^*, in a list of several elements, where each element has the same amplitude and is in a superposition state. It is worth noting that amplitudes are the square root of probabilities, because of which we have $o(\sqrt{N})$ speedup in time:

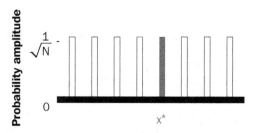

Figure 9.1 – Marked element in a list of several elements

Now we apply a unitary transformation to the superposition state such that $U_f|x > = (-1)^{f(x)}|x >$, which means that we flip the amplitude of the marked element, x^*, and the flipping operation can be carried out using a Z gate or, more specifically, by having a phase oracle.

Figure 9.2 shows the phase flip operation of the marked element, which results after that unitary transformation. This operation can constitute Grover's oracle, which in this case is the phase oracle:

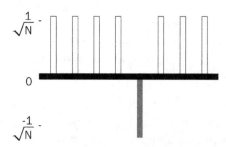

Figure 9.2 – Marked element is flipped

Now, the main process in Grover's algorithm is the technique of **amplitude amplification**, which happens through a mathematical operation known as **inversion about the mean**. In this operation, all the amplitudes of the quantum states are flipped about the average amplitude value and this operation utilizes the phenomena of quantum interference to achieve the best measurement result.

The mathematical operation of inversion about the mean is given as follows:

$$U_\psi = 2|\psi><\psi| - I_{2^N}$$

Figure 9.3 shows the result of the inversion about the mean operation:

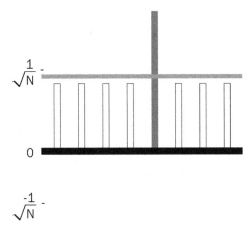

Figure 9.3 – Marked element is flipped

The step of inversion about the mean constitutes the **Grover diffusion operator** and this operation is a general step that needs to be applied after the Grover's oracle step increases the probability amplitude of the marked element. For the implementation part of the Grover diffusion, firstly Hadamards are applied to all the qubits to bring them into the state of superposition, and then the inversion about the mean operation, U_ψ, is performed, and finally, again, Hadamards are applied to all the qubits. You will see this implementation in Silq in the next section.

It is worth noting that all these quantum operations are performed in a single query and when N becomes large, then we need to repeat the step of Grover's oracle and the Grover diffusion together $\sqrt{N}$ times to find the marked element. To be more accurate, it takes around $\frac{\pi}{4}\sqrt{N} = 0.7854\sqrt{N}$ iterations to achieve the maximum probability of the marked element. Another important aspect to observe is that in our case, you can consider U_f as Grover's oracle and U_ψ as the Grover diffusion operator; so, $U_f U_\psi$ collectively constitutes Grover's search algorithm.

Since the Grover diffusion step is an operator, we can describe it using the matrix notation. A general Grover diffusion operator is provided as follows:

$$U_\psi = \begin{bmatrix} \frac{2}{N} - 1 & \frac{2}{N} & \cdots & \frac{2}{N} \\ \frac{2}{N} & \frac{2}{N} - 1 & \cdots & \frac{2}{N} \\ \vdots & \vdots & \ddots & \vdots \\ \frac{2}{N} & \frac{2}{N} & \cdots & \frac{2}{N} - 1 \end{bmatrix}$$

With Grover's algorithm covered, we are now ready to dive into the Silq implementation of the algorithm in the next section.

Grover's search for one solution using Silq programming

In this section, let's start coding Grover's search algorithm using the Silq programming language and you will see that the uncomputation of Grover's oracle and the Grover diffusion circuit happens automatically. Because of this advantage of automatic uncomputation, the Grover code is very simple and concise and intuitive.

Let's start coding the Grover diffusion operator first because that operator is generic and can be used by any kind of Grover's oracle. Open a new Silq file, name it groverDiffusion.slq, and save it inside a folder called helpers. Then, inside this file, insert the following code:

```
def groverDiffusion[n:!π](cand:uint[n])mfree: uint[n]{
    for k in [0..n) { cand[k] := H(cand[k]); }
    if cand!=0{ phase(π); }
    for k in [0..n) { cand[k] := H(cand[k]); }
    return cand;
}
```

Let's try to understand what is happening in the preceding code. In the n code variable is the number of elements that you want to have in the list. Also note that n is of type ! ℕ which means that it is classical natural number type. The cand variable is an unsigned array of size n that stores the marked element that is our candidate solution and we want this candidate solution to have the maximum probability amplitude so that when we measure the candidate state, we get this solution easily. First, Hadamard gates are applied to all the elements of cand to create an equal superposition. Then, it is checked that cand is not 0, we flip the phase of the candidate solution by π in cand, and then again apply the Hadamard gates to all the elements present in the cand variable to create a balanced superposition state. Finally, we return cand.

Now, let's see the code for Grover's algorithm, which consists of the Grover's oracle call and the Grover diffusion operator being called to find the marked element. Make a new file outside the helpers folder and name it groverSimple.slq and save that file in the same location where you stored the helpers folder. This is necessary because we are going to import the Grover diffusion function from the groverDiffusion.slq file. In the groverSimple.slq file, insert the following code:

```
import helpers.groverDiffusion;

def grover[n:!N](f: const uint[n] !→ lifted B):!N{
    nIterations:= round(π / 4 * sqrt(2^n));
    cand:=0:uint[n];
    for k in [0..n) {cand[k] := H(cand[k]);}
        for k in [0..nIterations) {
        if f(cand){
            phase(π);
        }
        cand:=groverDiffusion(cand);
    }
    return measure(cand) as !N;
}
```

In the preceding code, the `grover` function takes Grover's oracle f as an input. The `const` is used because f preserves its argument (it is not consumed) and `uint[n]` describes the fact that f takes a parameter in $[0, 2^n]$. The `!-> lifted B` suggests that f consists of classical operations (does not introduce nor destroy superposition) and returns a Boolean $\mathbb{B}$. The `:!N` indicates that the return type of the function is a classical integer. The number of iterations is defined by the $\frac{\pi}{4}\sqrt{N}$ relation, which you have already seen in the previous section. `nIterations:= round(π/ 4 * sqrt(2^n));` defines the number of iterations according to the formula $\frac{\pi}{4}\sqrt{N}$. Then, the `cand` unsigned array is defined for n bits and a Hadamard operation is applied to all the n bits in the `cand` variable to create a superposition of all the elements present in the `cand` variable.

Now, a `for` loop is initiated, which goes until the number of iterations means `nIterations`, and `f(cand)` is checked to see whether the marked element, which is the candidate solution, is found or not. If a solution is found, meaning `f(cand)` is 1, then the phase of that marked element is flipped by π and the Grover diffusion function is called to act on the `cand` variable, which now contains the flipped version of the candidate solution. Finally, the function returns the measurement of `cand`, which is the marked element:

```
def main() {
    f := λ(x:uint[5])lifted:𝔹{return x==3;}; // creates an
                        // oracle which outputs one only when x=3
    x := grover(f);
    assert(x==3); // verifies that grover finds the right
                  // solution
}
```

In the previous code, inside the `main` function, you can see the definition of Grover's oracle f, where we mark element 3 as our solution and then provide it to the `grover` function. Observe that λ can be used to create a **lambda function** in Silq, which is quite compact in size and is easy to decipher. It is important to note that Grover's oracle is of the `lifted` type because its arguments are constant and it does not create or destroys superposition. The output for this code can be found here: `https://github.com/PacktPublishing/Quantum-Computing-with-Silq-Programming/tree/main/Chapter09`

With the one solution for Grover's algorithm method covered, we are now ready to dive into a case where there can be multiple marked elements, which means we can have multiple solutions to find, and you will see that Grover's algorithm performs well in that case too. Let's go to the next section for Grover's search with multiple solutions.

Grover's search for multiple solutions using Silq programming

Until now, we have looked into Grover's search for finding only one solution, which we termed as the marked element. But Grover's algorithm can also be used to find **multiple solutions**, which means multiple marked elements. The number of iterations in the case of multiple solutions is around $\frac{\pi}{4}\sqrt{\frac{N}{M}} \approx 0.7854\sqrt{\frac{N}{M}}$, where M is the number of marked elements.

Let's now start with the extensive mathematical treatment for the case of multiple solutions in the next section.

Mathematical treatment of Grover's search for multiple solutions

Consider that the number of marked elements is M such that $1 \leq M \leq N$; so, therefore, we start with state $|\beta> = \frac{1}{\sqrt{M}} \sum_{f(x)=1} |x>$, which is the superposition of all the M marked elements.

We also have our original state prepared, which is $|\psi> = \frac{1}{\sqrt{N}} \sum_{x=1}^{N-1} |x>$. Now, the original state can be written in terms of N and M as coefficients by a bit of mathematical manipulation, as follows:

$$|\psi> = \frac{\sqrt{N-M}}{\sqrt{N}} \left(\frac{1}{\sqrt{N-M}} \sum_{f(x)=0} |x> \right) + \frac{\sqrt{M}}{\sqrt{N}} \left(\frac{1}{\sqrt{M}} \sum_{f(x)=1} |x> \right)$$

To simplify the preceding expression, you can consider the values inside the brackets as follows:

$$|\alpha> = \frac{1}{\sqrt{N-M}} \sum_{f(x)=0} |x> \ and \ |\beta> = \frac{1}{\sqrt{M}} \sum_{f(x)=1} |x>$$

Then, state $|\psi>$ can now be written as follows:

$$|\psi> = \frac{\sqrt{N-M}}{\sqrt{N}} |\alpha> + \frac{\sqrt{M}}{\sqrt{N}} |\beta>$$

Considering the simple $|\psi> = cos\theta \,|\alpha> + sin\theta \,|\beta>$ relation, we can define the Grover's algorithm operation as $G = U_\psi * U_f$, where U_f is Grover's oracle (phase oracle), which flips the phase of state $|\beta>$. The phase flip operation gives us the following:

$$U_f|\psi> = cos\theta \,|\alpha> + sin\theta \,|\beta> = cos\theta \,|\alpha> - sin\theta \,|\beta>$$

After some k iterations of Grover's algorithm, we become closer to finding the multiple solutions and the final state can be written as follows:

$$G^k|\psi> = \cos(2k+1)\theta \,|\alpha> + \sin(2k+1)\theta \,|\beta>$$

Consider a situation where we have a large database or array to search for the multiple solutions; then, $M << N$ and therefore, $\theta \approx sin\theta \approx \dfrac{\sqrt{M}}{\sqrt{N}}$ and $(2k+1)\theta = \dfrac{\pi}{2}$.

Finally, the equation becomes the following:

$$(2k+1)\frac{\sqrt{M}}{\sqrt{N}} = \frac{\pi}{2} \Rightarrow k \approx \frac{\pi}{4}\sqrt{\frac{N}{M}}$$

This proves that the number of iterations for searching multiple elements using Grover's search is indeed $\dfrac{\pi}{4}\sqrt{\dfrac{N}{M}}$.

With the background of the mathematics covered, we are now ready to dive into the Silq implementation of Grover's search for multiple solutions in the next section.

Silq implementation of Grover's search for multiple solutions

The Silq implementation of Grover's algorithm for multiple solutions is very similar to that of the one solution that you have learned about already; it just has some minor modifications to the code. But regardless of that, we will still go through the code.

The code for the Grover diffusion won't be explained again because it is going to be the same for every case. Let's start by looking at Grover's function. Open a new file called groverMultiple.slq and save it in the location where the helpers folder is present. The code is as follows:

```
import helpers.groverDiffusion;
```

```
def grover_multiple[n:!N](f: const uint[n] !→ lifted B, M:!N
        ):!N{
    nIterations:= round(((π/4) * sqrt(2^n/M));
    cand:=0:uint[n];
    for k in [0..n) { cand[k] := H(cand[k]); }

    for k in [0..nIterations){
        if f(cand){
            phase(π);
        }
        cand := groverDiffusion(cand);
    }
    return measure(cand) as !N;
}
```

In the preceding code, you can clearly observe that the grover_multiple function takes an extra parameter, which is the number of solutions, *M*, to search. M:!N is the number of solutions of f as parameter and it is a classical integer. The rest of the function definition is same as that of the grover function case we discussed in the previous section. You can clearly see that the number of iterations is $\frac{\pi}{4}\sqrt{\frac{N}{M}}$, as we proved, and the rest of the code section is the same as that of Grover's search for one solution, which we discussed before.

The main function is provided in the following code:

```
def main(){
    f := λ(x:uint[5])lifted:B{ return x==4 || x==5 || x==6; };
    // creates an oracle which outputs one only when x is in
    // {4,5,6}

    x := grover_multiple(f, 3);

    assert(x==4 || x==5 || x==6);
    // verifies that grover_multiple finds one of the right
    // solutions
}
```

In the previous code, you can see that in Grover's oracle, f, we are now marking three elements, 4, 5, and 6, to search using Grover's algorithm. The output for this code can be found here: https://github.com/PacktPublishing/Quantum-Computing-with-Silq-Programming/tree/main/Chapter09

You can see the intuitive implementation of the multiple solutions case and the simplicity in programming that Silq provides along with automatic uncomputation.

Now, in the next section, let's examine Grover's search algorithm when the number of solutions is not known to us, or in other words, they are random.

Grover's search for an unknown number of solutions using Silq programming

Grover's search for one solution and multiple solutions was fairly straightforward to understand and implement using the Silq programming language. However, there are cases where we are not sure of the number of solutions that we want to search for and we want our Grover's algorithm to search for those **unknown number of solutions** that we have in our mind. The case of finding an unknown number of solutions is a bit of a complex task and we will be implementing an algorithm for this purpose.

Due to the complex nature of the mathematical segment for this section, we recommend you go through the resources mentioned in the *Further reading* section, which will give you an idea of the mathematics behind the unknown number of solutions problem. The algorithm that we will be implementing is provided in *Figure 9.4*:

Algorithm 2 Quantum search with number of solutions **unknown**

Input: O_f with $f(x) = 1$ iff. $x \in A$. $\lambda = 6/5$.
Output: $x \in A$, a marked item.
 1: Initialize $m = 1$.
 2: **while** $m \leq \sqrt{N}$ **do**
 3:    pick uniformly random $k \leftarrow \{1, \ldots, m\}$.
 4:    apply k times the basic Grover iteration G on initial state $|h\rangle = \sum_x \frac{1}{\sqrt{N}} |x\rangle$.
 5:    measure and obtain x. If $x \in A$, output x and abort. Otherwise set $m \leftarrow \lambda m$.
 6: **end while**

Figure 9.4 – Grover's algorithm for an unknown number of solutions

Let us go through this algorithm in detail. When the number of solutions is not known, it is impossible to know the exact optimal number of iterations needed for Grover's algorithm to find a solution. To get around this, we use the fact that if we pick random integer $k \in \{0, ..., m-1\}$ uniformly, then, with the value of m big enough applying k iterations of Grover's algorithm and measuring will give one of the solutions with probability greater than 1/4. In order to quickly find the region in which this works, we start with m=1 and increase it exponentially (multiplying it by a factor λ in each iteration).If we denote by : $m^* < \sqrt{(2^n/M)}$, the critical point after which the probability of measuring a solution is greater than 1/4 and if we take $\lambda=6/5$ as exponential factor, then the algorithm takes less than 6m* to reach the critical point and less than 10m* to find a solution once m is in the right region. Thus, it finds a solution in $O(\sqrt{(2^n/M)})$.

You can find this algorithm in the *Further reading* section resource titled *Early days following Grover's Quantum search algorithm*, and for the mathematical section, refer to the title *Tight bounds on quantum searching*. To learn more about Grover's algorithm, have a read of the original paper that was published by Grover, with the title *A Fast Quantum Mechanical Algorithm for Database Search*.

Let's now move on to the Silq implementation of this algorithm in the next section.

Silq implementation of Grover's search for an unknown number of solutions

Let's study the Silq implementation of the unknown solutions problem. You will see that the code for this is very intuitive and similar to that of the previous cases that we discussed for Grover's search and follows the algorithm that we have discussed already closely:

```
import helpers.groverDiffusion;
import helpers.rand;

def grover_unknown[n:!N](f: const uint[n] !→ lifted B):!N{
    m := 1:!Q;
    l := 6/5;

    while (m <= 2^(n/2)) {
        nIterations := uniformInt(floor(m) coerce !N) + 1;

        cand := 0:uint[n];
        for k in [0..n) {cand[k] := H(cand[k]);}
```

```
        for k in [0..nIterations) {
            if f(cand) {
                phase(π);
            }
        }
        cand:=groverDiffusion(cand);
        }


        x := measure(cand);


        if f(x) {return x as !N;}
        else {m=l*m;}
    }


    return 0;
}
```

In the preceding code, `helpers.rand` imports a function called `uniformInt`, which gives a quantum random number for the selection of the number of iterations. Closely following the algorithm, you can observe that m has been initialized to 1 and l (λ) has been initialized to 6/5. Then, we start a `while` loop, which goes to $\sqrt{N}$, and we perform the steps of Grover's algorithm that we have already studied in the previous sections on one solution and multiple solutions cases. The only difference here is that after Grover's algorithm, we check for the solution, x, after measuring it. If we have found the solution, we simply return it; otherwise, we set $m \leftarrow \lambda m$ as provided in the algorithm.

The following code shows the `main` function implementation through which the `grover_unknown` function is being called to execute its operations:

```
def main() {
    f := λ(x:uint[5])lifted:B{ return x==1 || x==2 || x==5 ||
                              x==8; };
    // creates an oracle which outputs one only when x is in
    // {1,2,5,8}


    x := grover_unknown(f);


    assert(x==1 || x==2 || x==5 || x==8);
    // verifies that grover_unknown finds one of the right
```

```
      // solutions
  }
```

Observe Grover's oracle carefully and see that f has some random solutions, such as the numbers 1, 2, 5, and 8 being encoded, and whenever Grover's algorithm finds any one of those, its job is finished. The output for this code can be found at this link `https://github.com/PacktPublishing/Quantum-Computing-with-Silq-Programming/tree/main/Chapter09`

With all the Grover's algorithm cases covered – one solution, multiple solutions, and an unknown number of solutions – we are now ready to dive into Simon's algorithm in the next section.

Introducing Simon's algorithm

Simon's algorithm is one of the most important algorithms, which provides us with an intuition about the periodicity of a particular function; in other words, it helps us to find when a function repeats itself. Simon's algorithm is also called the **periodic quantum algorithm** and it provides an exponential speedup as compared to classical period-finding algorithms.

The main goal of Simon's algorithm is to find whether a given function is one-to-one or two-to-one, for which they are defined as having the following properties:

- **One-to-one**: This function will map unique inputs to unique outputs, such as $f(1) \rightarrow 1, f(2) \rightarrow 2$.

- **Two-to-one**: This function will map two inputs to a unique output, such as $f(1) \rightarrow 1, f(3) \rightarrow 2$.

For the two-to-one mapping process, we have a secret bit string, b, which helps to check whether the function is two-to-one or not. The condition is that if $f(x) = f(y)$ then $x \oplus y = b$.

In Simon's algorithm as well, we will use an oracle or black-box model, U_f, to encode our secret bit string, which will tell us whether the function is one-to-one or two-to-one. If you tried to solve this classically, then you would have to go through at least half plus 1 of the input values in order to find whether the given function is one-to-one or two-to-one.

Figure 9.5 shows the general circuit for Simon's algorithm, with the first register having n qubits and the second register having n qubits as well:

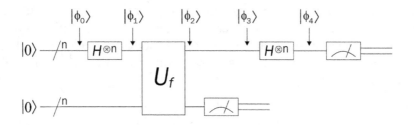

Figure 9.5 – Simon's algorithm circuit

Let's start understanding this circuit more carefully by calculating the quantum states formed at each stage of the circuit:

- First of all, the n qubits of the first register and second register are initialized to $|0>$. This means that $|\phi_0> = |0>^{\otimes n} |0>^{\otimes n}$.

- Then, Hadamard gates are applied to the first-register n qubits and x denotes first-register qubits. We get the state as $|\phi_1> = (H^{\otimes n} I^{\otimes n})|\phi_0> = \frac{1}{\sqrt{2^n}} \sum_{x \in \{0,1\}^n} |x> |0>^{\otimes n}$.

- Let's denote the second register as $|y> = |0>^{\otimes n}$ and oracle U_f is applied, which encodes our secret string, s. The oracle performs the $U_f|x> |y> = |x, y \oplus f(x)$ operation, where $f(x)$ is the oracle function that we wish to determine whether it is one-to-one or two-to-one. The state that we get is $|\phi_2> = U_f|\phi_1> = \frac{1}{\sqrt{2^n}} \sum_{x \in \{0,1\}^n} |x> |f(x)>$.

- Now we make a measurement of the second register and we will be observing a certain value of $f(x)$, which is not important, but there will be an impact on the first register due to this measurement process. If our secret string $s = 0^n$, then the first register will remain in equal superposition and regardless of the $f(x)$ value measured, x can be any bit string in $\{0,1\}^n$ with equal probability. Now, if our secret string $s = \{0,1\}^n$, then there are limited values for the first register, which we can denote by $f(z)$, and $f(z)$ will take only z or $z \oplus s$ as values. Due to this, the state of the first register becomes $|\phi_3> = \frac{1}{\sqrt{2}}(|z> + |z \oplus s>)$.

- Now we apply Hadamards in the first register again and after some simplification, we get the state as follows: $|\phi_4> = H^{\otimes n}|\phi_3> = \frac{1}{\sqrt{2^{n+1}}} \sum_{y \in \{0,1\}^n} (-1)^{z \cdot y}(1 + (-1)^{(s \cdot y)})|y>$.

- From state $|\phi_4>$, we measure n qubits of the first register and you will see that there can be two possibilities: either $s.y = 0$ or $s.y = 1$. If $s.y = 1$, then you will get $|\phi_4> = 0|y>$, which means the second register will always be 0. If $s.y = 0$, then you will get $|\phi_4> = \dfrac{1}{\sqrt{2^{n+1}}} \displaystyle\sum_{y\in\{0,1\}^n} (-1)^{z.y}|y>$, which means that you will always get an equal superposition of y.

Let's now start making the circuit of this algorithm and verify Simon's algorithm in the next section.

The Silq implementation of Simon's algorithm

For the Silq implementation of Simon's algorithm, we will consider our secret bit string to be 011 and therefore, we will require *2n* qubits to construct our quantum circuit. Here, *n* is the number of input qubits, which is 3 in our case, and therefore, we will require six qubits to work with. Let's start with the code, which is as follows:

```
def Simon(){
    // Initializing Qubits for Inputs - a,b,c and Oracle - d,e,f
    a:=0:𝔹;
    b:=0:𝔹;
    c:=0:𝔹;
    d:=0:𝔹;
    e:=0:𝔹;
    f:=0:𝔹;
    // Applying Hadamard to Inputs
    a:=H(a);
    b:=H(b);
    c:=H(c);
```

We can see that a `Simon()` function is defined and then inside that, six qubits – a, b, c, d, e, and f – are being initialized to construct the Simon's algorithm quantum circuit. Then, Hadamard gates are applied to the input qubits – a, b, and c. In the next snippet of code, let's see the encoding of the 011 secret bit string using the oracle:

```
    // Encoding 011 secret key in the Oracle
    if b{
        d := X(d);
    }
    if b{
```

```
        e := X(e);
    }
if c{
        d := X(d);
    }
if b{
        f := X(f);
    }
if c{
        e := X(e);
    }
if c{
        f := X(f);
    }
}
```

In the preceding code, you can see that we encode the 011 secret bit string using CX gates in the oracle and the construction is such that we take the b qubit as the control and choose d, e, and f as targets. Similarly, we choose c as the control and choose d, e, and f as target qubits. This is done because our bit string is a, b, c, which is 0, 1, 1. It means that a is 0, b is 1 and c is 1, so we make the b and c as controls with the d, e and f as targets. In a similar fashion, you can encode other bit strings as well. Next, we will return our outputs:

```
// Applying Hadamard to Inputs
a:=H(a);
b:=H(b);
c:=H(c);
// Measure the d,e,f qubits for variable consumption
md:=measure(d);
me:=measure(e);
mf:=measure(f);
return (a,b,c,md,me,mf);
}
```

After the creation of the oracle, we apply the Hadamard gates to the input qubits and measure the d, e, and f qubits so that they get consumed. If you do not consume the d, e, and f qubits, then you will get errors in your code. Finally, we return the a, b, c, md, me, and mf qubits, which gives the solution.

The `main` function is provided in the following code:

```
def main() {
    return Simon();
}
```

From the `main` function, we call the `Simon` function, which runs the `Simon` function and returns the output as shown in *Figure 9.6*:

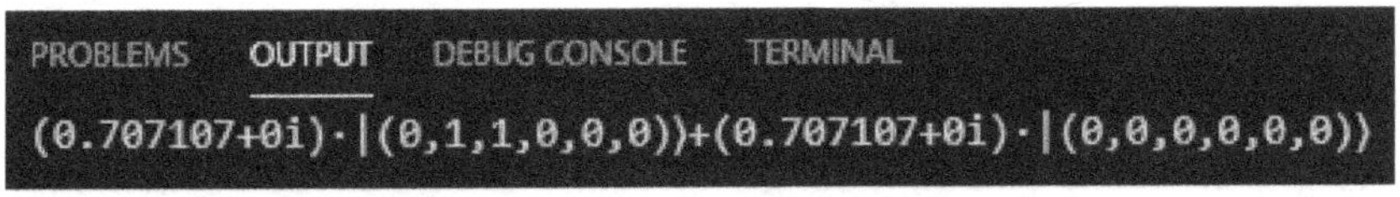

| PROBLEMS | **OUTPUT** | DEBUG CONSOLE | TERMINAL |

`(0.707107+0i)·|(0,1,1,0,0,0))+(0.707107+0i)·|(0,0,0,0,0,0))`

Figure 9.6 – Output of Simon's algorithm

The output shows that state `011` is present with state `000` as well. If you run the circuit several times, then you will see that state `011` comes quite often, which gives us proof that Simon's algorithm is able to detect the `011` bit string. This means that the given oracle function is two-to-one. If the most occurring state was `000`, then the function would have been one-to-one.

Now, you might be thinking that if the probability amplitude of both the `011` and `000` states are the same, how will you know whether it is accurate? Well, it turns out that this circuit is proven to give accurate results; to gain a better understanding of the statistics involved for this circuit, check out the book *Learn Quantum Computing with Python and IBM Quantum Experience*, mentioned in the *Further reading* section, which explores these issues in detail.

Summary

In this chapter, you learned about the notion of searching algorithms and how they are different for both classical and quantum cases. You gained the programming skills to construct Grover's algorithm using Silq for one solution, multiple solutions, and an unknown number of solutions. You will now be able to appreciate the mathematics behind Grover's algorithm and its intuitive implementation using Silq. Finally, you also learned about another important algorithm – Simon's algorithm – and learned how to implement a Simon's oracle circuit and verify its results.

In the next chapter, we will start looking at one of the most important quantum computing concepts, known as the **quantum Fourier transform**, and the **phase estimation algorithm**.

Further reading

- Fang Song, *Early days following Grover's quantum search algorithm*, arXiv, September 2017. Available at `https://arxiv.org/abs/1709.01236`.

- Michel Boyer, Gilles Brassard, Pete Hoyer, & Alain Tapp, *Tight bounds on quantum searching*, arXiv:quant-ph/9605034, 1996. Available at `https://arxiv.org/abs/quant-ph/9605034`.

- Lov K. Grover, *A fast quantum mechanical algorithm for database search*, arXiv:quant-ph/9605043. Available at `https://arxiv.org/abs/quant-ph/9605043`.

- Robert Loredo, *Learn Quantum Computing with Python and IBM Quantum Experience: A hands-on introduction to quantum computing and writing your own quantum algorithms with Python*, Packt Publishing, 2020.

- Dr. Christine Corbett Moran, *Mastering Quantum Computing with IBM QX: Explore the world of quantum computing using the Quantum Composer and Qiskit*, Packt Publishing, 2019.

- Robert S. Sutor, *Dancing with Qubits: How quantum computing works and how it can change the world*, Packt Publishing, 2019.

- David McMahon, *Quantum Computing Explained*, Wiley, 2017.

10

Quantum Algorithms III – Quantum Fourier Transform and Phase Estimation

The concept of periodicity has a huge impact on various applications that we use today. Periodic functions that repeat their value after certain regular intervals of time are used in important applications, such as the study of signals, systems, and communications. They are also used in studying wave mechanics in physics and vibrations. Apart from this periodicity, it has an impact on the analysis of the factorization process of numbers. It is because of so many useful applications that it becomes necessary to explore and take advantage of periodicity in the quantum computing domain as well.

In this chapter, you will explore the concepts related to periodic-based quantum algorithms, which are very different from the oracle-based quantum algorithms we have discussed so far in previous chapters. This chapter will help you to understand the concepts related to the Fourier transform and implement the **Quantum Fourier Transform (QFT)** and phase estimation, as well as building it from scratch using the Silq language. We will cover the following topics in this chapter:

- Introducing the classical **Discrete Fourier Transform (DFT)**
- Exploring the QFT
- Implementing the QFT using Silq
- Getting started with the phase estimation algorithm
- Implementing phase estimation using Silq

Technical requirements

You can download the code samples and output results for this chapter from this book's official GitHub repository at: `https://github.com/PacktPublishing/Quantum-Computing-with-Silq-Programming/tree/main/Chapter10`.

Introducing the classical Discrete Fourier Transform (DFT)

Before we dive into the QFT, it is important to know about the DFT because the QFT is derived from the DFT. The DFT is known as the frequency domain representation of an input sequence. It is used in the spectral analysis of various signals, such as reducing the variance of a spectrum. It is also utilized in the lossy compression of image and sound data. Apart from the previous applications mentioned, the DFT is also used in mathematics, such as for solving partial differential equations and in polynomial multiplication as well. Since the **Discrete-Time Fourier Transform (DTFT)** of a sequence represents a continuous and periodic transformation of the input sequence, if we sample the DTFT at periodic intervals, we get the DFT of the input sequence.

Mathematically, the DFT is defined by the following equation:

$$F(\omega) = \sum_{j=0}^{N-1} e^{\frac{2\pi jik}{N}} x_j$$

From the mathematical equation of the DFT, it is clear that there is a mapping from the input domain, x_i, to the output domain, $F(\omega)$, which is the frequency domain of the input. N is the total number of input sequences. The preceding equation is the DFT transformation. Since the DFT is a transformation from one function to another, in a very similar manner, we can derive the quantum analog where we can transform a quantum state from one state to another state. If you remember from *Chapter 2, Quantum Bits, Quantum Measurements, and Quantum Logic Gates*, you have seen many different quantum state transformations (from the operators) when quantum logic gates are being applied to a particular quantum state.

In the next section, let's now take a look at the QFT itself.

Exploring the QFT

In the previous section, we saw that the classical DFT is a mapping process or a transformation of a function from one domain to another. In a very similar way, the QFT is a transformation of the quantum states from the Z basis to the X basis (the Hadamard basis). Now, you might recall that the Hadamard gate that you saw in *Chapter 2, Quantum Bits, Quantum Measurements, and Quantum Logic Gates*, did the same operation. Yes, you are absolutely right in thinking that because the Hadamard operation is the one-qubit QFT!

The QFT performs a DFT operation but not on a classical sequence, rather on a quantum state. The QFT is an important algorithm to study as it is used as a subroutine for other quantum algorithms, such as the quantum phase estimation algorithm, which we will be discussing later in this chapter.

Mathematically, the QFT transformation is defined as follows:

$$|\psi> = \sum_{j=0}^{N-1} x_j |j> \xrightarrow{QFT} \sum_{j=0}^{N-1} y_j |j>$$

Now, the formula for y_j is provided as follows:

$$y_j = \frac{1}{\sqrt{N}} \sum_{k=0}^{N-1} x_k e^{\frac{2\pi jki}{N}}$$

In the equations provided here, $N = 2^n$, where n is the number of qubits, and if we let $\omega = e^{\frac{2\pi i}{N}}$ and $i = \sqrt{-1}$, then we will get the complete formula for calculating the QFT as follows:

$$QFT\,(|\psi>) = \frac{1}{\sqrt{N}} \sum_{j=0}^{N-1} \sum_{k=0}^{N-1} x_k \omega^{jk} \,|j>$$

As you saw, that put $\omega = e^{\frac{2\pi i}{N}}$ and the reason behind this is that $\omega = e^{\frac{2\pi i}{N}}$ is the primitive N^{th} root of unity, which is present in the QFT relation. Now, since you know the formula for the QFT, you will be able to calculate the one-qubit QFT, and you will be able to verify that it is indeed the Hadamard gate operation. Similarly, for a QFT of three qubits, you can take a look at *Figure 10.1*:

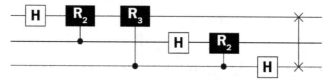

Figure 10.1 – The QFT of three qubits

From *Figure 10.1*, you can see that first, the Hadamard gate (one-qubit QFT) is applied to the first qubit, then the subsequent qubits are taken as control qubits, and rotation gates with respect to the z axis in the Bloch sphere are applied. Here, R_2 corresponds to $\frac{\pi}{2}$ z-axis rotation and R_3 corresponds to $\frac{\pi}{4}$ z-axis rotation. Since this circuit is for three qubits, in the first qubit, the rotation gates go up to R_3, and then in the second qubit, it goes to R_2 after Hadamard, and finally, in the last qubit, only Hadamard remains. In the end, the SWAP gate is applied in order to reverse the order of the qubit states.

Now, for four qubits, a very similar pattern to what you saw in the three-qubit case will repeat. In the four-qubit case, in the first qubit, the rotation gates will go up to R_4 ($\frac{\pi}{8}$ z-axis rotation), then in the second qubit, it goes to R_3 after Hadamard, then in the third qubit, the rotation will go up to R_2, and finally, in the last qubit, only Hadamard will remain. In the end, two SWAP gates will be applied – interchanging the first and fourth qubits and the second and third qubits.

Apart from the QFT, we sometimes also require computing the inverse QFT for some algorithms such as the phase estimation algorithm, which you will see later in the *Implementing phase estimation using Silq* section.

The formula for the inverse QFT is provided as follows:

$$QFT^{-1}(|\psi>) = \frac{1}{\sqrt{N}} \sum_{j=0}^{N-1} \sum_{k=0}^{N-1} x_k \omega^{-jk} |j>$$

The inverse QFT operation is completely valid, and it is the computation of the QFT but in a reversible way. Since quantum operations are unitary in nature, the inverse QFT operation holds without any problems. To gain more background on the QFT, it would be best to check out *Dancing with Qubits* by Robert S. Sutor, which explains the process of the QFT in much more detail with its proper mathematical derivation.

With the QFT covered, we are now ready to implement the QFT in the Silq language in the next section.

Implementing the QFT using Silq

In this section, you are going to learn how to implement the QFT algorithm from the very beginning, considering all the mathematics that we have gone through in the *Exploring the QFT* section.

In *Figure 10.2*, you can see a diagram of the QFT. This diagram is a generalized version of the QFT circuit that you saw for the three-qubits case in *Figure 10.1* in the preceding section:

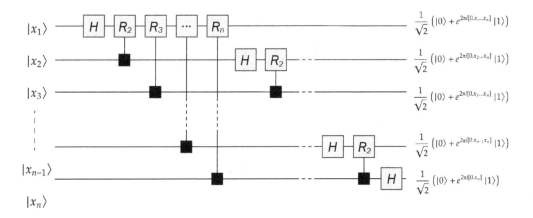

Figure 10.2 – QFT circuit for n qubits

Our code for the QFT will be based on *Figure 10.2*. The Silq implementation of the QFT is fairly intuitive and is very concise in size. Using Hadamard and controlled phasing, we generate the state corresponding to the circuit with the qubits in reverse order. Thus, the reversing of the qubits is done in anticipation at the beginning of the function so that, after applying Hadamard and phasing them, the qubits are outputted in the correct order. The code is as follows:

```
def QFT[n:!N](ψ: int[n])mfree: int[n]{
    for k in [0..n div 2]{
        (ψ[k],ψ[n-k-1]) := (ψ[n-k-1],ψ[k]);
    }
    for k in [0..n]{
        ψ[k] := H(ψ[k]);
        for l in [k+1..n]{
            if ψ[l] && ψ[k]{
                phase(2*π * 2^(k-l-1));
            }
        }
    }
    return ψ;
}
```

The code can be seen to be very compact in size and implements the QFT formula summations using the for loop. Now, in the preceding code, you can see that n qubits are taken and a quantum state of ψ is taken as the input on which the QFT is being applied [n:!] is a generic parameter to parameterize the arguments and return type of the function. Here mfree indicates that the function doesn't do measurements. Finally, int[n] defines the return type of the function which is a n-bit integer..

The QFT action can be rewritten as follows:

$$QFT(|x_1x_2...x_n>)$$

$$= \frac{1}{\sqrt{N}}\left(|0> + e^{2\pi i[0...x_n]}|1>\right) \otimes \left(|0> + e^{2\pi i[0...x_{n-1}x_n]}|1>\right) \otimes \cdots$$

$$\otimes \left(|0> + e^{2\pi i[0x_1x_2...x_n]}|1>\right)$$

In the preceding equation, $[0.x_1x_2\ldots x_n] = \sum_{k=1}^{n} x_k 2^{-k}$. Using Hadamard and controlled phasing, it is possible to generate the previous state with the qubits in reverse order. Let's take the example of the following code:

```
for k in [0..n div 2) {
        (φ[k],φ[n-k-1]) := (φ[n-k-1],φ[k]);
}
```

The reversing of the qubits is done in anticipation at the beginning of the function so that after applying the Hadamard and phasing them, the qubits are outputted in the correct order:

```
for k in [0..n) {
        ψ[k] := H(ψ[k]);
        for l in [k+1..n) {
            if ψ[l] && ψ[k] {
                phase(2*π * 2^(k-1-1));
```

The preceding code implements the process that is shown in *Figure 10.1*. In the very first for loop, we start by applying Hadamard operations to our qubits. Then, in the second for loop, the next qubits are taken as control qubits and the phase operation ($R_2, R_3,$ and so on in *Figure 10.2*) is applied to the qubit where Hadamard was applied before. This phasing is done according to *Figure 10.2*, where we take the control qubit as the next qubit and the target as the qubit where Hadamard was first applied.

After the reversing operation, the for loop is initiated for the n qubits and the superposition state of state ψ is created. After that, controlled phasing is applied through which the QFT operation is implemented. To look at the outputs of QFT, please refer to this link: https://github.com/PacktPublishing/Quantum-Computing-with-Silq-Programming/tree/main/Chapter10

With the QFT covered, let's now move on to the phase estimation algorithm, which uses the QFT as a separate subroutine.

Getting started with the phase estimation algorithm

The concept of the QFT that we have learned about in the previous sections will now help us to understand the **quantum phase estimation** algorithm, which utilizes the QFT as a subroutine block. The quantum phase estimation algorithm is an important algorithm as it is used in several other quantum algorithms, such as Shor's factorization algorithm and in the quantum algorithm for linear systems of equations.

Quantum phase estimation is used to estimate the phase (or eigenvalue) of an eigenvector of a unitary operator. This unitary operator can be any quantum transformation or any quantum gate as well. In a more mathematical sense, if we have the $|\psi>$ quantum state as the eigenvector of a unitary operator U with an eigenvalue of $e^{2\pi i\theta}$, then the phase estimation is used to estimate the value of θ with a high probability. The $U|\psi> = e^{2\pi i\theta}|\psi>$ eigenvalue equation holds true for the phase estimation technique.

If we increase the number of qubits, then it is easier to estimate the value of θ with a high probability and a finite level of precision. To estimate the phase, we take the controlled version of the U operator and apply it to all our qubits.

The steps that are used in the phase estimation are provided as follows:

1. We initialize our quantum state $|\psi>$ as the second register and initialize our first register (ancilla) with n qubits to state $|0>$.

2. We create a superposition of the first register n qubits (ancilla) by applying Hadamard gates to all of the n qubits.

3. The controlled-U gate operation is applied, where the first-register n qubits (ancilla) are the control and the second register with state $|\psi>$ is the target qubit. Again, remember that this U operator can be any quantum transformation or a quantum gate.

4. After the controlled-U operation, we apply the inverse QFT operation to the n qubits in the first register.

5. Finally, we measure the n qubits of the first register to obtain our result.

With the steps of the phase estimation algorithm covered, it will now be very easy to code this process in the Silq language in the next section.

Implementing phase estimation using Silq

In this section, you are going to learn how to implement the phase estimation algorithm from scratch using the algorithmic steps we have gone through in the *Getting started with the phase estimation algorithm* section. Since the steps of the phase estimation algorithm are defined in the previous section, you will now be able to understand the coding of the algorithm in Silq in a very easy manner.

Take a look at *Figure 10.3*. It is always better to visualize the circuit because it helps in understanding the internal workings of the algorithm. The following diagram shows the phase estimation circuit:

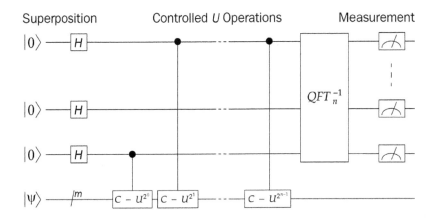

Figure 10.3 – Phase estimation circuit

From *Figure 10.3*, it becomes clear that the controlled-*U* operations are applied as we have implemented in the code and the inverse QFT is being performed at the very end of the circuit. Finally, measurement is taken for the first-register *n* qubits, which provide an estimated value of the phase associated with state $|\psi>$.

The Silq implementation of the quantum phase estimation will be based on *Figure 10.3*. You will find the implementation very intuitive and simple to understand because it is performed step by step according to *Figure 10.3* and the steps that you learned in the previous section.

Let's look at the implementation:

```
import qft;

def phaseEstimation[k:!ℕ] (
    U:int[k] !->mfree int[k],
    u:int[k],
    precision:!ℕ) {

    ancilla := 0:int[precision];
    for i in [0..precision) { ancilla[i] := H(ancilla[i]); }

    for i in [0..precision) {
        if ancilla[i] {
            for l in [0..2^i) {
                u := U(u);
```

```
            }
         }
      }

   ancilla := reverse(QFT[precision])(ancilla);
   result := measure(ancilla);
   measure(u);
   return result;
}
```

The code starts with the import of `qft` because as you saw, the QFT is used in the phase estimation algorithm. The phase estimation algorithm takes the U operator, u as the $|\psi>$ state, and the `precision` value (depending on the number of qubits) of the θ estimate as the input. This means that given a unitary operator U and an eigenvector $|u>$ such that $U|u> = e^{2\pi i\theta}|u>$, with $0 \leq \theta < 1$, the phase estimation algorithm outputs the phase θ of $|u>$ with a given level of precision which is ! N. u is an eigenvector of U. U and u are defined as `int[k]` where k is a generic parameter (defined here `[k:! ]`). The `!->mfree` signifies that there are classical operations with no measurements..

The `ancilla` register is the first register with `precision` value qubits (n qubits, if you recall the algorithm) and we apply the Hadamard gate to all the `ancilla` qubits, which creates a superposition according to the algorithm in the following line of the code: `for i in [0..precision) { ancilla[i] := H(ancilla[i]); }`.

After creating the superposition, we iterate through our precision value, set the `ancilla` qubits as the control, and apply the U operator to u ($|\psi>$ state) in the `u := U(u);` line. This is called controlled-U because we apply the U operator depending on the value of a control bit, in this case, one of the `ancilla` qubits. After the controlled-U operation is finished, we perform an inverse QFT operation in the `ancilla :=` `reverse(QFT[precision])(ancilla);` line to all our first register n qubits.

Finally, we measure our `ancilla` qubits and state u and return the result. You can clearly observe that the code is fairly simple to understand and concise due to the syntax of the Silq language. To look at the outputs of Quantum phase estimation algorithm, please refer to this link https://github.com/PacktPublishing/Quantum-Computing-with-Silq-Programming/tree/main/Chapter10

Summary

In this chapter, you learned about the concept of period-based algorithms and their implementation in the Silq language. You will now be able to appreciate the differences between the oracle-based algorithms covered in the previous chapters and period-based algorithms, which are unique and important classes of algorithms.

The most important fact to recognize is that the quantum algorithms, whether oracle- or period-based, are an important part of other, bigger quantum algorithms used in various industries for different applications; for example, in quantum finance, phase estimation, the QFT, and Grover's algorithm are utilized as subroutines and are a part of a large algorithm.

With all the important quantum algorithms covered, in the next chapter, we will start looking at one of the most important quantum computing applications, known as **quantum error correction**.

Further reading

- Robert Loredo, *Learn Quantum Computing with Python and IBM Quantum Experience: A hands-on introduction to quantum computing and writing your own quantum algorithms with Python*, Packt Publishing, 2020

- Dr. Christine Corbett Moran, *Mastering Quantum Computing with IBM QX: Explore the world of quantum computing using the Quantum Composer and Qiskit*, Packt Publishing, 2019

- Robert S. Sutor, *Dancing with Qubits: How quantum computing works and how it can change the world*, Packt Publishing, 2019

- Dr. Makhamisa Senekane, *Hands-On Quantum Information Processing with Python: Get up and running with information processing and computing based on quantum mechanics using Python*, Packt Publishing, 2021

- David McMahon, *Quantum Computing Explained*, Wiley, 2017

Section 4:
Applications of
Quantum Computing

In this part, you will explore the various cutting-edge applications of quantum computing. The key applications that this chapter will focus on are quantum error correction, quantum cryptography, and quantum machine learning. You will get hands-on coding experience in Silq to develop these applications, and this will enable you to apply quantum computing in the near future.

This section comprises the following chapters:

- *Chapter 11, Quantum Error Correction*
- *Chapter 12, Quantum Cryptography – Quantum Key Distribution (QKD)*
- *Chapter 13, Quantum Machine Learning*

11
Quantum Error Correction

Most of the data storage and communication systems we use can be represented as models where information travels from a sender to a receiver. While information is being transmitted through a channel, it may suffer from interference arising from the imperfections of the communication medium. While already crucial in classical systems, in quantum ones, it is essential that we design such corrective code because qubits can easily get corrupted by noise, either during storage or transmission. Entangled states, for example, are inherently fragile as a single qubit decoherence is enough to make the whole system collapse.

Even though quantum error correction cannot imitate its classical counterpart directly, the processes share many concepts, and knowing about the classical techniques is more than useful for understanding the quantum ones.

In this chapter, we are going to cover the following main topics:

- Introducing classical error correction techniques
- Understanding quantum error correction

You are going to learn the basics of classical error correction and how to correct an error occurring on a single bit during transmission through a noisy channel. You will study the simple bit-repetition codes and their generalization, the linear codes where you will be able to represent the messages, the errors and the encoding methods in a vectorial space, and then learn how to manipulate them. Then, you will discover the quantum techniques that are used for error correction on a single qubit. You will start by learning about the bit-flip and phase-flip codes and how to implement them in Silq. Finally, you will implement some code that combines these two in order to correct any arbitrary error occurring on a single qubit – the Shor code.

Technical requirements

To run the algorithms presented in this chapter, you need to have Silq installed. Please refer to the Silq website to learn how to download it: `https://silq.ethz.ch/`.

The code for the algorithms, as well as the examples, in this chapter can be found in this book's GitHub repository: `https://github.com/PacktPublishing/Quantum-Computing-with-Silq-Programming/tree/main/Chapter11`.

Introducing classical error correction technique

Communication channels are intrinsically unreliable because of the impossibility to completely prevent noise from interfering with information bits. Throughout the history of computers, this has led to various techniques being created for error correction, to ensure the integrity of a transmitted message.

In this section, we will look at how to detect and correct errors in classical computing. This will serve as an introduction to quantum error correction techniques, which we will discuss in the next section.

Let's start with one of the simplest classical error correction techniques, which is useful for correcting a single bit-flip error.

Redundancy and majority vote

First, we will introduce the central idea behind most error correction processes, which consists of introducing redundant bits of information and keeping only the majority value. We will explore how to use this on an example error model to design error-correcting code that effectively reduces the error rate of a noisy communication channel.

Error model

Let's consider the **Binary Symmetric Channel** (BSC$_p$) a model where a transmitter wishes to send bits to a receiver through a noisy channel. This channel is parameterized by p, the probability for any transmitted bit to be flipped independently during its passage. For example, if the bit 0 is sent, the receiver has probability p of receiving the flipped bit 1 and probability $1-p$ of receiving the correct bit 0, with p generally considered to be low. We will see that it is possible to send the same information bit several times so that a bit-flip is likely to be detected.

Encoding with redundancy

Now, let's move on to the key part of error correction – introducing redundancy to detect and, in the best case, correct errors. We will see that detection and correction can be conducted using a method known as **syndrome computation**. The simplest way to introduce redundancy is to repeat the information bit a given amount of times. We will start by introducing this method which is known under the name repetition code.

Two-bit repetition code

First, to detect if an error has occurred, we must have the sender encode each bit of information they want to transmit as a pair of two bits, adding an *ancillary* bit equal to the first one. Now, if the receiver gets a pair of differing bits (either 01 or 10), they know that one of the two bits was flipped. On the contrary, if they receive a pair where the two bits match (00 or 11), they only have to remove the ancillary bit to retrieve the first one containing the correct information (0 or 1, respectively).

Even though this **two-bit repetition code** is enough to detect a bit-flip error, it is not sufficient to correct it. Indeed, if the sender transmits bit 0 encoded as 00, the receiver will receive 01 if one of the bits gets flipped and 10 if the other bit gets flipped; the same would happen if the transmitted bit were 1. Thus, upon receiving 10 or 01, it is impossible to determine if the original bit was 0 or 1, so it is necessary to improve this method so that it can correct these errors.

Three-bit repetition code

Now, let's take a look at **three-bit repetition code**, where not only one but two ancillary bits are added by the sender to the information bit they wish to transmit. Thus, 0 is encoded as 000 and 1 is encoded as 111 since the receiver knows that a bit-flip error has occurred when the three bits they receive are not all identical. Furthermore, they can correct the error by taking a majority vote with the three qubits so that 001, 010, and 100 are mapped to 0 and 110, 101, and 011 are mapped to 1, thus effectively recovering the initial information.

Syndrome computation

One way of describing the error in the case of three-bit repetition code is by using a pair of bits called a **syndrome**, which consists of checking the *similarity* of the first and second bits and the first and third bits, respectively. If the received bits are $b_0 b_1 b_2$, we compute the syndrome using the XOR operation $\oplus$, as follows:

$$syndrome = (b_0 \oplus b_1)(b_0 \oplus b_2)$$

This is useful for finding out which correction we need to apply to the received bits to retrieve the error-free information. For example, if we receive 001, the syndrome is 01 because the first and second bits are identical but the first and third are different. Thus, a syndrome of 01 corresponds to the third bit being erroneously flipped. Here, we must flip it back to its initial value.

In our simple model, the syndrome can take four values, all of which are mapped to the appropriate correction:

- **00**: No correction
- **01**: Flip third bit
- **10**: Flip second bit
- **11**: Flip first bit

The idea of computing a syndrome to find out which correction to apply will be central in the next section, when we look at quantum error correction techniques.

Dealing with the introduction of more errors

While adding redundancy, we have also increased the probability of an error occurring because now, each bit is encoded as several bits. Each independently has the same probability p of transmission failure. Indeed, the probability of having zero errors during a single bit transmission in the case of three-bit repetition code is now equal to $(1 - p)^3$, which is lower than the previous value of $1 - p$ because $0 < 1 - p < 1$. However, what we are interested in is when two or more errors occur on the same encoded bit because, thanks to the encoding, we are now able to correct a single error. The following table breaks down the different probabilities for 0 to 3 errors:

NUMBER OF ERRORS	0	1	2	3
PROBABILITY	$(1-p)^3$	$3p(1-p)^2$	$3p^2(1-p)$	p^3

Figure 11.1 – Probabilities for the numbers of errors for transmitting a single bit in the three-bit repetition code

Here, we can see that the probability of having two errors is $3p^2(1-p)$. Indeed, factor $p^2(1-p)$ comes from the fact that we want one correct bit and two errors; factor 3 comes from the repartition of the two errors among the three bits. If p is sufficiently small, the probability of having two errors is approximate to $3p^2$ by dropping the higher power of p. Thus, the probability of having two or three errors can be written as follows:

$$P(two\ errors\ or\ more)\ \approx\ 3p^2+p^3$$

The error correction process is worth it if this probability is inferior to the previous error probability, which was equal to p. Once again, this is true if we assume that p is relatively small, which seems reasonable considering we have channels of communication with low noise.

In conclusion, even though adding more bits implies that more errors occur overall, the ability to correct single errors, which are by far the most common ones, is sufficient to decrease the failure probability of a low-noise channel when using three-bit repetition code.

Repeating the information bits is not the only way to add redundancy to a message, and this approach can be generalized by a superset of repetition codes known as linear codes.

Linear codes

In the previous section, we looked at repetition codes, which encode one-bit information into a two or three-bit message. Here, we are introducing **linear codes**, which are a generalization of this encoding process and transform n-bit information into m-bit messages, where m and n are two integers so that m is greater than n. For example, the three-bit repetition code is linear code with $m\ =\ 3*n$.

Let's begin by describing how the initial information and the encoded messages are represented as vectors.

Codewords

The different messages of size m that the sender can send after encoding the information are called **codewords**. In the case of three-bit repetition code, the information was a single bit – 0 or 1 – and the corresponding codewords were 000 and 111. If the transmission becomes corrupted, the receiver could get any one of the codewords in the set {000, 001, 010, 100, 111, 110, 101, 011} and would potentially have to resort to majority voting to retrieve the correct codeword and the initial bit of information.

Correct codewords can be generated from information bits using matrix computation with binary arithmetic:

$$c_i = \begin{bmatrix} 1 \\ 1 \\ 1 \end{bmatrix} b_i \; for \; i \in \{0,1\}$$

Here, b_i is the bit to encode as a 1x1 column vector, c_i is the codeword as a 3x1 column vector, and the 3x1 matrix $[1 \quad 1 \quad 1]^T$ represents the encoding operator and is called the **generator matrix**. Since all operations are done modulo 2, addition is equivalent to the logical XOR and multiplication is equivalent to the logical AND.

Let's look at another example called **Hamming(7,4)**, one of the most famous linear codes that's part of a family of error correcting codes. It was introduced by the mathematician Richard Hamming in 1950. As its name suggests, it encodes four-bit information as seven-bit codewords by adding three parity bits to the initial data so that it can detect and correct single-bit errors. Its generator matrix is as follows:

$$G = \begin{bmatrix} 1 & 1 & 0 & 1 \\ 1 & 0 & 1 & 1 \\ 1 & 0 & 0 & 0 \\ 0 & 1 & 1 & 1 \\ 0 & 1 & 0 & 0 \\ 0 & 0 & 1 & 0 \\ 0 & 0 & 0 & 1 \end{bmatrix}$$

Now, if we want to find the seven-bit codeword c associated with a given four-bit message b, we can compute it as follows:

$$c = G\,b$$

For example, if $b = 0110$, the generated codeword is $c = 1100110$.

Parity-check matrix

The tool that's used by the receiver to decode a codeword is called a **parity-check matrix**. It synthetizes the linear combinations to apply to the bits of the codeword to detect the presence of an error. The goal is to design the matrix H so that a codeword c is correct if – and only if – $H\ c = \mathbf{0}$.

Here, $\mathbf{0}$ is a column of zeros of size $m - n$ corresponding to the amount of redundancy that's added during the encoding: the difference between the sizes of the encoded and the original messages. In the case of three-bit repetition code, the encoding adds two bits, and we expect to have the three same bits at the reception. Thus, a parity check can be done by verifying that both the first and second and the first and third bits have the same parity, given the following parity-check matrix:

$$H = \begin{bmatrix} 1 & 1 & 0 \\ 1 & 0 & 1 \end{bmatrix}$$

If a codeword is correct, then the three bits have the same parity and conversely, if the first and second and the first and third bits have the same parity, then they are all identical. To see that a non-altered codeword necessarily gives $\mathbf{0}$ when it's multiplied by the parity-check matrix, we can compute its product with the generator matrix:

$$H\ G = \begin{bmatrix} 1 & 1 & 0 \\ 1 & 0 & 1 \end{bmatrix} \begin{bmatrix} 1 \\ 1 \\ 1 \end{bmatrix} = \begin{bmatrix} 1*1 \oplus 1*1 \oplus 0*1 \\ 1*1 \oplus 0*1 \oplus 1*1 \end{bmatrix} = \begin{bmatrix} 0 \\ 0 \end{bmatrix}$$

The parity-check matrix for the Hamming (7,4) code is as follows:

$$H = \begin{bmatrix} 0 & 0 & 0 & 1 & 1 & 1 & 1 \\ 0 & 1 & 1 & 0 & 0 & 1 & 1 \\ 1 & 0 & 1 & 0 & 1 & 0 & 1 \end{bmatrix}$$

If we take the codeword we generated in the previous section, $c = 1100110$, we can verify the following:

$$H\ c = \begin{bmatrix} 0 & 0 & 0 & 1 & 1 & 1 & 1 \\ 0 & 1 & 1 & 0 & 0 & 1 & 1 \\ 1 & 0 & 1 & 0 & 1 & 0 & 1 \end{bmatrix} \begin{bmatrix} 1 \\ 1 \\ 0 \\ 0 \\ 1 \\ 1 \\ 0 \end{bmatrix} = \begin{bmatrix} 0 \\ 0 \\ 0 \end{bmatrix}$$

More generally, we know that any correct codeword is annulated when it's multiplied by the parity-check matrix by verifying the following:

$$HG = \begin{bmatrix} 0 & 0 & 0 & 1 & 1 & 1 & 1 \\ 0 & 1 & 1 & 0 & 0 & 1 & 1 \\ 1 & 0 & 1 & 0 & 1 & 0 & 1 \end{bmatrix} \begin{bmatrix} 1 & 1 & 0 & 1 \\ 1 & 0 & 1 & 1 \\ 1 & 0 & 0 & 0 \\ 0 & 1 & 1 & 1 \\ 0 & 1 & 0 & 0 \\ 0 & 0 & 1 & 0 \\ 0 & 0 & 0 & 1 \end{bmatrix} = \begin{bmatrix} 0 & 0 & 0 & 0 \\ 0 & 0 & 0 & 0 \\ 0 & 0 & 0 & 0 \end{bmatrix}$$

Indeed, because the product of the parity-check matrix that was created by the generator matrix is the zero matrix, we can ensure that any correct codeword $c = G\, b$ ensures that $H\, c = H\, G\, b = 0$.

Representing errors

In this vectorial structure, bit-flip errors are represented by vectors of unit length so that adding them to a codeword modifies it accordingly. Thus, on a codeword of length n, a bit-flip error on the i-th bit corresponds to a vector with n-1 zeros and a single one on the i-th row. We denote this error vector as e_i since the modified version of the codeword c is the codeword $c' = c + e_i$. Now, recall that multiplying a correct codeword c by the parity-matrix H gives the zero vector:

$$H\, c = 0$$

Thus, if we apply the parity-check matrix to the altered codeword, we get the following:

$$H\, c' = H\, c + H\, e_i = H\, e_i$$

The output of applying the parity-check matrix to a codeword is, in fact, an error syndrome, which is useful for detecting and correcting errors, if any. If this syndrome equals **0**, we know that no error has occurred; otherwise, it equals $H\, e_i$ and we know that the i-th bit was flipped and that we must flip it back to correct the error.

For three-bit repetition code, we have the following error vectors:

$$e_1 = \begin{bmatrix} 1 \\ 0 \\ 0 \end{bmatrix}, e_2 = \begin{bmatrix} 0 \\ 1 \\ 0 \end{bmatrix}, e_3 = \begin{bmatrix} 0 \\ 0 \\ 1 \end{bmatrix}$$

The error syndromes associated with these error vectors are as follows:

$$H\, e_1 = \begin{bmatrix} 1 \\ 1 \end{bmatrix}, H\, e_2 = \begin{bmatrix} 1 \\ 0 \end{bmatrix}, H\, e_3 = \begin{bmatrix} 0 \\ 1 \end{bmatrix}$$

Here, we can see that we have the exact same syndromes that we had when we first computed them at the beginning of this section.

To detect a given error e, we need to have $H\,e \neq 0$, so that it is distinguishable from a correct codeword c for which $H\,c = 0$. If we want to correct it, we also need $H\,e$ to be different from the other potential error syndromes so that its value gives us, without a doubt, the correction to apply.

Now that we have seen the rudiments of classical error correction, we will look at its quantum counterpart, along with its similarities and differences.

Understanding quantum error correction

In this section, we are going to introduce three error-correcting codes for quantum computation and their implementation in Silq: **bit-flip code**, **phase-flip code**, and **Shor code**. These codes are essential because qubits are particularly prone to errors as they are inherently fragile. Whether the qubits suffer from unexpected decoherence or go through faulty quantum gates, quantum computation is not reliable, and one goal of quantum error correction is to achieve fault-tolerance.

At first glance, it seems that mirroring classical error correction by adding redundancy to our system is doomed to fail because the **no-cloning theorem** prevents us from copying a given quantum state. However, we will see that with *entanglement*, it is possible to encode the information in one qubit into a state of several qubits in order to detect and correct errors.

Working with bit-flip code

We will start by introducing **bit-flip code**. This is a quantum error-correcting code that's used to detect and correct single bit-flip errors. It does this by using entanglement to encode the information and then uses syndrome measurement to decode the received state.

In this section, we will describe how the encoding and decoding processes work by using a simple error model, and we will learn how to implement bit-flip code in Silq.

Error model

We consider an error model a model where a transmitter wishes to transmit a single qubit to a receiver through a noisy channel. The input state is denoted as $|\psi\rangle = \alpha|0\rangle + \beta|1\rangle$ and the channel flips this state with probability p. Thus, the receiver will receive the correct state $|\psi\rangle$ with probability 1-p and the flipped state $\alpha|1\rangle + \beta|0\rangle$ with probability p.

Encoding to a three-qubit state

Because of the no-cloning theorem, it is not possible to directly copy the information of an unknown qubit state into other qubits to add redundancy in our system, as in the classical version of the three-bit repetition code. However, it is possible to add two *ancillary* qubits to the system and entangle them with the information qubit so that $|0\rangle$ is mapped to $|000\rangle$ and $|1\rangle$ is mapped to $|111\rangle$. This can be done by initializing the ancillary qubits to $|0\rangle$ and applying two CNOT gates with the information qubit to control them. If the information qubit is $|1\rangle$, then the state of the ancillary qubits is flipped to $|1\rangle$, and if the information qubit is $|0\rangle$, then the ancillary qubits stay in state $|0\rangle$. Thus, our initial state $|\psi\rangle = \alpha|0\rangle + \beta|1\rangle$ is now mapped to the entangled state $|\psi'\rangle = \alpha|000\rangle + \beta|111\rangle$.

As for the classical three-bit repetition code, we consider that the channel acts independently and equally on each qubit so that we have the probability repartition described in *Figure 11.1*. Thus, if we manage to detect and correct the most probable type of errors, which is when there is only a single bit-flip, then the error code has improved the fidelity of the transmission.

Syndrome computation

Now that we have our three-qubit encoding, we would like to detect if one of the three qubits were flipped during the transmission. We can do this by checking the parity between the qubits, just like we did in the classical version. However, it is not possible to do this directly. This is because measuring the state to obtain the parity of its qubits would lead to its collapse and the loss of our information qubit state. In order to overcome this technical difficulty, we will introduce two new ancillary qubits, with the objective of manipulating them so that the outcome of their measurement is the syndrome, which gives us the correction to apply if an error has occurred. We can measure them without fear of losing any information as long as the three-qubit information state is not disturbed while doing so.

The parity of two qubits is obtained by initializing a qubit to $|0\rangle$ and applying two CNOT operations to this qubit, with the others used as controls so that it will end in state $|0\rangle$ if the parity is even and state $|1\rangle$ if the parity is odd. Thus, we can project the pairwise parity of our three-qubit state onto the ancillary qubits. Their measurement gives us exactly the error syndrome we were looking for, without us needing to destroy any information.

As in the classical case, if the syndrome is $|00\rangle$, we know no bit-flip occurred. If the syndrome is $|01\rangle$, then the first and second qubits have the same parity but the third differs from the others. We can correct this information by flipping the third qubit. Similarly, if the syndrome is $|10\rangle$ or $|11\rangle$, we flip the second or the first qubit to retrieve the original state, respectively.

Now that we have seen the theory behind the bit-flip code for quantum error correction, let's learn how to practically encode it in Silq.

Implementing bit-flip code in Silq

Let's learn how to implement the whole circuit of quantum error correction with bit-flip code in Silq. The goal is to create a function that takes a qubit to be transmitted and a noisy channel as input and returns the received qubit after detecting and correcting the error.

Encoding

First, we need a function to encode a single qubit into the three-qubit entangled state, where $|\psi\rangle = \alpha|0\rangle + \beta|1\rangle$ is mapped to $|\psi'\rangle = \alpha|000\rangle + \beta|111\rangle$. This function, encode, is described in the following code snippet:

```
def encode(ψ:𝔹) mfree {
     return (dup(ψ), dup(ψ), ψ);
}0
```

Even though the built-in dup function used here duplicates the information qubit, it does not break the no-cloning theorem. It simply entangles a new qubit with the one passed as a parameter in the same way as the following code does with the CNOT operator X:

```
aux := 0:𝔹;
if ψ {
aux := X(aux);
}
```

Note that the encode function is annotated as mfree so that it can be reversed. This helps decode the state once the error has been transmitted and corrected.

Syndrome computation and error correction

Next, we will define the correct function, which takes the three-qubit state as input. This may be modified during the transmission. It computes the syndrome and applies the appropriate correction to the state before returning it, freed of bit-flip errors:

```
def correct(ψ: 𝔹^3) {
     p1 := measure(ψ[0] ⊕ ψ[1]);
     p2 := measure(ψ[0] ⊕ ψ[2]);

     if (p1 && p2) {
```

```
    ψ[0] := X(ψ[0]);
    } else if (p1) {
    ψ[1] := X(ψ[1]);
    } else if (p2) {
    ψ[2] := X(ψ[2]);
    }
    return ψ;
}
```

In this function, the pair *(p1, p2)* corresponds to the measurement of the syndrome taking the information of the parities regarding the first and second and the first and third qubits, respectively. We can measure the syndrome without destroying information because the XOR operation $\oplus$ creates a separate ancillary qubit that the parity computation is made on. We then apply the relevant correction, depending on the syndrome value: flip the first, second, or third qubit if the syndrome is 11, 10, or 01, respectively. Notice that if the syndrome is 00, which means that no error was detected, the three-qubit state is returned unchanged.

Defining the bit-flip code function

Now that we have all the individual bricks, we can construct the `bit_flip_code` function. It takes a qubit to be transmitted and a channel as input and returns the qubit after simulating its passage through the whole error-correcting process. The channel acts on three-qubit states and potentially induces a flip on one of the three qubits of the state:

```
def bit_flip_code(ψ: B, channel: B^3 !→ B^3) {
    ψ := encode(ψ);
    ψ := channel(ψ);
    ψ := correct(ψ);
    ψ := reverse(encode)(ψ);
    return ψ;
}
```

In the preceding code, the qubit ψ is encoded as a three-qubit state using the `encode` function before passing through the `channel` function, which potentially flips one of the three qubits. The `correct` function then computes the syndrome and applies the appropriate correction to retrieve the three-qubit state before the transmission. Finally, we recover the original qubit by reversing the encoding function, which is basically equivalent to discarding the qubits that were added for the encoding.

Testing the bit-flip code function

Let's look at an example call for our `bit_flip_code` function. It is defined in the `main` function so that we can easily test it. In the following code, the qubit to transmit is initialized to |1⟩ and the channel is defined as a function that, as input, takes a three-qubit state and returns it with the first qubit flipped. To check that the error has been corrected, we must assert that the qubit is in the right state by trying to forget its assumed value. If not, we would get a *bad forget* error because we would be trying to uncompute an erroneous equality:

```
def channel(ψ:𝔹^3) {
    ψ[0] := X(ψ[0]);
    return ψ;
}


def main() {
    ψ := 1:𝔹;
    φ := bit_flip_code(ψ, channel);
    forget(φ = 1);
}
```

We can check that our `bit_flip_code` function effectively corrects all single bit-flip errors by changing the `channel` function, so that the second or third qubit gets flipped instead of the first. It is also possible to test the correct transmission of a quantum superposition of states by initializing the qubit to transmit to $H|0\rangle = \frac{|0\rangle + |1\rangle}{\sqrt{2}}$, and then verifying that applying the Hadamard transform to the received qubit outputs the state |0⟩ (recall that H^2 is the identity). The `main` function described in the following code shows one example of bit-flip error detection and correction for quantum information:

```
def main() {
    ψ := H(0:𝔹);
    φ := bit_flip_code(ψ, channel);
    forget(H(φ) = 0);
}
```

Unlike what happens in classical computers, bit-flip errors are not the only errors to occur on qubits that can also suffer from phase-flip errors, where a qubit in state α|0⟩ + β|1⟩ gets transformed into the state α|0⟩ − β|1⟩.

Working with phase-flip code

In this section, we'll look at **phase-flip code** and its Silq implementation. It is an error-correcting code that relies on the same mechanisms as the bit-flip code, but uses syndrome computation and entanglement to recover the original state.

In this section, we will describe how the encoding and decoding processes work in a simple error model, and we will learn how to implement phase-flip code in Silq.

Error model

Let's consider an error model where a transmitter wishes to transmit a single qubit to a receiver through a noisy channel. The input state is denoted as $|\psi\rangle = \alpha|0\rangle + \beta|1\rangle$ and the channel flips this state with probability p. Thus, the receiver is assured to receive the correct state $|\psi\rangle$ with probability $1-p$ and the flipped state $\alpha|0\rangle - \beta|1\rangle$ with probability p.

Encoding to a three-qubit state

The encoding for phase-flip code begins exactly like it does for bit-flip code – we add two *ancillary* qubits to the system and entangle them with the information qubit by using CNOT operators X so that $|0\rangle$ is mapped to $|000\rangle$ and $|1\rangle$ is mapped to $|111\rangle$. As for the bit-flip code, our initial state $|\psi\rangle = \alpha|0\rangle + \beta|1\rangle$ becomes the entangled state $|\psi'\rangle = \alpha|000\rangle + \beta|111\rangle$. Directly sending this encoded state through the noisy channel is not useful because we would receive the state $\alpha|000\rangle - \beta|111\rangle$ with probability p, and we would not be able to reconstruct state $|\psi\rangle$ from it.

To reuse the decoding part of the bit-flip code, we must know that a phase-flip in the Hadamard basis $(|+\rangle, |-\rangle) = \left(\dfrac{|0\rangle + |1\rangle}{\sqrt{2}}, \dfrac{|0\rangle - |1\rangle}{\sqrt{2}} \right)$ is equivalent to a bit-flip in the standard basis $(|0\rangle, |1\rangle)$. Indeed, if you consider the state $|\varphi\rangle = \alpha|+\rangle + \beta|-\rangle$ and apply a phase-flip to it, you get the state $|\varphi'\rangle = \alpha|-\rangle + \beta|+\rangle$, which is similar to applying a bit-flip to the state $|\psi\rangle = \alpha|0\rangle + \beta|1\rangle$. Thus, the last operation before transmitting the encoded state through the channel is to apply Hadamard transforms to each of the qubits so that $|\psi'\rangle = \alpha|000\rangle + \beta|111\rangle$ becomes $|\psi''\rangle = \alpha|+++\rangle + \beta|---\rangle$. Now, if the channel flips the phase of, for example, the third qubit, we receive the state $|\Phi\rangle = \alpha|++-\rangle + \beta|--+\rangle$ after transmission. Applying another round of Hadamard transforms to each qubit outputs the state $|\Phi'\rangle = \alpha|001\rangle + \beta|110\rangle$. This change that's made by applying Hadamard transforms right before and right after transmission has converted the phase-flip into a bit-flip that we can now correct with the same syndrome computation and error correction method described in the *Working with bit-flip code* section.

Now, let's learn how to implement phase-flip code in Silq.

Implementing the phase-flip code in Silq

The implementation of the phase-flip code is highly similar to the implementation of the bit-flip code, since the encoding and error correcting parts are identical. Because of this, we will reuse the `encode` and `correct` functions we defined in the previous section.

Defining the phase-flip code function

The `phase_flip_code` function takes, as inputs, a qubit to be transmitted and a channel and returns the qubit after simulating its passage through the whole error-correcting process. The channel acts on three-qubit states and potentially flips the phase of one of the three qubits of the state:

```
def phase_flip_code(ψ: 𝔹, channel: 𝔹^3 !→ 𝔹^3) {
    ψ := encode(ψ);
    for k in [0..3] {ψ[k] := H(ψ[k]);}
    ψ := channel(ψ);
    for k in [0..3] {ψ[k] := H(ψ[k]);}
    ψ := correct(ψ);
    ψ := reverse(encode)(ψ);
    return ψ;
}
```

The only difference with the bit-flip code is that we apply Hadamard transforms to each of the three qubits immediately before and after it's transmitted through the noisy channel. So, if a phase-flip error occurred, it is converted into a bit-flip error, which is then corrected accordingly.

Testing the phase-flip code function

Let's look at an example call for our `phase_flip_code` function. It is defined in the `main` function so that we can easily test it. In the following code, we will try to transmit a qubit in state $|0\rangle$ through a channel that flips the phase of the second qubit of a three-qubit state. To check that the error is effectively corrected, we will assert that the qubit is in the right state by trying to forget its assumed value. If not, we would get a *bad forget* error because we would be trying to uncompute an erroneous equality:

```
def channel(ψ:𝔹^3) {
    ψ[1] := Z(ψ[1]);
    return ψ;
```

```
    }
```

```
def main() {
    ψ := 0:𝔹;
    φ := phase_flip_code(ψ, channel);
    forget(φ = 0);
}
```

We must test that quantum superpositions are also robust against phase-flip errors by initializing the qubit so that it transmits to the state $H|0\rangle = \dfrac{|0\rangle + |1\rangle}{\sqrt{2}}$, and also asserting that the received qubit is in the correct state. This example call can be found in the following code:

```
def main() {
    ψ := H(0:𝔹);
    φ := phase_flip_code(ψ, channel);
    forget(H(φ) = 0);
}
```

We now know how to correct single bit-flip or single phase-flip errors, but we would like to correct either one without knowing which one is occurring beforehand. Even better, is it possible to design quantum error-correcting code that detects and corrects a combination of both types of errors? In the next section, we will present the code, which can correct arbitrary single qubit errors!

Working with Shor code

In this section, we will look at **Shor code**. It is an error-correcting code that synthetizes the techniques that are used for the bit-flip code and the phase-flip code into a unique code. This can correct arbitrary single-qubit errors using syndrome computation and entanglement to recover the original state.

In this section, we will describe how the encoding and decoding processes work in a simple error model, and we will see how to implement Shor code in Silq.

Error model

Let's consider an error model where a transmitter wishes to transmit a single qubit to a receiver through a noisy channel. The input state is denoted as $|\psi\rangle = \alpha|0\rangle + \beta|1\rangle$ and the channel arbitrarily alters this state with probability p. Thus, the receiver is assured to receive the correct state $|\psi\rangle$ with probability $1-p$ and an arbitrary modified state with probability p.

Encoding to a nine-qubit state

Shor code consists of a nine-qubit encoding for correcting either a bit-flip error, a sign-flip error, or both on a single qubit. As these errors are represented by the **Pauli matrices**, which form the basis for the unitary transforms space, being able to correct them is equivalent, due to their linearity, to being able to correct any given error on a single qubit. The nine-qubit encoding transforms state $|\psi\rangle = \alpha|0\rangle + \beta|1\rangle$ into the following state:

$$|\psi'\rangle = \frac{\alpha}{2\sqrt{2}}(|000\rangle + |111\rangle)^{\otimes 3} + \frac{\beta}{2\sqrt{2}}(|000\rangle - |111\rangle)^{\otimes 3}$$

We can obtain this entangled state by performing the following steps:

1. Create two duplicates of the initial qubit with CNOT gates, as we have seen for the bit-flip and phase-flip codes:

$$\alpha|000\rangle + \beta|111\rangle$$

2. Apply a Hadamard transform to each of the qubits:

$$\alpha\left(\frac{1}{\sqrt{2}}\right)^3 (|0\rangle + |1\rangle)^{\otimes 3} + \beta\left(\frac{1}{\sqrt{2}}\right)^3 (|0\rangle - |1\rangle)^{\otimes 3}$$

3. Create two duplicates of each of the three qubits to form the nine-qubit state:

$$\frac{\alpha}{2\sqrt{2}}(|000\rangle + |111\rangle)^{\otimes 3} + \frac{\beta}{2\sqrt{2}}(|000\rangle - |111\rangle)^{\otimes 3}$$

The first two steps encode the qubit so that it's robust against phase-flip errors by switching to the Hadamard basis $(|+\rangle, |-\rangle) = \left(\frac{|0\rangle + |1\rangle}{\sqrt{2}}, \frac{|0\rangle - |1\rangle}{\sqrt{2}} \right)$, as we saw for the phase-flip code. To also correct bit-flip errors, each of these three qubits are encoded as three qubits that the bit-flip error correction is applied to. Thus, the first, fourth, and seventh qubits (and, by extension, the three groups $(1, 2, 3)$, $(4, 5, 6)$, and $(7, 8, 9)$, which are considered as three inputs) are used for detecting and correcting a phase-flip error. Moreover, syndrome analysis is conducted on each of the three groups of qubits – $(1, 2, 3)$, $(4, 5, 6)$, and $(7, 8, 9)$ – to detect and correct a bit-flip error.

Now, let's learn how to implement Shor code in Silq.

Implementing Shor code in Silq

Let's learn how implement Shor code in Silq by designing a function that models the whole error-correcting process.

The implementation of Shor code in Silq has similarities with the implementations of the bit-flip and phase-flip codes but due to the 3x3 structure of its encoding, we need to begin by defining a function that will help us apply a given function to each element of a three-tuple or triple.

Helper function

Let's define a function, `applyToEach`, that takes a triple of elements of generic type τ and a function $f : \tau! \rightarrow \tau'$ that we want to apply to each element of the triple as input. The following code describes the implementation of this function, where the triple is broken down into its three elements and a new triple with the function that's applied to each element is returned:

```
def applyToEach[τ,τ'](triple:τ^3, f: τ! → τ') {
    (h0,h1,h2) := triple;
    fTriple := (f(h0),f(h1),f(h2));
    return fTriple;
}
```

We use generic types τ and τ' because, depending on the context, we will need to apply this function to a triple of qubits (of type $\mathbb{B}\text{^}3$) or a triple of triple of qubits (of type $(\mathbb{B}\text{^}3)\text{^}3$).

With this helper function implemented, we are now ready to encode the information qubit into a nine-qubit state.

Encoding

We have already seen that encoding is done in three steps:

1. Triplicating the original qubit.

2. Applying a Hadamard transform to each of the three qubits.

3. Triplicating each of the qubits once more.

Let's start by defining a triplicating function that uses the built-in dup function in the same manner as it's used in the bit-flip code encoding:

```
def triplicate(ψ:𝔹) mfree {
    ψ := (dup(ψ), dup(ψ), ψ);
    return ψ;
}
```

Now, we can define our encoding function using the triplication and the three steps description, as follows:

```
def encode(ψ: 𝔹) {
    ψ := triplicate(ψ);
    ψ := applyToEach(ψ, H);
    ψ := applyToEach(ψ, triplicate);
    return ψ;
}
```

The first two lines, which contain the first triplication and the application of Hadamard transforms, correspond to the encoding for correcting a phase-flip error, while the third line, which contains the second triplication, corresponds to the encoding for correcting a bit-flip error.

Error correction

To correct a bit-flip error on a triplet of qubits, we must reuse the `correct` function we defined for the bit-flip code, which measures the syndrome and applies the correction. Here, we want to design a `correctBitFlip` function that corrects a bit-flip error on the nine-qubit state (of type $(\mathbb{B}\wedge 3)\wedge 3$). For that, we need to apply the `correct` function to the three groups of three qubits, thanks to the `applyToEach` function, as follows:

```
def correctBitFlip(ψ: (𝔹^3)^3) {
    ψ := applyToEach(ψ, correct);
    return ψ;
}
```

To correct a phase-flip error, we need to reverse the second triplication in order to recover the first, fourth, and seventh qubits that were switched to the Hadamard basis during the encoding. Now, we can get back to the standard basis by applying Hadamard transforms to each of the qubits, and then use the `correct` function to detect and correct a phase-flip error that's been converted into a bit-flip error:

```
def correctPhaseFlip(ψ: (𝔹^3)^3) {
    ψ := applyToEach(ψ, reverse(triplicate));
    ψ := applyToEach(ψ, H);
    ψ := correct(ψ);
    return ψ
}
```

We now have all the tools necessary to design a function that helps transmit a qubit encoded with Shor code.

Defining the Shor code function

The following `shor_code` function takes, as input, a qubit ψ to be transmitted and a `channel` function that acts on a nine-qubit state of type $(\mathbb{B}\wedge 3)\wedge 3$ and returns the qubit after simulating its passage through the whole error-correcting process. The noisy channel can induce an arbitrary error on a single qubit and can also flip both a qubit and its phase:

```
def shor_code(ψ:𝔹, channel: (𝔹^3)^3 !→ (𝔹^3)^3) {
    ψ := encode(ψ);
    ψ := channel(ψ);
    ψ := correctBitFlip(ψ);
    ψ := correctPhaseFlip(ψ);
    ψ := reverse(triplicate)(ψ);
```

```
    return ψ;
}
```

In the preceding code, the qubit ψ is encoded as a nine-qubit state using the `encode` function before it's passed through the `channel` function, which potentially flips one of the nine qubits, its phase, or both. We then corrected the bit-flip and the phase-flip errors and, finally, recovered the original qubit by reversing the `triplicate` function. Note that we do not reverse the whole `encode` function because steps 2 and 3 of the encoding were already reversed during the phase-flip error correction. Thus, the original qubit is obtained simply by reversing the first step of the encoding, which consisted of a triplication.

Testing the Shor code function

Let's look at an example call for our `shor_code` function. It is defined in the `main` function so that we can test it easily. In the following code, the qubit to transmit is initialized to |1> and the channel is defined as a function that takes, as input, a nine-qubit state of type $(\mathbb{B}\verb|^|3)\verb|^|3$ and flips one of the qubits and its phase (the second qubit of the first group, in this case). Applying the Y gate to a qubit is equivalent to successively applying the X and Z gates to the same qubit. To check that the error is effectively corrected, we must assert that the qubit is in the right state by trying to forget its assumed value. If not, we would get a *bad forget* error because we would be trying to uncompute an erroneous equality:

```
def channel (ψ: (𝔹^3)^3) {
    ψ[0][1] := Y(ψ[0][1]);
    return ψ;
}


def main() {
    ψ := 1:𝔹;
    φ := shor_code(ψ, channel);
    forget(φ=1);
}
```

It is possible to test that the implementation is correct on a quantum input by changing the qubit so that it's transmitted to a superposition (for example, ψ := H(1:𝔹)). You can also modify the channel to induce any given error on a single qubit and check that the Shor code correctly recovers the initial value.

Summary

Over the course of this chapter, we have seen the rudiments of classical error correction, where introducing redundant information is key to recovering from errors, provided they occur with a low-enough probability. We introduced simple bit-repetition models that corrected bit-flip errors, thanks to syndrome computation and measurement and their generalization – linear codes.

Then, we dived into quantum error computation and saw that even though the no-cloning theorem prevents us from directly duplicating a state, it is still possible to encode a qubit by entangling it with other qubits, thus introducing redundancy without breaking any quantum law. Moreover, using ancillary qubits, it is possible to compute a syndrome and measure it without interfering with the quantum information that we wish to transmit.

After introducing two simple error correction codes for correcting either a bit-flip or a phase-flip error, we looked at Shor code, which can, by combining the previous approaches, correct an arbitrary error that occurs on a single qubit.

Finally, we implemented these quantum error correction codes in Silq by taking advantage of the high-level design of the language.

In this chapter, you learned the basics of both classical and quantum error-correction theories, as well as how to implement three error-correction functions in Silq. You consolidated your knowledge about quantum phenomena such as entanglement, superposition of states, and measurement. You can now use built-in constructs and generic types to design complex yet easy-to-read functions. You also know how to design tests to verify the outputs of the functions you implement.

In the next chapter, you will learn about quantum cryptography and, more specifically, quantum key distribution.

12
Quantum Cryptography – Quantum Key Distribution

A few decades ago, cryptographic techniques were mainly used by governments and military forces to exchange messages during wartime when information was key. Now that huge amounts of data are transmitted over the internet, it has become crucial to design strong cryptographic algorithms to ensure data security and integrity.

To protect your private data, such as banking information and passwords, these algorithms typically use a key to transform it into unreadable scrambled text so that only someone who knows the key can decrypt it and access the information.

Classical cryptographic algorithms rely on the assumption that an attacker only has access to a limited power of computation, but the rise of quantum computing could break this assumption. This has led to the creation of quantum cryptographic techniques that make use of quantum mechanics to encrypt and decrypt data in order to design unhackable algorithms.

In this chapter, you are going to learn the basics of classical cryptography with an introduction to simple techniques such as the Caesar cipher and the one-time pad. You will get an overview of the techniques used for encrypting data that are divided into two categories: symmetric and asymmetric cryptography. Then, you will dive into quantum cryptography and you will study the quantum key distribution protocol. Finally, you will be able to implement quantum key distribution in Silq.

In this chapter, we are going to cover the following main topics:

- Introducing classical cryptography techniques
- Understanding quantum key distribution

Technical requirements

In order to run the algorithms presented in this chapter, you need to have Silq installed. Please refer to the Silq website to see how to download it: `https://silq.ethz.ch/`.

The code for the algorithms, along with examples, can be found in our GitHub repository: `https://github.com/PacktPublishing/Quantum-Computing-with-Silq-Programming/tree/main/Chapter12`.

Introducing classical cryptography techniques

From the earliest algorithms that are easily hackable to the recent ones that rely on hard-to-solve mathematical problems, cryptographic techniques have evolved over the decades to become stronger against attacks.

In this section, we will look at how cryptography works in classical computation. This will serve as an introduction to quantum cryptography in the next section.

Let's begin by introducing the basics and the vocabulary of classical cryptography.

The basics of cryptography

First things first, what is **cryptography** and why is it needed? Suppose you want to send a secret message to someone. If you do not possess a secure communication channel with this person, whether physical or virtual, then whatever means of communication you use, your message has a chance of being intercepted by a third party. This third party, also called an *adversary*, *eavesdropper*, or *Eve*, may take various forms and interfere at any point of the communication, whether by hacking your computer, intercepting a letter, or overhearing a conversation. The point is that if your message is written in a form that is understandable by anyone and an adversary gets their hands on it, then the information that it contains becomes compromised.

The way to prevent anyone intercepting your message from understanding its content is to transform it into an unintelligible form, and this conversion process is known as **encryption**. The original and encrypted messages are known respectively as the **plaintext** and the **ciphertext**. The reverse operation, **decryption**, thus consists of converting ciphertext back into plaintext. Cryptography consists of the study and application of various algorithms used for providing secure communication that is robust against adversaries. These algorithms, known as **ciphers**, define the procedures to follow to perform the encryption and decryption of a message. They typically make use of **keys**, which are secret pieces of information used either to encrypt plaintext or to decrypt ciphertext. If the same key is used for both encryption and decryption, we talk about **symmetric-key** algorithms and, conversely, if the keys differ, we talk about **asymmetric-key** algorithms.

Now that we have defined cryptography and introduced some useful vocabulary, let's take a look at one of the simplest and most famous examples, the Caesar cipher.

Caesar cipher

Also known as the shift cipher, the **Caesar cipher** merely substitutes each letter of the plaintext by shifting the alphabet by a given number of positions. The key for this cipher is the number of positions to shift the plaintext by, or equivalently, the letter representing this number in the alphabet (where A=0, B=1, ..., Z=25). Thus, if the key is F, or 5, the ciphertext is obtained by shifting every letter in the plaintext by 5: A becomes F, B becomes G, ..., Z becomes E. Note that a key of A, or 0, corresponds to not encrypting the plaintext at all.

For example, if we encode the word *SILQ* with the key S, we need to shift each letter of the plaintext by 18 positions in the alphabet, and we obtain the ciphertext *KADI*. To decrypt a ciphertext encrypted with the Caesar cipher, we just need to know the encryption key and apply the reversed shift operation to retrieve the original plaintext. If we have the ciphertext *KOUHNOG* and we know that it was encrypted thanks to a Caesar cipher with the key U, then by shifting each letter by 20 positions to the left (or equivalently 6 to the right), we obtain the plaintext *QUANTUM*. Here, the same key can be used to encrypt or decrypt a message, thereby the Caesar cipher falls into the category of symmetric encryption methods.

Caesar ciphers, although very simple to use, are also quite easy to crack. Firstly, if an attacker knows that a Caesar cipher has been used, they can easily compute all shifting possibilities and try to work out the original plaintext because the computational power needed is relatively low. Furthermore, if the encrypted text is sufficiently long, it is possible to use **frequency analysis** to compare the number of occurrences of a letter in the ciphertext to its frequency in general in the language. Indeed, Caesar ciphers do not modify the occurrence frequencies of letters and, as such, the most common letters in the ciphertext are likely to be shifted from the most common letters in the language.

In order to be robust against frequency analysis, it is necessary to use an encryption technique that does not encode each letter uniquely. We are going to introduce one such process that is theoretically uncrackable, the one-time pad.

One-time pad

The **one-time pad** encryption method requires that both the sender and the receiver share a key that is at least as long as the plaintext to encrypt. To obtain the ciphertext, the sender converts the plaintext and the key into a sequence of numerical values where A is 0, B is 1, ..., Z is 25. He then combines the two sequences by adding them value and taking each result by value modulo 26. Finally, he converts the numerical values back into letters to compute the ciphertext.

For example, if we want to encrypt the word *CRYPTO* with the key *SKJCIX*, we start by converting both to a sequence of numerical values: *CRYPTO* becomes 2/17/24/15/19/14 and *SKJCIX* becomes 18/10/9/2/8/23. Then, we add both sequences term by term and take the result modulo 26 as follows:

$$
\begin{array}{rccccccccccc}
   & 2 & \cdots & 17 & \cdots & 24 & \cdots & 15 & \cdots & 19 & \cdots & 14 & \mid message \\
 + & 18 & \cdots & 10 & \cdots & 9 & \cdots & 2 & \cdots & 8 & \cdots & 23 & \mid key \\
 = & 20 & \cdots & 27 & \cdots & 33 & \cdots & 17 & \cdots & 27 & \cdots & 37 & \\
 = & 20 & \cdots & 1 & \cdots & 7 & \cdots & 17 & \cdots & 1 & \cdots & 11 & \mid ciphertext \\
\end{array}
$$

Finally, by converting the obtained sequence to letters, we obtain the ciphertext *UBHRBL*. Retrieving the original message from the ciphertext is an easy task if you possess the encryption key. Indeed, you only need to apply the reverse operation, a subtraction term by term modulo 26, to the ciphertext to recover the plaintext. For our example, the calculation is as follows:

$$20 \cdots \quad 1 \cdots \quad 7 \cdots 17 \cdots \quad 1 \cdots \quad 11 \quad | \, ciphertext$$
$$- \; 18 \cdots \; 10 \cdots \quad 9 \cdots \; 2 \cdots \quad 8 \cdots \quad 23 \quad | \, key$$
$$= \quad 2 \cdots -9 \cdots -2 \cdots 15 \cdots -7 \cdots -12$$
$$= \quad 2 \cdots \; 17 \cdots \; 24 \cdots 15 \cdots \; 19 \cdots \quad 14 \quad | \, message$$

Here we see that with the one-time pad, frequency analysis cannot help us with a ciphertext because a given letter from the plaintext may (and probably will) be encoded differently each time it appears. In the same manner, two different letters can be encoded as the same one in the ciphertext: this is the case with the letters *R* and *T* of *CRYPTO*, which both get ciphered to *B*.

Furthermore, the one-time pad is **information-theoretically** secure in the sense that, even with infinite computing power, an adversary would not be able to gain any type of information about the plaintext by studying the ciphertext alone. Suppose that the intercepted ciphertext is *JLBCWN*. With infinite time, the adversary would be able to find that it could be the word *ATTACK* ciphered with the key *JSICUD*, but he would also find that it could be the word *DEFEND* ciphered with the key *GHWYJK* or even any other plausible 6-character messages using the suitable key. In short, the only information that the eavesdropper would get is the maximum possible length of the message, and not even its exact length because additional characters could be added to the plaintext to hide it.

Despite being provably uncrackable, the one-time pad is not widely used in cryptography; in fact, less secure but easier-to-employ methods are generally preferred. One of the reasons for this is that the one-time pad is limited by the fact that it needs a key at least as long as the message to cipher to be generated and transferred through a secure communication channel, which is not an easy task to implement in practice. However, we will see in the next section that in quantum cryptography the one-time pad is still one of the most widely used techniques.

We will now introduce some widely used encrypting methods in modern classical cryptography.

Overviewing the main types of encryption algorithms

Cryptographic methods are principally divided into symmetric and asymmetric algorithms, which we are going to see later on in this section. But first, let's define hashing, a concept that is widely used in various cryptographical settings.

Hashing

Hashing is a cryptographic method that transforms data of arbitrary size into a fixed-length string called the **hash value**, or simply, the **hash**. It is designed as a one-way function so that it is easy to compute a hash from an input message but impossible to reverse the operation and retrieve the data from a given hash value. Moreover, hash functions rely on three key properties:

- Determinism: A given input message will always generate the same hash.

- Unicity: Two different hash values necessarily come from two different messages.

- Avalanche effect: A slight change to the input will significantly modify the hash.

Hashing is different from encrypting because, by design, it obviates any possibility of decryption. In cryptography, hash functions are typically used for the verification of data integrity or as a digital signature. Suppose you want to receive a file through an insecure communication channel. The sender will compute the hash value of the file before transmission, and you will do the same after transmission. By comparing the two values, you will know if the file was altered during the process because, due to the avalanche effect, even the slightest change will induce disparities in the computed hashes.

The most common and widely used hashing functions today are *MD5* from the Message Digest standard, and *SHA-1* and *SHA-256* from the Secure Hash Algorithm standard.

Now, let's get back to encryption-decryption algorithms. These are mainly separated into two categories, known as symmetric and asymmetric cryptography, and we will start by introducing the former.

Symmetric cryptography

The most traditional and intuitive encryption algorithms lie in the category of **symmetric cryptography**. They are designed such that the same key is used both for encryption and decryption. Caesar ciphers and the one-time pad that we presented in the previous section of this chapter are classical examples of symmetric cryptography: it is sufficient for the receiver to know the key used by the sender to be able to decipher a message:

Figure 12.1 – Symmetric cryptography representation

The main advantage of this type of algorithm is that only an encryption technique and a unique key are needed to safely exchange data between two parties, and this low complexity goes hand in hand with fast implementation. The first standardized cipher was the **Data Encryption Standard (DES)**, and the most widely used symmetric encryption algorithm in modern cryptography is the **Advanced Encryption Standard (AES)**. Both standards are known as **block ciphers** because their encryption methods operate on fixed-length blocks of data. Typically, AES encrypts 128-bit blocks of data with 128-, 192-, or 256-bit keys.

However simple it is to use, symmetric encryption is not very practical on its own as it requires the secure exchange of keys. It is thus often coupled in real-world applications with the other main category of cryptographic processes: asymmetric-key algorithms.

Asymmetric cryptography

As opposed to its symmetric counterpart, which uses the same key for encryption and decryption, **asymmetric cryptography** requires the use of two different keys to perform the processes. This pair of keys consists of a **public key**, which anyone can access, and a **private key**, which only its owner can access. As such, asymmetric cryptography is also often referred to as public-key cryptography.

This part of cryptography is qualified *asymmetric* because it provides a one-way form of communication: anybody can encrypt a message with the public key but only the owner can decrypt a cipher with their private key. For that to work, the generation of the pair of keys is based on mathematical problems that are assumed sufficiently hard to solve, so that an attacker cannot break the encryption without having access to the key:

Figure 12.2 – Asymmetric cryptography representation

Because asymmetric encryption is slower than symmetric encryption, they are often used in combination: a key is safely exchanged between two parties thanks to an asymmetric protocol, and then this key is used for a symmetric-key algorithm. This is, for example, the case for **Hypertext Transfer Protocol Secure (HTTPS)**, which is the secure version of **HTTP**, the protocol used to exchange data between a website and a browser. It uses the **Transport Layer Security (TLS)** protocol to ensure the safety of the communication by first generating and exchanging keys using an asymmetric protocol and then using these keys to encrypt the data with symmetric algorithms. The asymmetric part of TLS is known as the **TLS handshake** and takes place each time you connect to an HTTPS website to establish the security of the connection.

Let's now dive into how key exchange using asymmetric encryption works with one of the first public-key protocols invented: Diffie-Hellman.

Diffie-Hellman key exchange

Diffie-Hellman key exchange is a method for generating shared secret keys for two parties communicating over an insecure channel. It is one of the first examples of public-key cryptography implementation and it is still used today in various cryptographic models, notably in the TLS protocol.

The general idea of the Diffie-Hellman key exchange is based upon the mathematical theory of groups. At the beginning of the process, the two parties, which we will call Alice and Bob, publicly agree on a generator g of a finite cyclic multiplicative group G of order n. Then, they follow these steps:

1. They both choose at random a secret natural number, a for Alice and b for Bob.

2. They both raise g to the power of their secret number. Alice computes g^a and Bob computes g^b.

3. They exchange their results. Alice receives g^b from Bob and Bob receives g^a from Alice.

4. They raise the received result to the power of their secret number. Alice computes $(g^b)^a$ and Bob computes $(g^a)^b$.

At the end of the process, Alice and Bob share a common secret g^{ab} thanks to the associative property of groups. This secret is safe and can be used as a key for further exchanges between Alice and Bob even though it was generated on an insecure communication channel. The security of the process comes from the fact that it is technically difficult for an attacker to retrieve the power an element it is raised to. In short, knowing g^a does not help us to find the value a, and it is therefore impossible computationally to deduce g^{ab} from the public values only. This problem is known in mathematical theory as the **discrete-logarithm problem** and the security of numerous algorithms in asymmetric cryptography relies on the assumption that it is hard to solve as long as the group is chosen with care.

Let's take a practical example to better understand how key exchange works. Typically, the group G chosen is the multiplicative group of integers modulo p for p a prime number, denoted as $(\mathbb{Z}/p\mathbb{Z})^{\times}$. Suppose Alice and Bob publicly agree on using $p = 29$ and $g = 8$ as the generator of $(\mathbb{Z}/29\mathbb{Z})^{\times}$. The resulting Diffie-Hellman key exchange consists of the following steps:

1. Alice chooses $a = 3$ at random, Bob chooses $b = 5$ at random.

2. Alice computes $8^3 \bmod 29 = 19$, and Bob computes $8^5 \bmod 29 = 27$.

3. Alice sends her result, 19, to Bob, and Bob sends his result, 27 to Alice.

4. Alice computes $27^3 \bmod 29 = 21$, and Bob computes $19^5 \bmod 29 = 21$.

At the end of the process, Alice and Bob both share the secret value 21 and an eavesdropper only knows the values exchanged 19 and 27, as well as p and g. In practice, p is a sufficiently large prime number so that retrieving the secret values a and b from g^a and g^b is assumed impossible with the computational power at our disposal today.

Now that we have seen various techniques for data encryption in the classical world, we will see how quantum cryptography works, and especially one protocol, quantum key distribution.

Understanding quantum key distribution

Most widely used classical cryptographic algorithms rely on the assumption that an attacker cannot easily solve hard mathematical problems due to the limitation of their computational power. However, some quantum algorithms, such as Shor's factorization of integers, could break this assumption should a large enough quantum computer be built one day.

The goal of quantum cryptography is thus to design new cryptographic techniques that make use of the properties of quantum mechanics, such as the no-cloning theorem and the Heisenberg uncertainty principle, to build secure systems. Thus, unlike its classical counterpart, quantum cryptography does not need computational assumptions to defend against attacks, but relies instead on the laws of quantum physics.

Several protocols have been defined to tackle quantum key distribution, the two most famous being **BB84** introduced by Charles H. Bennett and Gilles Brassard in 1984 and **E91** introduced by Artur Ekert in 1991. In this section, we will study BB84 and refer to it as the quantum key distribution protocol.

Let's start by describing the quantum key distribution protocol, which allows two parties that do not share prior information to safely exchange a secret key by sending qubits over a quantum channel.

Describing the quantum key distribution protocol

For the **quantum key distribution** protocol, we consider two parties, Alice and Bob, wishing to exchange some information over a quantum channel in order to generate a shared secret that cannot be gleaned by an eavesdropper, Eve. The first party, Alice, chooses a random sequence of bits and, for each bit, she either encodes it in the Hadamard basis $(|+\rangle, |-\rangle) = \left(\frac{|0\rangle + |1\rangle}{\sqrt{2}}, \frac{|0\rangle - |1\rangle}{\sqrt{2}} \right)$ or in the standard basis $(|0\rangle, |1\rangle)$, once again at random.

She then sends the sequence of qubits to Bob. Upon receiving Alice's qubits, Bob measures each of them in the random basis of his choice (independently of Alice) and obtains a sequence of bits. In theory, at least half of those bits are similar to Alice's: the ones for which Alice and Bob chose the same basis. The other half have lost their information when measured in the wrong basis because they have randomly collapsed to 0 or 1.

After this first exchange over a quantum channel, Alice and Bob share some information, the bits for which they chose the same basis, but they need to communicate in order to identify those bits. The subsequent discussion takes place on a public channel that may be subject to a passive eavesdropper. Alice and Bob identify the bits for which they chose the same basis, and without alteration, they are supposed to be identical and constitute the secret shared information between the two parties. However, if Eve has measured the qubits during the transmission from Alice to Bob, she may have tampered with them by measuring them in the wrong basis because she also has to randomly guess the bases when doing her measurements.

In order to verify that no eavesdropping took place, Alice and Bob publicly compare some of the bits they share that are supposed to be the same. There is thus a trade-off between revealing enough bits so that the detection of the eavesdropper, if present, is likely and keeping as much shared secret information as possible. If some of the revealed bits differ, Alice and Bob know that someone has altered the qubits and that the secrecy of the shared bits is compromised, so they discard them and retry the process from the beginning. On the contrary, if the comparisons agree, they assume that no eavesdropper has seen their exchanged data and that the remaining hidden bits constitute secret shared information between them. They can then use these bits as a one-time pad key over the public channel to secure their communications:

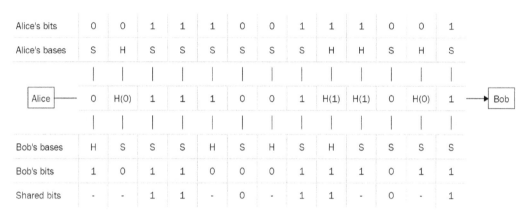

Figure 11.3 – Quantum key distribution protocol

As an example, let's suppose Alice chooses a random sequence of bits, 0011100111001, and a random sequence of bases, SHSSSSSSHHSHS, where S and H respectively correspond to the standard basis ($|0\rangle, |1\rangle$) and the Hadamard basis

$(|+\rangle, |-\rangle) = \left(\dfrac{|0\rangle + |1\rangle}{\sqrt{2}}, \dfrac{|0\rangle - |1\rangle}{\sqrt{2}}\right)$. She then sends to Bob the bits encoded as qubits in the

corresponding basis:

Bits	0	0	1	1	1	0	0	1	1	1	0	0	1
Bases	S	H	S	S	S	S	S	S	H	H	S	H	S
Qubits	$\|0\rangle$	$H\|0\rangle$	$\|1\rangle$	$\|1\rangle$	$\|1\rangle$	$\|0\rangle$	$\|0\rangle$	$\|1\rangle$	$H\|1\rangle$	$H\|1\rangle$	$\|0\rangle$	$H\|0\rangle$	$\|1\rangle$

Table 11.1 – Alice sends qubits generated from randomly chosen bits and bases to Bob

Bob computes his own random sequence of bases, HSSSHSHSHSSSS, and uses it to measure the received qubits:

Qubits	$|0\rangle$	$H|0\rangle$	$|1\rangle$	$|1\rangle$	$|1\rangle$	$|0\rangle$	$|0\rangle$	$|1\rangle$	$H|1\rangle$	$H|1\rangle$	$|0\rangle$	$H|0\rangle$	$|1\rangle$
Bases	H	S	S	S	H	S	H	S	H	S	S	S	S
Bits	1	0	1	1	0	0	0	1	1	1	0	1	1

Table 11.2 – Bob measures Alice's qubits in randomly chosen bases

Now Alice and Bob publicly compare their sequence of bases to find out which bits they supposedly share:

Bases A	S	H	S	S	S	S	S	S	H	H	S	H	S
Bases B	H	S	S	S	H	S	H	S	H	S	S	S	S
Bits A	0	0	1	1	1	0	0	1	1	1	0	0	1
Bits B	1	0	1	1	0	0	0	1	1	1	0	1	1

Table 11.3 – Alice and Bob compare their sequence of bases to retrieve the shared information

Finally, they compare some of the bits from the ones they share and verify that they are the same:

Shared bits	1	1	0	1	1	0	1
Checked bits			0				1

Table 11.4 – Alice and Bob reveal some bits at random to detect the presence of an eavesdropper

The remaining bits, 11110, constitute the shared information that they can then use as a one-time pad key for subsequent communications. If an eavesdropper had measured the qubits during the transmission from Alice to Bob, it would probably have been detected when Alice and Bob compared some of the bits they were supposed to agree on. This is because quantum laws force the eavesdropper to be active by measuring the qubits to gain information about them and, in doing so, to become detectable because the eavesdropper affects the following measurements.

Here, we are taking a theoretical approach, and we consider that apart from the interference of an eavesdropper, the quantum transmission is perfect even though this is obviously not the case in a practical context. In a real-life setting, Alice and Bob should use error-correction methods on top of the quantum key distribution protocol to ensure the integrity of the shared key.

Let's now see how to implement the quantum key distribution protocol in Silq.

Implementing the quantum key distribution in Silq

We describe here a simple implementation of the Quantum Key Distribution in Silq where two parties, Alice and Bob, share some secret information over a quantum channel and check whether an eavesdropper has interfered with their communication. To generate the random sequences of bits and bases, we will use the helper function `rand` to generate a random bit. It is defined as the measure of $H|0\rangle$ so that it randomly outputs 0 or 1:

```
def rand(){
    return measure(H(false));
}
```

Let's start on Alice's side with the generation of her random bits and bases.

Preparing the state (Alice)

We have seen that the process of quantum key distribution begins with Alice generating qubits to send to Bob from bits and bases chosen at random. We implement this first step in the `prepareState` function, which takes an integer $n \in \mathbb{N}$ as input and returns the random sequences of n bits and bases that Alice chose, as well as the corresponding qubits that she sends to Bob.

Alice's bits and bases are initialized as classical n-bit integers, and each bit is set to a random value using the helper function `rand`. The standard basis corresponds to 0 and the Hadamard basis to 1. Then, the qubits are computed directly from the bits by applying a Hadamard transform to them, for which the corresponding basis is 1. The implementation of `prepareState` can be found in the following snippet of code:

```
def prepareState(n:!N) {
    bitsA := 0:!int[n];
    basesA := 0:!int[n];
    for i in [0..n){
        bitsA[i] = rand();
        basesA[i] = rand();
```

```
    }
    qubitsA := bitsA:int[n];
    for i in [0..n]{
        if basesA[i] {qubitsA[i] = H(qubitsA[i]);}
    }
    return (bitsA, basesA, qubitsA);
}
```

Here, we keep a trace of the bits and bases generated by Alice because we will need to compare them with the ones generated by Bob later on in the process.

Measuring the qubits (Bob)

Alice has sent her qubits to Bob, who needs to measure them in random bases to obtain his own version of the initial bits. This is done in the `measureB` function, which takes the qubits sent by Alice as an n-bit integer as input and returns the random bases chosen by Bob and the corresponding measured bits as classical n-bit integers. In the same manner as Alice, the bases are computed at random with the `rand` function and the qubits undergo a Hadamard transform before measurement if and only if the corresponding basis is set to 1. The implementation of `measureB` is as follows:

```
def measureB[n:!ℕ](qubitsA:int[n]) {
    basesB := 0:!int[n];
    for i in [0..n]{
        basesB[i] = rand();
        if basesB[i] {qubitsA[i] := H(qubitsA[i]);}
    }
    bitsB := measure(qubitsA);
    return (bitsB, basesB);
}
```

At this point, we have the original bits and bases chosen by Alice and the bases chosen by Bob, as well as the bits he computed with them. From there, we implement the public discussion between both parties to generate a safe shared secret.

Comparing the bases

First, Alice and Bob need to know which of the bits they share are identical, and these correspond to the bases that Bob guessed correctly. We thus implement a `compareBases` function that takes both sequences of bases as input and returns the indices where they coincide as a classical *n*-bit integer. This function also returns the quantity of shared information, which is the number of bits for which Alice and Bob chose the same basis. In the following implementation, we see that the indices are computed by taking the negation of the XOR of the two sequences of bases because it evaluates to 1 if and only if the inputs are identical:

```
def compareBases[n:!N](basesA:!int[n], basesB:!int[n]) {
    indices := 0:!int[n];
    nInfo := 0:!N;
    indices = ~(basesA ⊕ basesB);
    for i in [0..n) {nInfo+=indices[i];}
    return (indices, nInfo);
}
```

The number of bits shared is computed in the `nInfo` variable by adding all indices: 0 when the bases differ, 1 when they are the same. We will use it later when determining the number of bits we need to reveal in order to detect the presence of an eavesdropper.

Computing the shared information

Now that we have computed the indices of the bases on which Alice and Bob agree, we need to keep only the corresponding bits and discard the others because measuring them has destroyed their worth. In order to do that, we first implement the `computePotentialSharedInfo` function, which takes the number of matching bases, `nInfo`, their indices, and Alice's and Bob's bit sequences as input and returns the potential shared information for both parties as classical integers with `nInfo` bits. In the following snippet of code, you can see that we are in a `while` loop scanning `indices` until the `nInfo` 1 are found, and we gather the corresponding bits from Alice and Bob in `infoA` and `infoB` respectively:

```
def computePotentialSharedInfo[n:!N](
                        indices:!int[n], nInfo:!N,
                        bitsA:!int[n], bitsB:!int[n]) {

    infoA := 0:!int[nInfo];
    infoB := 0:!int[nInfo];
```

```
    count := 0:!N;
    i := 0:!N;
    while (count < nInfo) {
        if indices[i] {
            infoA[count] = bitsA[i];
            infoB[count] = bitsB[i];
            count+=1;
        }
        i+=1;
    }
    return (infoA, infoB);
}
```

Next, we need a function implementing the sacrifice by Alice and Bob of some of their shared bits to check whether they are indeed identical, and no eavesdropper has interfered during transmission. This is done with the checkEavesdropper function, which takes nSharedBits, the number of bits to keep secret, and the two integers of presumably shared information as input and returns the indices of the bits that remained secret and whether an eavesdropper was detected when comparing some of the information bits. The absence of an eavesdropper is computed in the boolean noE, which is initialized to true and set to false as soon as two compared bits are different, a sign that the data has been interfered with.

We initialize the number of bits checked, bitsRevealed, to 0 and loop until it reaches the required number of bits, which is the total number of bits shared minus the number of bits we want to keep secret: $n - nSharedBits$ To ensure that we reveal different bits each time, we initialize a variable called notAlreadyChecked to the value $2^n - 1$ so that it is an n-bit integer with all bits set to 1, which keeps track of the indices of the as yet unchecked bits. Every loop, we choose at random a new bit to reveal using the uniformInt function, which outputs a random number in a given range, and we verify that it has not been already checked. If not, we update the boolean noE by checking whether Alice and Bob effectively reveal the same bit or not, we switch the corresponding notAlreadyChecked bit to 0, and we increase the number of bits revealed by 1. Otherwise, we simply retry a new random index:

```
def checkEavesdropper[n:!N](nSharedBits:!N,
                             infoA:!int[n], infoB:!int[n]) {
    bitsRevealed := 0:!N;
    noE := true;
    count := 0:!N;
```

```
    i := 0:!N;
    notAlreadyChecked := 2^n - 1 coerce !int[n];
    while (bitsRevealed < n - nSharedBits) {
        i = uniformInt(n);
        if notAlreadyChecked[i] {
            noE &= (infoA[i] == infoB[i]);
            notAlreadyChecked[i] = false;
            bitsRevealed+=1;
        }
    }
    return (notAlreadyChecked, noE);
}
```

Finally, we use these two functions to implement the next function, computeSharedInfo, which takes the bit sequences from Alice and Bob, the number of concordant bases, as well as their indices and the number of bits to remain secret at the end of the process, nSharedBits, as input. It then outputs the final secret shared information as an integer with nSharedBits bits and the absence of eavesdropping as the boolean noE. It starts by reducing the bit sequences of Alice and Bob to the bits corresponding to the correctly guessed bases using the computePresumablySharedInfo function. Then, it verifies the absence of eavesdropping by burning some bits with the checkEavesdropper function. This function also returns the bits that were not revealed in the notAlreadyChecked variable. The final secret shared information is thus computed by looping through the information bits of Alice (or equivalently Bob) and keeping only the ones for which notAlreadyChecked is set to true, meaning that they were not revealed:

```
def computeSharedInfo[n:!N](bitsA:!int[n], bitsB:!int[n],
                           indices:!int[n],
                           nInfo:!N, nSharedBits:!N) {

    (infoA, infoB) := computePresumablySharedInfo(indices,
                           bitsA, bitsB, nInfo);

    (notAlreadyChecked, noE) := checkEavesdropper(infoA,
                           infoB, nSharedBits);

    sharedInfo := 0:!int[nSharedBits];
    count := 0:!N;
```

```
    i := 0:!N;
    while (count < nSharedBits) {
        if notAlreadyChecked[i] {
            sharedInfo[count] = infoA[i];
            count+=1;
        }
        i+=1;
    }

    return (sharedInfo, noE);
}
```

We have now defined all the functions we need, and we are ready to implement the whole quantum key distribution process.

Implementing the quantum key distribution process

The quantum key distribution process is implemented in the qkd function, described next, that takes a channel modeling the transmission of qubits from Alice to Bob with potential interference from an eavesdropper as input. It starts with Alice choosing her bits and bases and preparing the qubits to send to Bob in the prepareState function. Then, the qubits pass through the channel before going to Bob, who chooses bases to measure them and obtain bits in the measureB function.

Finally, after the comparison of the bases with the compareBases function, Alice and Bob know how many bits of info they presumably share, and they *burn* one-third of them to check for the presence of an eavesdropper with the computeSharedInfo function. It returns whether an eavesdropper was detected, along with the number of secret bits successfully shared by Alice and Bob at the end of the process if there is no interference:

```
def qkd[n:!N](channel: int[n] !→ int[n]){
    (bitsA, basesA, qubitsA) := prepareState(n);

    qubitsA := channel(qubitsA);

    (bitsB, basesB) := measureB(qubitsA);
    (indices, nInfo) := compareBases(basesA, basesB);

    nSharedBits := floor((2/3)*nInfo) coerce !N;
    (sharedInfo, noE) := computeSharedInfo(indices, bitsA,
```

```
            bitsB, nInfo, nSharedBits);

      return (noE, nSharedBits);
}
```

Let's now see how to test our implementation.

Testing the quantum key distribution implementation

We define two tests for our quantum key distribution implementation. In the first one, testQKDnoE, there is no eavesdropping. The channel function is defined as the identity function and does not modify the qubits. We thus assert that the boolean noE is true after the process and the variable nSharedBits is the size of the secret key shared by Alice and Bob at the end. By computation, its value is equal to two-thirds of the number of bases chosen by both Alice and Bob because the remaining third is used to check for the presence of an eavesdropper:

```
def testQKDnoE() {
      n := 10;
      channel := λ(b:int[n]). b;
      (noE, nSharedBits) := qkd[n](channel);
      assert(noE);
      print(noE, nSharedBits);
}
```

In the second test, testQKDE, channel is defined as a function applying a Hadamard transform on all the qubits, modeling an eavesdropper that intercepts the qubits during transmission, and measures them in the Hadamard basis before sending altered qubits to Bob. Here, you can verify that noE is most of the time set to false as the presence of an eavesdropper is likely to be detected when Alice and Bob compare some of their shared bits. The probability of detection is not 100% because we are working on a relatively low number of bits, and there is a chance that the bits that are checked are identical even though an eavesdropper has gained information during transmission. If we increase the number of exchanged bits, there will be more correct basis guesses from Bob, more shared information between our two protagonists, more revealed bits to check for an eavesdropper, and thus less chance for the eavesdropper to remain unnoticed:

```
def testQKDE() {
      n := 10;
      channel := λ(b:int[n]){for i in [0..n) {b[i] := H(b[i])};
```

```
        return b; };
    (noE, nSharedBits) := qkd[n](channel);
    print(noE, nSharedBits);
}
```

Both tests can then be launched in the `main` function as follows:

```
def main() {
    testQKDnoE();
    testQKDE();
}
```

If you want, you can modify the tests to try different behaviors for the eavesdropper or increase the number of bits exchanged. You can also print the shared bits at different points of the process to see how it works more clearly.

Summary

Over the course of this chapter, we introduced the basics of classical cryptography, and you learned how to use encryption techniques from symmetric cryptography with the Caesar cipher or the one-time pad, and from asymmetric cryptography with Diffie-Hellman key exchange.

Then, we turned toward quantum cryptography and learned about quantum key distribution, which is a quantum protocol that facilitates secure key exchange for two parties that do not share any prior information.

Finally, you learned how to implement the entire process of quantum key distribution using Silq. You can now apply your newly acquired knowledge to implement another quantum cryptography process: quantum coin tossing.

In the next and final chapter, you will get an introduction to quantum machine learning.

13
Quantum Machine Learning

With the growth of classical computers in every industry and various applications, a lot of data has been generated over the past few years. The advent of powerful classical computing, through things such as **Graphics Processing Units (GPUs)**, has enabled many industries to work with large amounts of data efficiently in a small amount of time. But we have started to observe that the amount of data is growing rapidly, and it is going to increase further in the coming years, which will mean that classical computing methods will take longer to process and extract useful information from data. Quantum machine learning holds promise in this field, in that it can bring the power of quantum computing to the classical machine learning techniques used today due to the incredibly speedy parallel nature of the computation of quantum computers.

In this chapter, you will explore the concepts of classical machine learning methods and develop practical skills and familiarity with the nuances of quantum machine learning. You will also learn how to make comparisons between classical and quantum machine learning. We will cover the following topics in this chapter:

- Introducing classical machine learning
- Getting started with quantum machine learning
- Learning about the quantum K-means algorithm
- Exploring variational circuits
- The latest developments in quantum machine learning and quantum computing

By the end of the chapter, you will understand the concepts of classical machine learning and the basic foundations of quantum machine learning. You will feel confident in your knowledge of quantum machine learning algorithms such as variational circuits and quantum K-means and how they compare to their classical counterparts.

Introducing classical machine learning

Machine learning refers to the science and engineering of building intelligent machines that can perform different kinds of tasks without being explicitly programmed to do so. In other words, we can define machine learning as the study of algorithms and statistical models that are used to solve a particular problem without being programmed and that only rely on patterns and inferences from data. Since classical computers (operating on classical bits) are used to do machine learning, it is called **classical machine learning**.

With that definition of machine learning, you can see that the machine is not actually learning; rather, it searches for a mathematical relation in some input data that will result in an output called a **prediction**. *Machine learning* is a marketing term coined by Arthur Samuel from IBM in 1959 to attract potential industries and customers to use this technology. In essence, machine learning is nothing but a composition of mathematics of various branches, such as statistics, probability, linear algebra, calculus, and optimization. Often, machine learning is called **statistical learning**, because machine learning algorithms derive their methods from statistics, and therefore it is necessary to be familiar with various concepts related to statistics and other mathematical topics.

Since this book is not about machine learning, we will not be diving deep into this field and its mathematical details. We will only focus on some specific classical machine learning algorithms whose quantum analog will be discussed in the following sections: *Getting started with quantum machine learning, Learning about the quantum K-means algorithm*, and *Exploring variational circuits*.

Let's get started with the various types of machine learning methods in the next section.

Types of learning

There are different types of learning when it comes to machine learning algorithms. The type of learning depends on the **type of data** that is involved in the training of the machine learning algorithms. There are four types:

- **Supervised learning**: In this type of learning, the dataset has labels associated with each of the data points. Labels act as supervisors to the machine learning algorithm and help the algorithm to learn the data in an efficient manner. There are two types of supervised learning – classification learning and regression learning. For example, if you have various images of dogs and cats, then the labels are *dog* and *cat* for those images you want your algorithm to classify. For the dogs and cats example, the labels are a discrete number of classes (or categories); hence, this is called **classification learning**. If, on the other hand, you have the labels as numerical values, which means they are continuous, then this is called **regression learning**. Some examples of supervised algorithms include linear regression, logistic regression, artificial neural networks, support vector machines, decision trees, and random forests.

- **Unsupervised learning**: In this type of learning, the dataset does not have any labels. Here the machine learning algorithm tries to capture the patterns and distribution present in the dataset rather than making predictions. Examples of unsupervised learning include principal component analysis for dimensionality reduction, K-means clustering, recommender systems using autoencoders, and outlier detection.

- **Semi-supervised learning**: As can be understood from the name, here the dataset contains both labeled and non-labeled examples, and the machine learning algorithm then tries to construct a model (as in supervised learning) from the non-labeled data points.

- **Reinforcement learning**: In reinforcement learning, the machine is an **agent** and it lives in an **environment**. The **state** of that environment is taken as a feature vector and the agent can perform various **actions** in that environment, which can result in rewards or penalties. The agent here tries to learn a **policy** (a function) that maximizes the average reward by choosing the most optimal actions. Common examples of reinforcement learning algorithms include Q-learning, deep Q-learning, Monte Carlo, SARSA, **trusted region policy optimization (TRPO)**, **proximal policy optimization (PPO)**, **twin delayed deep deterministic (TD3)** policy gradient, and the **asynchronous advantage actor critic (A3C)** algorithm.

Let's now look at the types of machine learning based on the **number of parameters** present in a machine learning algorithm. Each algorithm has its own set of parameters that can be tuned in order to get better predictions with higher accuracy for a particular dataset. The types of machine learning model based on the number of parameters are categorized as follows:

- **Parametric models**: In this type of model, there is a finite, fixed set of parameters present in the algorithm that does not scale with the training data. This means that no matter the amount of training data points thrown at the parametric algorithm, the number of parameters will remain fixed and only those same parameters will be used to make predictions. These models are very simple, require less training data to learn, and have a speedy training process. However, these models suffer from limited functional forms and poor data fitting. Examples of parametric algorithms include linear regression, logistic regression, perceptrons, naïve Bayes, and artificial neural networks.

- **Non-parametric models**: In this type of model, the number of parameters present for a machine learning algorithm grows with the size of the training dataset. This means that the amount of information that can be captured by non-parametric algorithms grows with the size of the dataset. Due to the growth in the number of parameters, these models provide flexibility, power, and performance but suffer from slower training speeds and overfitting issues. Examples of non-parametric algorithms include K-nearest neighbors, decision trees, random forests, and support vector machines.

We have seen the different types of algorithms based on the number of parameters present in machine learning algorithms. Let's now take a look at algorithms that are based on the **modeling of the distribution of data**; you will see many researchers using the following terms quite often in the research literature:

- **Discriminative model**: Suppose you call the data X and you call the labels associated with them Y. A discriminative model learns a **conditional probability distribution $P(Y|X)$** directly from the training data. These models model the decision boundary between various categories (or classes) present in the given dataset. Discriminative models are computationally cheaper, do not suffer from outliers present in the data, and are good for supervised machine learning tasks. These models generally cannot work with missing data and require more training data to learn. Examples of discriminative models include logistic regression, support vector machines, K-nearest neighbors, artificial neural networks, decision trees, and random forests.

- **Generative models**: Generative models learn the **joint probability distribution P(X,Y) = P(X|Y) P(Y)** of the data. They estimate the *P(X|Y)* and *P(Y)* parameters directly from the training data and use them to calculate *P(Y|X)* by utilizing Bayes' theorem. This is just like transforming *P(X,Y)* into *P(Y|X)* using Bayes' theorem. Generative models capture the actual distribution of each of the classes present in the dataset. Generative models are computationally expensive, suffer from outliers present in the dataset, and need less training data compared to discriminative models. These models are good for working with missing data and are good for unsupervised learning tasks. Examples of generative models include **linear discriminant analysis (LDA)**, naïve Bayes, Bayesian networks, hidden Markov models, and Markov random fields.

Now, with the types of machine learning algorithms covered in detail, let's now learn about some prominent classical machine learning algorithms whose quantum analogs will be discussed in the *Getting started with quantum machine learning, Learning about the quantum K-means algorithm*, and *Exploring variational circuits* sections. Forming an understanding of the classical algorithms will help you to appreciate the concepts of quantum machine learning algorithms. Let's get started with an unsupervised machine learning algorithm known as K-means clustering in the next section.

The K-means clustering algorithm

Clustering is a type of problem where we assign labels to a given dataset that does not have any labels associated with it. Clustering algorithms work by capturing and extracting the feature patterns present in the dataset and then making labels for the data. Clustering helps to analyze the structure of the data and helps to divide the data points into various clusters, where data points in each cluster have some similarity with each other. One of the simplest and most easy-to-understand clustering algorithms is known as the **K-means clustering algorithm**.

K-means is a clustering algorithm that divides the dataset into *K* non-overlapping clusters, where each of the data points is associated only with a single cluster. The K-means algorithm tries to minimize the sum of the squared distance between the data points and the cluster centroid, where the cluster centroid is the arithmetic mean of the data points present in the cluster.

The main steps to assign labels with K-means clustering are as follows:

1.   First, we choose K random points as cluster centroids. We can choose our K points initially as well.

2.   We assign each of the data points to its nearest cluster by calculating the Euclidean distance between the data points and the centroid point. Other distance measures include Manhattan distance and cosine distance.

3.   We compute the new centroids for the clusters by taking the average of all the data points that were assigned to the clusters.

4.   We keep repeating the process of calculating the Euclidean distance between data points and centroids and keep computing new centroids until the centroid locations do not change.

To give you a better understanding, *Figure 13.1* shows an example of the K-means clustering algorithm where you can observe that the plus signs, cross signs, and circle signs have their own non-overlapping subgroups (clusters):

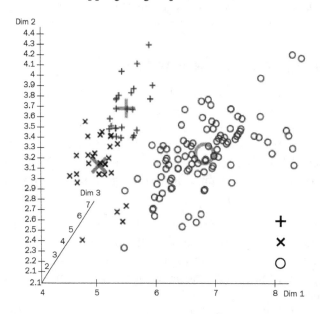

Figure 13.1 – K-means clustering applied to data

In this algorithm, the value of K is a hyperparameter that is tuned by a data analyst according to the requirements of a certain application in the industry. The central approach used by K-means is known as the **expectation maximization** (**EM**) algorithm. In EM, **E** is the assignment of data points to the cluster centroid and **M** is the computation of the centroids of each of the clusters.

Several evaluation metrics exist for the K-means performance measurement, such as the elbow method, silhouette analysis, the Dunn index, and the Davies-Bouldin score. K-means is used in document clustering, market segmentation, image compression, and segmentation. You will learn about the quantum version of the K-means algorithm in the *Learning about the quantum K-means algorithm* section.

With the K-means algorithm covered, let's now move onto another interesting machine learning aspect.

Artificial neural networks

Artificial neural networks are machine learning models that have been inspired by the biological neurons present in our human brains. Just as biological neurons act as information processing units, in a very similar manner, artificial neural networks consist of neurons, or computational units, and they perform the average of all the inputs provided to them. The connections between the neurons are known as **synapses**, and each of these synapses has weights associated, which can be tuned to make the neural network learn.

In *Figure 13.2*, you can see a pictorial representation of a simple neural network with a single hidden layer. As we add more and more hidden layers, the network becomes deeper, and then we call it a **deep neural network**. Any network with two or more layers we call a deep neural network:

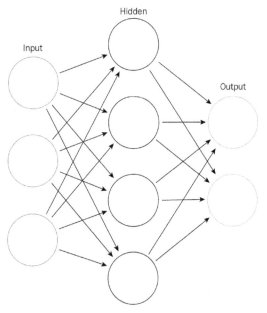

Figure 13.2 – Artificial neural network

To introduce non-linearity into a neural network, we use specific types of functions known as **activation functions**. Activation functions help a neural network to model the complex, non-linear data that we typically find in everyday datasets. Some of the most commonly used activation functions for neural networks are sigmoid, threshold, **rectified linear unit** (**ReLU**), and hyperbolic tangent functions. The ReLU activation function is used in the hidden layers of a neural network when the network is deep. It helps to model complex mathematical functions for the given dataset in a better way.

The output layer predicts classes (or continuous regression values) based on the dataset. The predicted classes (labels) are then fed into a loss function, where the true labels (the original labels that came with the dataset) are compared with the predicted labels. The value generated by the loss function is the measure of the network's error rate. This error value is then fed back into the neural network and the weights of the network are modified accordingly using optimization methods such as **gradient descent** or **stochastic gradient descent**. The optimization algorithm tries to reduce the error between the predicted values (labels) and the true values (labels), and there are many other optimization algorithms besides the gradient descent methods. The process of calculating the derivatives is known as **backpropagation** (**backprop** or **BP**). Backpropagation involves the computation of the gradient of the loss function with respect to the weights. The updating of the weights (parameters) is performed by optimization algorithms (such as **gradient descent**), which use the derivatives (calculated by backpropagation) to minimize the loss. In neural networks, weights are the varying (changing or **variational**) parameters of the network that get tuned by backpropagation to give us better predictions.

The process of passing data through the neural network (feedforward) and backpropagation with the tuning of weights is termed as a single **epoch** of training. These epochs are carried out in multiple iterations so as to reach a better accuracy score. In the *Exploring variational circuits* section, you will see that variational circuits are equivalent to a quantum neural network, and this whole process of training a neural network is carried out for variational circuits as well.

With neural networks covered, we will now move on to a very important topic known as the kernel-based support vector machine.

Kernel support vector machines (SVMs)

Support vector machines (**SVMs**) are a supervised learning algorithm that can perform both classification and regression. For our case, we will consider SVM as a classification algorithm to explain how it works. The main idea behind SVM is that it tries to find an optimal **hyperplane** that can separate the classes from each other. In a 2D case, we will have a simple line acting as a hyperplane that will be able to separate the data points from each other.

In *Figure 13.3*, you can see a 2D plane and three lines. The middle line is known as the **decision boundary** and the two other lines are the margins (the dotted lines at the bottom and the top) that need to be separated as far as possible (for the most accurate predictions):

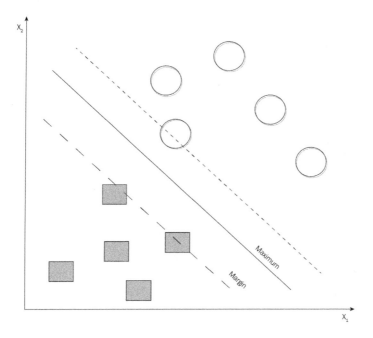

Figure 13.3 – SVM

The margin lines are created with the help of **support vectors**, which are data points that represent the classes present in a dataset. You can clearly see two boxes touching the bottom margin line and a circle touching the top margin lines. These two boxes and the circle form the support vectors.

Each data point in the 2D space is considered a vector because all the calculations of SVM take place in the 2D plane, which is a vector space. It is important to note that the margin lines can change if the position of the support vectors changes.

In brief, the SVM algorithm identifies two margin lines where there are no data points between the two margin lines. Then, it maximizes the distance between the margins and finally draws the decision boundary (halfway between the margins) to make a classification. The SVM algorithm that we have discussed until now is the linear SVM algorithm, but in the real world, we work with higher-dimensional feature spaces with a lot of data points, meaning linear SVM is not an ideal choice for separating the classes present in a high-dimensional dataset.

When we are faced with non-linear data such as what is shown in *Figure 13.4* in the left-hand graph, we use a mathematical trick known as a **kernel** trick to make our classification job easier:

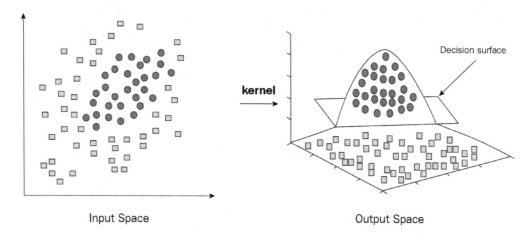

Figure 13.4 – Kernel trick for SVM

You can see that a circle can classify the boxes from the circle data points, but a circle is not a straight line. However, in the right-hand graph, you can see that by the use of the kernel trick, you can separate the boxes and circle with a 2D hyperplane in a 3D coordinate vector space. This 2D-to-3D transformation is virtual, not real!

The kernel method of SVM is a mathematical technique that helps to classify high-dimensional data in its original dimensional form without the computation of the coordinates of the data in higher dimensions. The kernel method helps to find similarities present in the data in high dimensions. This means that the transformation of going to a higher-dimensional space to classify the data is not needed, and the kernel trick allows us to do the computations in the original feature space. The various types of kernels that you can use are **radial basis functions** (**RBFs**), Gaussian kernels, polynomial kernels, sigmoid kernels, and Laplace RBF kernels.

The concept of kernel methods for SVM will be helpful for you to understand the Hilbert space-based method that we will discuss in the next section.

Getting started with quantum machine learning

In the previous section, you learned about the field of machine learning and the three most common algorithms used by machine learning researchers and by industries to accelerate growth. Every year, we are now witnessing a significant amount of growth of data worldwide, and the rate is going to increase even more in the near future. It has been estimated that about 60 zetabytes (10^{21}) has been accumulated by our planet!

Due to the growth of data and its associated features, the power of classical computers is becoming limited. We have powerful classical computers today that can deal with high-dimensional data, but a time is coming when classical computers won't be able to handle very high-dimensional data, and at that time **quantum machine learning** algorithms will have to step in.

The term **quantum machine learning** was coined by Lloyd, Mohseni, and Rebentrost in their paper *Quantum algorithms for supervised and unsupervised machine learning* in 2013. Since then, there has been a lot of research and growth happening in this cutting-edge field. Quantum machine learning is the merging of quantum algorithms with classical machine learning algorithms; it is also known as **quantum-enhanced machine learning**. There are a lot of developments happening currently regarding various applications of quantum machine learning, some of which include solving linear systems of equations, quantum-enhanced reinforcement learning, quantum neural networks, and quantum sampling techniques, which are used in various finance-related industries.

On the basis of the type of data and the data-processing device, there are four main categories for classifying quantum machine learning approaches. These categories are defined in *Figure 13.5* and you can clearly observe the classical elements:

Type of Processing Device → Type of Data ↓	Classical Device	Quantum Device
Classical Data	CC	CQ
Quantum Data	QC	QQ

Figure 13.5 – Approaches to quantum machine learning

For the **CC (Classical Data, Classical Device)** approach, we have classical data that is processed by classical computers, as we have already seen in the previous section. These are your classical machine learning algorithms. For the **QC** case, we see the usage of classical machine learning with quantum data, as in distinguishing between various quantum states and learning phase transitions in many-body quantum systems.

CQ and **QQ** are both quantum machine learning because here we deal with the quantum computer as the main processing device with both kinds of data – classical and quantum. Primarily, we are currently only dealing with the CQ case, where we have large classical datasets and we then use quantum computers to search for the latent underlying patterns present in the data or extract useful information from data and make inferences from it.

But you might be wondering now about how will we use classical data on a quantum computer – it's classical, right? It's not in a quantum state! Well, the good news here is that there exist encoding mechanisms that can help you to encode your classical data into a quantum state to then be processed by a quantum computer. In the next section, we'll look at some of the encoding schemes in brief to understand their processes.

Encoding classical data into a quantum state

There are various ways to encode classical information into a quantum state. We will briefly go through the techniques that are used for encoding. The main methods that we are going to see are basis encoding, amplitude encoding, angle encoding, higher-order embedding, and variational/trained embedding. Let's start with basis encoding.

Basis encoding

Basis encoding is a scheme where binary data (using 0s and 1s) is encoded as a superposition of the quantum states. For example, if we have the data points $x_1 = (0,1)^T$ and $x_2 = (1,1)^T$ as quantum states $|01>$ and $|11>$, then we can make a superposition state of 2 qubits, such as $\frac{1}{\sqrt{4}}(|00> + |01> + |10> + |11>)$ from which we can form the amplitude vector as $(0, \frac{1}{\sqrt{2}}, 0, \frac{1}{\sqrt{2}})$, because we only need the states $|01>$ and $|11>$. Therefore, the superposition state of encoding becomes $\frac{1}{\sqrt{2}}|01> + \frac{1}{\sqrt{2}}|11>$. You will observe that the more qubits there are, the more sparse the amplitude vector becomes, with lots of zeros, which is not very efficient.

Next, let's look at a better encoding scheme known as amplitude encoding.

Amplitude encoding

As the name suggests, **amplitude encoding** simply means encoding the classical information as the probability amplitude associated with the quantum states. For example, if we have the classical data $x_1 = (0.33, -0.45)^T$ and $x_2 = (-0.78, 0.22)^T$, then the quantum state vector will be $\frac{1}{\sqrt{4}}(0.33|00 > -0.45|01 > -0.78|10 > +0.22|11 >)$. In amplitude encoding, there is a chance that the data can get corrupted while quantum processing is carried out in the quantum states. This corruption can lead to inaccurate results and the training of the quantum model will be subjected to erroneous predictions. It is also worth noting that the 2-qubit quantum state can also be written as a column vector to represent the data.

Let's look at a better and more intuitive approach to data encoding that is known as angle encoding.

Angle encoding

The **angle encoding** method is very popular and is used heavily in many quantum machine learning models. In angle encoding, the data value is stored as rotations of quantum states, which means the amount of angle value by which a quantum state is rotated is equal to the value represented by the classical data. The number of qubits can be equal to the number of features present in the dataset. For example, the data $x_1 = (0.33, -0.45)^T$ and $x_2 = (-0.78, 0.22)^T$ can be stored using angle encoding with X-, Y-, and Z-axis rotations around the Bloch sphere, such as $R_y(0.33), R_z(-0.45)$ and $R_y(-0.78), R_z(0.22)$ separated by Hadamard gates.

Let's now take a look at a very different kind of encoding known as **higher-order encoding**.

Higher-order encoding

To understand **higher-order encoding**, you need to understand quantum feature maps. The **quantum feature map** is the quantum version of the classical kernel that you saw in the kernel SVM algorithm. This means that this quantum feature map should be hard to simulate classically so as to gain an advantage over classical kernels, as it provides the function of mapping data into a higher-dimensional feature space. So, in higher-order encoding, a classical dataset can be mapped onto the Bloch sphere using quantum feature maps, which act as quantum kernel functions. Higher-order encoding takes advantage of the high-dimensional quantum Hilbert space.

Let's now take a look at the last method of encoding, called variational encoding, which is gaining more and more attention in the research community of quantum computing researchers.

Variational/trained encoding

This method of encoding is very similar to higher-order encoding. The classical data points are represented as quantum states with the help of quantum feature maps. This is known as quantum embedding. This embedding is carried out with the help of a parameterized quantum circuit where the parameters of the quantum circuit can vary or be trained like a neural network! This kind of data encoding is the variational way of data encoding.

With the various encoding methods covered, let's now take a look at the kernel-based quantum machine learning model briefly. Since you are already familiar with the kernel SVM algorithm, it will be easy for you to understand.

Kernel-based quantum machine learning models

This section will be completely based on a tutorial by Maria Schuld titled *Quantum machine learning models are kernel methods*, which is referred to in the *Further reading* section if you want to dig deeper into this topic.

In the higher-order encoding and variational encoding methods, you saw that classical data is transformed to a high-dimensional Hilbert space (quantum feature space), which is done using a quantum feature map. It turns out that when we replace a machine learning model with a quantum circuit (quantum models), these quantum models analyze the data in higher-dimensional Hilbert spaces where only inner products are present, which can be accessed through measurements.

As you know, quantum computers are currently very noisy, and they need to be made fault-tolerant. This kernel-based quantum machine learning method will be suitable for both near-term quantum computers and fault-tolerant quantum computers, and the quantum models running on these quantum computers can be replaced with a kernel SVM algorithm whose kernel will calculate the distance between the data-encoded distance quantum states.

When classical data is encoded into quantum states, this encoded data lives in the quantum feature space, where the quantum models can be defined as a linear model whose decision boundary can be defined by a measurement. Also, it is worth noting that kernel-based training methods are guaranteed to find the optimal measurements if the loss function is convex in nature. Measurements will have the form of a linear combination of the training data points with some coefficients.

With the kernel methods covered, let's now move on to a quantum algorithm called the quantum K-means algorithm in the next section.

Learning about the quantum K-means algorithm

We have already discussed the classical K-means clustering algorithm, and that will now help you to understand the quantum version of the K-means algorithm. As you already know, with the increase in the dimensions of big data recently, classical computers are becoming slower at processing data, and the same applies to the K-means algorithm as well. It has been found that the classical version of K-means has a time complexity of $\log(NMK)$, where N is the number of features of the data points, M is the total number of input data points, and K is the number of clusters. However, with the quantum K-means algorithm, we get a time complexity of $\log(N)MK$ because only $\log_2(N)$ qubits are required to load the N-dimensional input data points using the amplitude encoding technique.

For the implementation of the quantum K-means algorithm, three main components are utilized – the swap test circuit, the distance calculation circuit, and Grover's optimization circuit. The swap test circuit is used to measure the overlap between two quantum states (inner product). You can recall from *Chapter 1, Essential Mathematics and Algorithmic Thinking*, that the overlap (inner product) measures the similarity between two quantum states, which will help in identifying the similar data points to be clustered together. In *Figure 13.6*, you can see the swap test circuit used for the K-means algorithm:

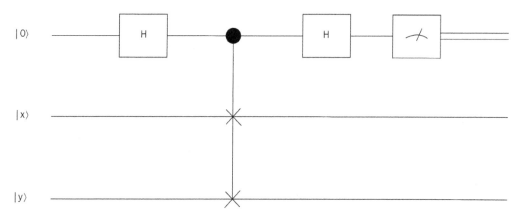

Figure 13.6 – Swap test circuit

Suppose you have prepared two quantum states:

$$|\psi> = \frac{1}{\sqrt{2}}(|0,x> +|1,y>)$$

$$|\phi> = \frac{1}{\sqrt{Z}}(|x||0> +|y||1>)$$

The value of $Z = |x|^2 + |y|^2$.

Then, you can calculate the distance using the overlap as follows:

$$Dist = 2Z < \psi|\phi >$$

The results of the SWAP test are such that if $|\psi> = |\phi>$, then we get state $|0>$ with high probability, and if $|\psi>$ *and* $|\phi>$ are not equal, then we get $|1>$ with probability ½. For a distance-based K-means algorithm, which we have discussed just now, the general quantum circuit can be seen in *Figure 13.7*, where $a_0, i_0, d_0,$ and c_0 represent the ancilla, index, data, and class qubits, respectively:

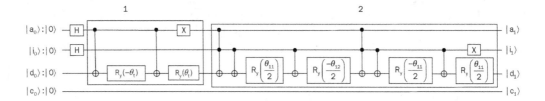

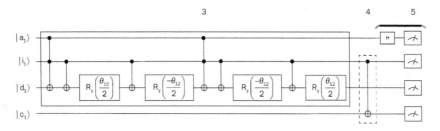

Figure 13.7 – Distance-based quantum K-means circuit

The circuit shown in *Figure 13.7* is a general quantum K-means circuit that uses the distance between a test vector and the training vectors (data points) provided in the circuit to cluster the data points. We start with the superposition state with the ancilla and index qubits using a Hadamard gate. In step 1, you can see the circuit for encoding the 2D test vector, and in steps 2 and 3, you can see the encoding for two training vectors, each being 2D. In step 4, the class labels for the training vectors are flipped, and finally, in step 5, the measurement is taken. θ_t is the value of the test vector and θ_{11} and θ_{22} are the values of the training vector corresponding to the classes c_1 and c_2.

As you can clearly observe, the encoding of the classical data into the Y-axis rotations is an essential part of the circuit and forms a great deal of the circuit mechanism. Finally, with the swap test at the end, in step 4, we achieve the K-means effect. With the K-means circuit covered, it will now be a good exercise for you to go through the additional reading resources and try constructing this circuit using Silq programming. You can refer to *Chapter 7*, *Programming Multiple Qubit Quantum Circuits with Silq*, to refresh your memory of the construction of quantum circuits.

With the quantum K-means covered, we are now ready to move on to the next section, where we will discuss variational circuits and their workings.

Exploring variational circuits

In this section, we will be diving into the concept of variational circuits, which form an integral part of today's quantum machine learning algorithms and research. We will be briefly looking into the three most common variational methods – **variational quantum classifier (VQC)**, **variational quantum eigensolver (VQE)**, and **quantum approximation optimization algorithm (QAOA)**. Let's start with VQC in the next section.

Variational quantum classifier (VQC)

VQC, as the name suggests, is a classifier that is composed of quantum circuits with variational parameters or trainable parameters. This is the basis for quantum neural networks. Since you are already familiar with the concepts of artificial neural networks, it will be easy for you to appreciate the nature of the variational circuit used for classifiers.

There are many different types of variational circuits available that can be used for quantum classifiers, and many of the circuit architectures have been defined in the paper *Expressibility and Entangling Capability of Parameterized Quantum Circuits for Hybrid Quantum-Classical Algorithms*, with the proper reasoning about the functioning of those circuits. This paper is available in the *Further reading* section if you want to dig deeper into this area of research. *Figure 13.8* shows a sample variational circuit from the paper mentioned previously:

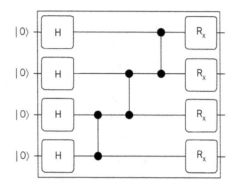

Figure 13.8 – Variational circuit

Before the variational circuit, we first encode the classical data into quantum states, and then we start putting layers of these variational circuits. Each layer of a variational circuit can be thought of as a hidden layer of the classical neural networks that you have already studied. The circuit shown in *Figure 13.8* consists of some Hadamard gates and then some controlled Z operations with parameterized X rotation gates whose values can be trained using classical optimization algorithms such as gradient descent.

In *Figure 13.9*, you can see a schematic of the workings of VQC in detail:

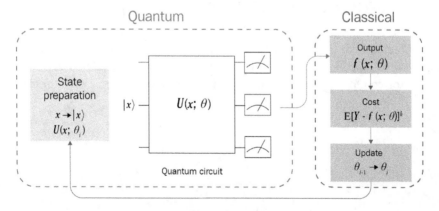

Figure 13.9 – Workings of VQC

The process for training a variational classifier is the same as that of an artificial neural network. First, the classical data is converted into quantum states $|x>$ using encoding and state preparation schemes. Then, the variational circuit block $U(x;\theta)$ is run and a measurement is taken, which predicts one of the class labels (since this is a classification problem). These predicted class labels are then compared with the true labels (output $f(x;\theta)$) with the help of a cost function ($\mathbb{E}[Y - f(x;\theta)]^k$), and the optimization algorithm is run to adjust the parameters of the variational circuit, and then this process is repeated as an epoch. This is the update process of the $\theta_{i-1} \rightarrow \theta_i$ parameters using optimization algorithms. Then, finally, the updated parameters are fed back into the state preparation routine and the variational circuit is run again with these new parameters. To include non-linearity in this case, we add it to the measurement step as it is the classical step and quantum circuits cannot be non-linear because they must always be unitary in nature.

Let's now take a look at another interesting quantum machine learning method known as the VQE.

Variational quantum eigensolver (VQE)

Before we look at **VQE**, it is important to understand the concept of a Hamiltonian, because it is used in VQE. The **Hamiltonian (H)** operator represents the total energy of a system, and total energy here refers to the sum of the kinetic and potential energy of a system. The set of measurement outcomes of a Hamiltonian operator represents the energy eigenvalues associated with this operator.

VQE is a hybrid quantum-classical algorithm that helps to find the energy eigenvalues associated with a large H operator (H matrix). VQE is one of the algorithms that are also suitable to run on the NISQ devices we have today. VQE has been utilized in the field of chemistry, including for simulating molecules and finding the ground states and excited states of hydrogen atoms. Imagine that you are trying to find the ground state of a hydrogen atom that corresponds to the lowest energy eigenvalue of the Hamiltonian operator. It is worth noting here that the Hamiltonian in the case of hydrogen will be the set of all the possible energy values of the hydrogen atom. Let's see how we can solve this problem.

Primarily, VQE consists of two steps that help to find the lowest energy of a hydrogen atom:

1. Creating an ansatz quantum circuit is a nice mathematical approach to the problem we are trying to solve. The quantum state that we get from this ansatz can be denoted by $|\psi(\theta) >$. It is worth noting that ansatz is parameterized by θ.

2. This $|\psi(\theta) >$ is then used to measure the Hamiltonian operator. The measurement is done using the expectation value $< \psi(\theta)|H|\psi(\theta)$.

Figure 13.10 shows the circuit for VQE that is used for the calculation of the energy states of a hydrogen atom. *Figure 13.10* is based on the paper *Scalable quantum simulation of molecular energies*, which is provided in the *Further reading* section:

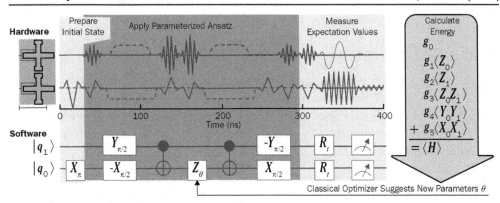

SCALABLE QUANTUM SIMULATION OF MOLECULAR ENERGIES   PHYS. REV. X 6, 031007 (2016)

Figure 13.10 – VQE for the energy state calculation of a hydrogen atom

After taking the measurement, we use classical non-linear optimization techniques to adjust the parameters of the ansatz and we keep iterating until we get our desired output. Now, you might be thinking, what happens if the expectation value becomes lower than the energy eigenvalue we are trying to find? The answer to this is that, luckily, we have a variational principle in quantum mechanics that is used in VQE, and it does not allow the calculated expectation value to go below the minimum energy eigenvalue of the H operator.

Since we have covered VQE, let's now take a look at QAOA in the next section.

Quantum approximate optimization algorithm (QAOA)

QAOA is an approximate optimization algorithm that can be used to solve combinatorial optimization problems such as the traveling salesman problem, which we introduced and explained in *Chapter 4*, *Physical Realization of a Quantum Computer*. Since QAOA is an involved algorithm, we won't be going very deep into the algorithm, but will instead only present the main idea behind the workings of the algorithm. QAOA is another hybrid quantum-classical algorithm.

In QAOA, unitary operators are applied to the superposition of quantum states, and at each iteration, a measurement is performed and a combinatorial optimization objective function is calculated. When this is carried out a certain number of times, the objective function value converges on an optimal desired value. The combinatorial objective function can be represented using a Hamiltonian operator. To get a better idea of the workings of QAOA, refer to the *Further reading* section, specifically the paper *A Quantum Approximate Optimization Algorithm*.

We have covered a lot of important algorithms in this section related to variational quantum algorithms. Now, let's dive into the next section, where we will briefly discuss the latest developments in the field of quantum computing and quantum machine learning.

The latest developments in the field of quantum machine learning and quantum computing

In this final section of this chapter and book, let's take a look at the major developments happening in the field of quantum computing and quantum machine learning.

As you know, quantum computing is slowly gaining prominence in the industry. As more and more research happens and more and more people come to recognize the power of quantum computing, the field will continue to progress in terms of education, awareness, and applications. A lot of research currently goes into finding various applications for quantum computing in domains such as finance, chemistry, transportation, medicine, drug development, aerospace, and artificial intelligence.

If you follow *Quantum World Association* (`http://quantumwa.org/`) and *Swiss Quantum Hub* (`https://www.swissquantumhub.com/`), then you will be able to keep track of the latest developments happening in the field of quantum computing and quantum information processing in general.

SpinQ Gemini (`https://arxiv.org/abs/2101.10017`) is one of the world's first commercially available desktop-like quantum computers that operates at room temperature and is based on **nuclear magnetic resonance** (**NMR**). This will be used for education and research purposes and will help many quantum enthusiasts to gain practical, hands-on experience with a real compact quantum computer. This is one of the examples of the research happening in the field of constructing portable and affordable quantum computers. SpinQ is a Shenzhen, China-based company working on quantum computers.

One very popular research area, related to the SpinQ quantum computer, is room-temperature quantum computing. Very recently, an Austrian quantum computing start-up named AQT demonstrated that it is possible to have the entanglement of 24 qubits at room temperature (`https://arxiv.org/pdf/2101.11390.pdf`). Quantum photonics is another new area where a lot of research is happening, and companies are focusing on the construction of photonics-based quantum computers (`https://www.xanadu.ai/`).

To keep track of the research happening in the field of quantum machine learning, it is best to follow *PennyLane* by *Xanadu* (`https://pennylane.ai/`), *Cambridge Quantum Computing* (`https://cambridgequantum.com/`), and *Zapata Computing* (`https://www.zapatacomputing.com/`). There is a lot of research on quantum machine learning focusing on the application of VQE and QAOA, which we discussed in the previous sections of this chapter. Quantum machine learning is also being applied in areas of finance, such as portfolio optimization, derivatives pricing, financial risk management, and financial modeling. Recently, there has been growing interest in quantum image processing and quantum natural language processing to achieve a quantum computing advantage over these classical and cutting-edge fields. There is active research going on in the field of quantum convolutional neural networks and quantum generative adversarial networks, as well as work going on in various parameterized quantum circuits, which can improve the efficiency of quantum machine learning algorithms.

Summary

In this chapter, you learned about the concept of machine learning and the various algorithms that hold importance in industries today. Then, we looked into the concepts of quantum machine learning and how it is different from classical machine learning. During the discussion of quantum machine learning, you learned about various encoding schemes, kernel-based quantum models, the quantum K-means algorithm, and variational circuits. Finally, we discussed the latest goings-on in the field of quantum computing, with some resources for you to keep yourself up to date on the latest developments in the field of quantum computing.

Heartiest congratulations to you as you have reached the end of this chapter and this book! We hope that you have gained some valuable knowledge in the new high-level quantum programming language Silq and that you will be able to apply that knowledge in your own research and make interesting quantum projects and applications.

We hope that you have enjoyed reading this book and learning about the main concepts of quantum computing with Silq. We wish you all the very best on your quantum journey!

Further reading

- Christopher M. Bishop, *Pattern Recognition and Machine Learning*, Springer, 2006.

- Maria Schuld, Francesco Petruccione, *Supervised Learning with Quantum Computers*, Springer (Vol17), 2018.

- Seth Lloyd, Masoud Mohseni, and Patrick Rebentrost, *Quantum algorithms for supervised and unsupervised machine learning*, arXiv:1307.0411v2, November 2013. Link to the publication: `https://arxiv.org/abs/1307.0411v2`.

- Dan Ventura and Tony Martinez, *Quantum Associative Memory*, arXiv: quant-ph/9807053, July 1998. Link to the publication: `https://arxiv.org/abs/quant-ph/9807053`.

- Maria Schuld, Mark Fingerhuth, and Francesco Petruccione, *Implementing a distance-based classifier with a quantum interference circuit*, arXiv:1703.10793, August 2017. Link to the publication: `https://arxiv.org/abs/1703.10793`.

- Yudong Cao, Gian Giacomo Guerreschi, and Alan Aspuru-Guzik, *Quantum neuron: an elementary building block for machine learning on quantum computers*, arXiv: 1711.11240, November 2017. Link to the publication: `https://arxiv.org/abs/1711.11240`.

- Vojtech Havlicek, Antonio D. Córcoles, Kristan Temme, Aram W. Harrow, Abhinav Kandala, Jerry M. Chow, and Jay M. Gambetta, *Supervised learning with quantum enhanced feature spaces*, arXiv: 1804.11326, June 2018. Link to the publication: `https://arxiv.org/abs/1804.11326`.

- Seth Lloyd, Maria Schuld, Aroosa Ijaz, Josh Izaac, and Nathan Killoran, *Quantum embeddings for machine learning*, arXiv: 2001.03622, February 2020. Link to the publication: `https://arxiv.org/abs/2001.03622`.

- Maria Schuld, *Quantum machine learning models are kernel methods*, arXiv: 2101.11020, January 2021. Link to the publication: `https://arxiv.org/abs/2101.11020`.

- Sumsam U. Khan, *Quantum K-means Algorithm*, diva2:1381305, August 2019. Link to the publication: `https://kth.diva-portal.org/smash/search.jsf?dswid=2934`.

- Sukin Sim, Peter D. Johnson, and Alan Aspuru-Guzik, *Expressibility and Entangling Capability of Parameterized Quantum Circuits for Hybrid Quantum-Classical Algorithms*, arXiv: 1905.10876, May 2019. Link to the publication: `https://arxiv.org/abs/1905.10876`.

- Joshua Goings, *Variational Quantum Eigensolver (VQE) Example*, August 2020. Link to the publication: `https://joshuagoings.com/2020/08/20/VQE/`.

- Peter J. J. O'Malley, et al., *Scalable quantum simulation of molecular energies*. Physical Review X 6.3 (2016): 031007.

- Edward Farhi, Jeffrey Goldstone, and Sam Gutmann, *A Quantum Approximate Optimization Algorithm*, arXiv: 1411.4028, November 2014. Link to the publication: `https://arxiv.org/abs/1411.4028`.

Packt.com

Subscribe to our online digital library for full access to over 7,000 books and videos, as well as industry leading tools to help you plan your personal development and advance your career. For more information, please visit our website.

Why subscribe?

- Spend less time learning and more time coding with practical eBooks and Videos from over 4,000 industry professionals

- Improve your learning with Skill Plans built especially for you

- Get a free eBook or video every month

- Fully searchable for easy access to vital information

- Copy and paste, print, and bookmark content

Did you know that Packt offers eBook versions of every book published, with PDF and ePub files available? You can upgrade to the eBook version at packt.com and as a print book customer, you are entitled to a discount on the eBook copy. Get in touch with us at customercare@packtpub.com for more details.

At www.packt.com, you can also read a collection of free technical articles, sign up for a range of free newsletters, and receive exclusive discounts and offers on Packt books and eBooks.

Other Books You May Enjoy

If you enjoyed this book, you may be interested in these other books by Packt:

Dancing with Qubits

Robert S. Sutor

ISBN: 978-1-83882-736-6

- See how quantum computing works, delve into the math behind it, what makes it different, and why it is so powerful with this quantum computing textbook

- Discover the complex, mind-bending mechanics that underpin quantum systems

- Understand the necessary concepts behind classical and quantum computing

- Refresh and extend your grasp of essential mathematics, computing, and quantum theory

- Explore the main applications of quantum computing to the fields of scientific computing, AI, and elsewhere

- Examine a detailed overview of qubits, quantum circuits, and quantum algorithm

Learn Quantum Computing with Python and IBM Quantum Experience

Robert Loredo

ISBN: 978-1-83898-100-6

- Explore quantum computational principles such as superposition and quantum entanglement
- Become familiar with the contents and layout of the IBM Quantum Experience
- Understand quantum gates and how they operate on qubits
- Discover the quantum information science kit and its elements such as Terra and Aer
- Get to grips with quantum algorithms such as Bell State, Deutsch-Jozsa, Grover's algorithm, and Shor's algorithm
- How to create and visualize a quantum circuit

Packt is searching for authors like you

If you're interested in becoming an author for Packt, please visit `authors.packtpub.com` and apply today. We have worked with thousands of developers and tech professionals, just like you, to help them share their insight with the global tech community. You can make a general application, apply for a specific hot topic that we are recruiting an author for, or submit your own idea.

Leave a review - let other readers know what you think

Please share your thoughts on this book with others by leaving a review on the site that you bought it from. If you purchased the book from Amazon, please leave us an honest review on this book's Amazon page. This is vital so that other potential readers can see and use your unbiased opinion to make purchasing decisions, we can understand what our customers think about our products, and our authors can see your feedback on the title that they have worked with Packt to create. It will only take a few minutes of your time, but is valuable to other potential customers, our authors, and Packt. Thank you!

Index

www.ingramcontent.com/pod-product-compliance
Lightning Source LLC
LaVergne TN
LVHW081335050326
832903LV00024B/1162